FOUR DOLLARS AND A DREAM

THE LIFE AND TIMES OF CINO CHEGIA

By Jeff Gilliland and Cino Chegia

Published by G Force Publications.

ISBN: 0692634002
ISBN-13: 978-0692634004

Front cover: Cino and his little brother Alberto, early 1940s.
Back cover: Cino in the 1990s.

For my father.

TABLE OF CONTENTS

ACKNOWLEDGMENTS

Jeff – First and foremost, I want to thank Jim Gilliland, who approached me with this project in 2011 and has been its legal advisor, proofreader, publisher, and above all its champion ever since. Thank you for giving me the opportunity to tell this sensational story! I would also like to thank Vickie Gilliland for always encouraging me, and for being my link to home as I wrote *Four Dollars and a Dream* from Los Angeles, Chicago, and Washington, DC. Finally, a huge thank-you to Cino himself, who let me into his life and entrusted me to tell his story.

My most sincere gratitude to the following people and institutions for their immense contributions to this work: Alberto Chegia; Faustina Chegia; Pino and Pina Chegia; Maura Chegia; Jimi Chegia; Cory and Eugenia Chegia; Anna Tosi and her family; my nonna, Madeline Petri; Tony Vignale; Giulietto Vignale; Leon Vignale; Lou Alberti; Bob Biasotti; Steve McKae; Jon Paasch, the map-master; The Oakland Public Library; *The Oakland Tribune*; The Historical Museum at Fort Missoula; Google Translate; and Wikipedia.

Last but not least, a shout-out to my sister, Lisa, who coined the title *Four Dollars and a Dream* and then graciously lent it to me (with interest) for the book!

Cino – I would like to thank all my relatives for supporting me, the American government for letting me come to this country, the American people for welcoming me with open arms, and all my friends and the people I've met for helping me along every step of the way.

We hope you enjoy the book!

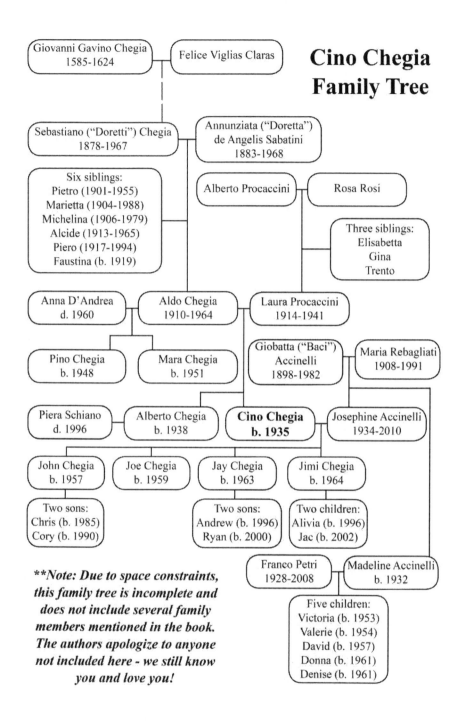

Cino Chegia Family Tree

Giovanni Gavino Chegia
1585-1624

Felice Viglias Claras

Sebastiano ("Doretti") Chegia
1878-1967

Annunziata ("Doretta")
de Angelis Sabatini
1883-1968

Six siblings:
Pietro (1901-1955)
Marietta (1904-1988)
Michelina (1906-1979)
Alcide (1913-1965)
Piero (1917-1994)
Faustina (b. 1919)

Alberto Procaccini

Rosa Rosi

Three siblings:
Elisabetta
Gina
Trento

Anna D'Andrea
d. 1960

Aldo Chegia
1910-1964

Laura Procaccini
1914-1941

Pino Chegia
b. 1948

Mara Chegia
b. 1951

Giobatta ("Baci")
Accinelli
1898-1982

Maria Rebagliati
1908-1991

Piera Schiano
d. 1996

Alberto Chegia
b. 1938

**Cino Chegia
b. 1935**

Josephine Accinelli
1934-2010

John Chegia
b. 1957

Joe Chegia
b. 1959

Jay Chegia
b. 1963

Jimi Chegia
b. 1964

Two sons:
Chris (b. 1985)
Cory (b. 1990)

Two sons:
Andrew (b. 1996)
Ryan (b. 2000)

Two children:
Alivia (b. 1996)
Jac (b. 2002)

Franco Petri
1928-2008

Madeline Accinelli
b. 1932

Five children:
Victoria (b. 1953)
Valerie (b. 1954)
David (b. 1957)
Donna (b. 1961)
Denise (b. 1961)

***Note: Due to space constraints,
this family tree is incomplete and
does not include several family
members mentioned in the book.
The authors apologize to anyone
not included here - we still know
you and love you!*

Map of Italy – Important Points

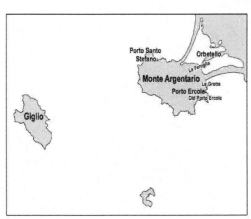

.

PROLOGUE

April 24, 2012. A crowd gathers on the prow of the *Maregiglio* ferry, pointing and laughing in a world of languages. Before them, an emerald island juts out from the opal sea, shimmering in the afternoon sunlight. They fall hushed, and focus their lenses. But their target is not the steep granite hillsides, nor the red-roofed village clustered around the island's small port—it is the gleaming white cruise ship capsized just offshore, impaled on the rocks like a mile-long Moby Dick. This is Giglio Island, sleepy home of fishermen and diving enthusiasts, a stone's throw from the Tuscan coast. This is the *Costa Concordia*, infamous victim of one of the worst boating disasters in Italy's proud maritime history. As the *Maregiglio* nears port, it's as if you can reach out and touch the wreck: hear the shriek of steel on stone, feel the fear of four thousand souls set adrift by an ill fated sail-by. Camera bulbs flash; tourists crow.

Just off the bow, apart from the crowd, an aging man with a wirebrush mustache gazes out at the wreckage. Tufts of whiting hair peek out from his green, flat-brimmed cap, and he zips his windbreaker against the salt spray. Though many others cling to the railing for support, he rocks naturally with the buck of the ocean. Next to him, his niece—dark-haired, with the same ruddy complexion and broad smile—chuckles. "You know, if we were back home, they'd be selling pieces of this ship like souvenirs instead of trying to get rid of it."

"Unbelievable," the man says. His smile never breaks, but his singsong voice thickens for a moment. This place, once his home, is now a black mark on the good name of his people.

Hours later, the *Maregiglio* drops anchor back where it began: Porto Santo Stefano, on the northern tip of the tiny promontory of Monte Argentario, Tuscany, Italy. Once a small fishing village, Santo Stefano has transformed into a thriving city, a destination for wealthy Europeans and backpackers seeking adventure and safe harbor for their yachts. Climb high enough up the Via Panoramica and you can see how the city has clawed up and out, the port at its heart now dwarfed by apartment buildings and luxury hotels carved out of the hillside. By day, Porto Santo Stefano is a cheery cacophony of pastel stucco and bright blue shutters; by night, the lights slink out from the waterfront bars to dance on the dark water. Cranes and cell phone towers stretch out over La Fortezza, the city's stone fortress, built by the Spanish during their brief occupation in the sixteenth century. They seem to peer at it, the cranes do, amused and indifferent like children examining a relic in a museum.

On the dock, a lone man waits, impassive and unspeaking like the sea. The fading sun glints off his wireframe glasses; his hands, clasped behind his back, never move. Unlike his brother, he has no need to see the *Costa Concordia* up close. Unlike his brother, he was there the night of its foundering—watching from shore as friends raced to their boats, as weeping families huddled under blankets and cast about for the things they had lost. Unlike his brother, he saw the emergency tents rise, like the *cappanne*[1] that huddled in the *olivetti*[2] back when they were boys. As the old men walk slowly along the *lungomare*,[3] he does not glance behind him, not once. One thing about Italians is: they rarely look where they don't want to see.

This story, in part, is about things unseen, things lost and reshuffled. It's about how that which is hard can be the most pure, and about how the tide of war sullies everything it does not destroy. It's about two families, three cities, fifty years and six thousand miles; a terrible fright, an old hospital ship; vows made and then broken; trash turned to treasure. But most of all, it's about the unbreakable bond of family—ever-changing but fundamental and gravitational, like the sea—that brought two old men back together again on the shores of their homeland.

---

[1] Huts
[2] Olive groves
[3] Seafront promenade

CHAPTER ONE: ENTER CHINAMAN

"Ha' capito?"[4]
- Italian colloquialism

October 13, 1935. A crowd gathers outside *L'Ospizio*,[5] peering in doorways and windows to glimpse the commotion tearing through the first-floor apartment. Neighbors laugh and shake their heads. This could go on for a while.

"Sebastiano is a strong name—a proud name!" shouts Doretti, slightly slurred. He runs his hand through his hair and drains his wine in a gulp, licking the last drops from his drooping mustache.

"Can you not say the same of Alberto?" roars his counterpart, Alberto Procaccini. Blue-eyed and nearly bald, he towers over the much smaller Doretti. "Call him Alberto, you make him a Procaccini—and the Procaccini fought alongside Garibaldi and

---

[4] "You understand me?"
[5] The Hospice: the name of the apartment building where the Chegias lived.

Mazzini in the *Risorgimento*.[6] We have a street named after us in Milan, for God's sake. There was even a Procaccini onboard with Gabriele d'Annunzio during the *Beffa di Buccari*,[7] you know!"

"But he is *not* a Procaccini; he is a Chegia!" retorts Doretta, really the only one who can go toe-to-toe with Alberto. "His people are fishermen and pirates, not professors and painters like you. He will be named after his father: Aldino, maybe. Or Alcide, like his uncle."

"Oh no, no," says Alcide, stooped and stewing. "Don't bring me into this. You want him called *Il Gobbetto*[8] too, just because we share a name? Don't make the child suffer like that."

The debate rages like a hurricane, whipping the tiny living room into a froth. In the eye of the storm sits Laura Procaccini Chegia, quietly rocking the baby boy. She is tired; she will say nothing. Let the voices seethe and swirl around her, and see what warped wood or polished stone they deliver to her doorstep.

Finally, the hot winds calm. Something has caught them, billowing out like a sail. Curious, they lap at the thing, prod it, test it for seaworthiness. From the doors and windows of L'Ospizio, the neighbors lean in for a better view.

"Cino," repeats Vittorio, with finality. "Cino Alberto Chegia."

"Cino," the winds echo back. A twinkling gleam jumps from one to another as they assess the name. It's memorable, it's unique, it's bound to give the boy trouble—and it will drive his father crazy when he comes back from duty to meet his firstborn. It's perfect.

---

[6] The Italian War of Independence, which unified the nation in the 1860s.
[7] The Bakar Mockery: a World War I escapade in which three Italian torpedo boats—one carrying nationalist poet Gabriele d'Annunzio—slipped through Austro-Hungarian defenses, attacked a shipping hub and escaped unscathed.
[8] The Hunchback

"To Cino!" the families cheer, glasses aloft.

The neighbors carry word out like the wind: through the courtyard, past the old olive tree, into the twilit streets of Le Grotte. Laura snuggles her suckling newborn. Driftwood or gemstone, the storm has delivered, and now it's time for the boy to live with the consequences.

The problem, of course, was that Aldo wasn't around. In those days in Italy, it was up to the father to name his children: when a baby was born, the father said, "I will name my child such-and-such," and that was that. But when Cino came along, Aldo Chegia was a world away, floating through the South China Sea on the deck of a warship called the *Trento*. He was halfway through his twenty-six-month stint in the Royal Navy—military service was mandatory for all able-bodied Italian men until 2004—and the families had no way to reach him. So that's how all nine Chegias—Doretti, Doretta, Pietro, Alcide, Vittorio, Marietta, Michelina, Faustina, and their spouses and kids—plus Laura's kin, the Procaccinis—Alberto, Rosa, Betta, Gina, Trento, etc., etc.—wound up in Doretti and Doretta's apartment in L'Ospizio trying to out-din the din.

Ultimately, the decision for what to name the boy came down to three of the things Italians prize most: a strong sense of history, hearty stock (for soup and for people), and a good joke. The Chegias and Procaccinis took care of the first two, so all that was left was the joke—and calling the boy Cino was a damn good joke. It sounded like the popular name "Gino," but just different enough to confuse people and lead to hilarious misunderstandings. It evoked thoughts of cartoonish adventure, thanks to the well-known comic strip *Cino e Franco.*[9] But what made the name a good joke is that "Cino" (pronounced "Chino") is Italian for "Chinese man"—a fitting name for a boy whose father was in China when he was born!

The kid wouldn't even need a nickname, like his grandfather Sebastiano ("Doretti"); his grandmother Annunziata ("Doretta"); his uncles Pietro ("Lascia Fa"), Alcide ("Il Gobbetto"), and Piero ("Vittorio"); his aunt Marietta ("L'Anticipiata"); or his mother Laura ("La Rossa," for her fair skin and red hair). Cino's real name was a nickname in and of itself, and it would surely dog him for the rest of his life. Aldo would be furious when he found out; they all knew that. But there wasn't anything he could do about it. And that made the joke even better.

---

[9] The Italian translation of American comic strip *Tim Tyler's Luck*, which depicted two young orphans who travel around Africa and later fight in World War II.

Chapter Two: The Rising Tide

"A quei tempi, non c'era niente."[10]
- Cino Chegia

February, 1930. A crowd gathers in Porto Recanati, watching with morbid curiosity as the man flails against his captors.

"Hold still!" the Blackshirts demand, forcing the spoon into the man's mouth. The castor oil slips, viscous and amber-hued, down his gullet. His skin turns pale and he clutches his throat, backing away to hide the shame of what is to come. The Blackshirts laugh and sneer.

Suddenly, in strides a large, blue-eyed man, carrying his authority like a cloak on his shoulders. The people part to let him through.

"Let the man go," he says, his eyes fixed on the Fascist oppressors. "He can barely read, let alone sign this pledge of allegiance to your godforsaken party."

---

[10] "In those days, there was nothing here."

The crowd gasps. The Blackshirts turn his way, drawing clubs and brass knuckles from their belts. "And what are you going to do about it?"

The man breathes deeply, balls his fists, and charges into the fray. His mighty swings knock a few of the Blackshirts off their feet, but in the end he is no match for their weapons and numbers. Their blows fall heavy on his prone body; the crowd murmurs in anger and helplessness, watching their beloved son felled by these cruel, wanton men. In the confusion, the castor oil victim slips away to retch and void his bowels in peace.

After the crowd clears, Alberto Procaccini heaves his bloodied body off the street. He drags himself back home, meeting his shocked wife and kids at the door. "Pack up your things," he says. "It's time to go. We'll be safe in Porto Ercole."

———————————

There is no silver on Monte Argentario. Despite the name, which translates loosely to "Silvery Mountain", the little Tuscan promontory holds no precious metals inside its rock walls. What it holds instead is the same thing held within the myriad towns and cities where Italians gather to share their lives: a much better story.

"It's the olive trees, see," say natives like Doretti and Doretta, salty seafolk who trace their local lineage back hundreds of years. "Their leaves glint like silver in the sun. So when sailors would pass by, they would say, 'Hold on now! There's silver on that mountain!' And when the Spanish came they said, 'We better protect all this silver from the pirates,' so they built all these forts here. Never found a flake of the stuff, but they sure ate some good olives."

"Nonsense," say the transplants and new arrivals—the educated, like Alberto Procaccini. "It was named after the *Argentarii*." Back in the second century B.C., they will tell you,

Rome was at war with Carthage. In need of emergency military funds, the Republic turned to its Argentarii, or moneylenders. One of these early financiers, Domitius Aerobarbus, gave Rome the money it needed. In exchange, Rome gave him a massive plot of nearly uninhabited land on the Tuscan coastline, misleadingly dotted with olive trees. Moneylender Mountain was born.

If the transplants are versed in geological history, too, they will tell you that Monte Argentario was once an island, part of the Tuscan archipelago along with Giglio Island and Elba, where Napoleon was once exiled for 300 days. Over millennia, however, currents from the Tyrrhenian Sea and Albegna River formed two land strips called *tomboli*, connecting Monte Argentario's east coast to the Tuscan mainland. The northern tombolo, the Tombolo di Giannella, is the main artery from the promontory to the nearest mainland city, Orbetello. The southern tombolo, the Tombolo di La Feniglia, is one of the longest uninterrupted stretches of beach in Western Europe. In between the tomboli lies Lake Orbetello, a brackish saltwater lake protected from the tide by the strips of land on either side.

Monte Argentario's jagged coastline is marked with steep cliffs and secluded coves, which teem with small fish like anchovies and sardines. The wooded hills rise to a peak in the promontory's center: Punta Telegrafo, just over 2,000 feet high. Settled first by the ancient Etruscans, it was eventually claimed by Rome, bequeathed to Domitius Aerobarbus, and then passed around to Emperor Constantine, the Catholic Church, and King Ladislaus of Naples and Siena. None of them paid it any mind.

In 1557, however, Monte Argentario fell to the Spanish, who for the first time settled the region as if it had a purpose. That purpose likely did not involve silver, but it most certainly did involve pirates: the Spanish were planning to build a client state in Tuscany, a region then notorious for bloody raids from Barbary

Coast pirates seeking Christian slaves for the Ottoman Empire. With its natural bluffs and full view of the Tyrrhenian Sea, Monte Argentario would provide the perfect protection against foreign invasion and pirate raid.

So, they built fortresses—and fortresses, and more fortresses. In the north, La Fortezza, overlooking the peninsula's largest bay. To the west, just south of La Feniglia, Forte Filippo and La Rocca guarded the north and south ends of a rocky cove. In the middle, higher up on the mountainside, Forte Stella watched over them all. These low, hulking edifices still stand: home to museums and luxury condos, monuments to Italy's lived history.

As these bastions of protection arose, small villages sprang up beneath them. La Fortezza gave birth to Porto Santo Stefano, Forte Filippo to Le Grotte, and La Rocca to Porto Ercole, which huddled behind the rock wall that runs from its battlements down to the sea. The first settlers were fishermen, drawn by the abundance of sea creatures and the shelter of Spanish cannons. Different clans settled in different areas: Ligurians and Sardinians made homes in Porto Santo Stefano and Le Grotte, while Porto Ercole consisted mostly of Southerners who had come up from Calabria and Naples. Eventually, others followed: Spanish nobility, many of whose bodies still lie in crypts beneath the region's oldest churches; Sardinian soldiers, sent to Monte Argentario to fight pirates; even, as local folklore holds, some of the pirates themselves.

Among the first Le Grotteans was a Sardinian soldier named Giovanni Gavino Chegia, who in 1617 married Felice Viglias Claras and settled down to a life by the sea. Like many, Giovanni and his family began fishing the Tyrrhenian waters, sending their *menaita*[11] out every night to catch anchovies and sardines by the light of the moon. For 250 years, an unending string of Giovanni and Giovanna Chegias farmed the sea, catching enough to make do

---

[11] Lamp-fishing boat (plural: *menaite*)

and passing their profound knowledge of the craft down from generation to generation. In the late 19th century, Sebastiano Chegia—who reminded his friends of the singer Doretti—met Annunziata de Angelis Sabatini, a strong woman with a wide brow and intelligent features. Though she could be short-tempered, he found her sweet and friendly, the heart and soul of the town. They were married in 1900—Doretti found his Doretta, and our story began.

By the turn of the twentieth century, Monte Argentario's tiny villages had grown into tiny towns, complete with small ports for their boats, a cannery for their fish, and a train that hauled people and goods from Porto Santo Stefano to Orbetello. Though the Spanish were long gone and the region subsumed into the Italian government's Province of Grosseto, life still felt like it did generations ago: so simple, so softly rhythmic that nobody thought it would ever change. But it did change, and changed fast—from the steady, slow lull of the sea, to the martial beat of war's drum and fife.

It began with the *Risorgimento*. After the fall of Rome, the Italian peninsula fractured into city-states, vying with each other for power and routinely invaded by foreign powers like France and Austro-Hungary. In the mid-nineteenth century, Italian nationalists began a movement to reunite what was once the most powerful nation in the known world. Led by the Giuseppes—Mazzini and Garibaldi—a ragtag band of freedom fighters became a revolutionary army, that marched north from Sicily and pushed all foreign rulers, including the Spanish, out of Italian lands. Despite the opposition of the Catholic Church—which had itself ruled much of Italy for hundreds of years—the people rallied for the cause of unification. Their battle cry was "Viva VERDI": on its surface a tribute to famed composer Giuseppe Verdi, but beneath it a call for the reign of *Vittorio Emanuele, Rey D'Italia*—Victor Emanuel, King of Italy. In 1869, the Kingdom of Italy was established, and his reign began.

Born again in the modern world, Italy began the work of forming into a modern nation. Yet the political, ethnic and ideological divides that had split the country into city-states did not simply disappear: they bubbled just below the surface, under a thin veneer of national identity. Rivalries between former independent powers like Venice and Genoa, and between the trade hubs on the coasts and poor farming communities inland, led to bitter arguments over wealth distribution. Moreover, few could agree on how to govern the country: though a constitutional monarchy was seen as the strongest foundation, many intellectuals—including Mazzini—called for a full Republic, and rising Socialist voices in the south demanded a complete overhaul of the system. As absolutist monarchies across Europe began to crumble under the weight of their own empires, the young Kingdom of Italy struggled to hold itself together.

It all came to a head in the Great War. At first, Italy kept its distance from the conflict: fresh off its own revolution, the country was too weak and its military too small to match up against the major powers. After a few years, however, nationalists like Gabriele D'Annunzio began clamoring for intervention: to them, the Great War was a chance to rally Italians behind one banner, and to assert the nation's presence on the international stage. Anarchist and Socialist counterprotests immediately sprang up, decrying the bourgeios intentions of those hoping to resurrect the glory of Rome. Fearing that the demonstrations would dissolve into riots and possibly civil war, in 1915 Italy declared war on the Triple Alliance of Germany, Austria-Hungary, and the Ottoman Empire.

Three years later, nearly one million Italian soldiers lay dead in the sands of North Africa and the snows of the Alps. Technically, Italy emerged victorious from the war, regaining control over the disputed territories of Trentino and Trieste. But the losses at home far outweighed the gains on the front. The country's morale was broken, its military shattered—and the worst was still to come. Immediately following the war, an unprecedented economic depression swept through Europe. In Germany, inflation rose so much that by 1923 the exchange rate of German marks to American dollars was over four billion to one. The Austro-Hungarian and Ottoman Empires were disbanded, and the new countries that emerged fell into years of poverty and ethnic violence. In Russia, the Communist October Revolution deposed Czar Nicholas II and established the Bolshevik government that would later become the Soviet Union.

In Italy, the violent unrest picked up right where it left off. As the country defaulted on its war loans, strikes broke out in factories and farming communities. Seeking to capitalize on the chaos, extremist militias from every part of the political spectrum clashed in the streets, gunning each other—and many innocent bystanders—down. Fearing a complete breakdown in the rule of law, the government turned to the only man who seemed able to stamp out these rebellions: Benito Amilcare Andrea Mussolini, a socialist-turned-nationalist whose *Fasci Rivoluzionari d'Azione Internazionalista*[12] was quickly becoming one of the most visible, and most feared, political groups in the country. Calling themselves *Fascisti*, or Fascists, Mussolini's followers were led by gangs of former soldiers in black shirts, who ruthlessly pursued and defeated Socialist revolutions across the country.

By 1922, Mussolini had consolidated so much power, and intimidated or assassinated so many of his opponents, that he was ready to make his move. He and his Blackshirts marched on Rome,

---

[12] Fasci of Revolutionary Action. In Latin, the "Fasces" is a bundle of sticks, symbolizing strength through unity—the central tenet of Fascism.

seizing control of the government at the points of their guns. From there, Mussolini began a long campaign of political alliance and profound, impassioned propaganda, to convince the Italian people that he was the only man who could lead them. It worked: by 1925, Mussolini had eradicated all opposition, and named himself *Sua Eccellenza Benito Mussolini, Capo del Governo, Duce del Fascismo e Fondatore dell'Impero.*[13] He was bigger than the King, bigger than the Pope—the new father of the Fatherland. Across Italy, average citizens sang songs to their Supreme Leader, and carried chants of *Credere, Obeddire, Combattere*—Believe, Obey, Fight—to every nook and cranny of the nation. As it soon would in Germany, Fascism took hold of Italy, and would not release its grip until millions more had died.

For many years, the Mussolini regime seemed to be steering Italy in the right direction. Guided by his dictatorial hand, the trains began running on time: a notable change for a country long used to general chaos and frequent strikes. His Battles for Grain, Land, and Lira increased Italy's self-sufficiency, improved its economy and regulated inflation; his Battle for Births prompted a population boom that helped Italy measure up against other Western European nations. Through group calisthenics, marching, and chanting, he encouraged "national cohesion"—cohesion, naturally, around the cult of his own personality. Underneath it all was a constant call for *spazio vitale*: "living space", room for Italy to grow into the great nation it was under Julius Caesar, and could once again be under Benito Mussolini. With complete—and deft—control over the media, Mussolini proclaimed his message throughout Italy and convinced most of the country that he was their key to glory.

Despite Mussolini's vehement support from many Italians, there were still some dissenters he could not muzzle. Most were

---

[13] His Excellency Benito Mussolini, Head of Government, Duke of Fascism, and Founder of the Empire

intellectuals and writers, teachers and politicians who still remembered the dream of Giuseppe Mazzini: a true Republic, free from foreign and domestic tyranny. These local thought-leaders shaped the opinions of their communities, and in them Mussolini found the first true challenge to his authoritarian rule. He knew that he could not simply make them "disappear"—the more popular figures he carted away, the more the masses would rise up against him. Dead Socialists the Italian people could handle; seeing their best and brightest clubbed in the streets was a recipe for revolution.

So Mussolini set out on a new quest: get Italy's intellectuals to pledge their loyalty to him. From Venice to Naples, he sent his propagandists to the homes of those who spoke out against him, extolling the virtues of Fascism and exhorting them to sign on the dotted line. If that didn't work, he sent the Blackshirts, armed with the weapons of coercion: threats, innuendoes, humiliating punishments like castor oil force-feeding, which causes extreme vomiting and diarrhea. If even that had no effect, he sent them back with real weapons, and a simple command—leave town or suffer the consequences.

The Fascists rationalized these exilings as "relocations," sending leaders from one region to a place where their talents would be of more use. These places often happened to be on the other side of the country, far from the dissenter's sphere of influence. The method worked: organizers and mobilizers gaining a following in one town suddenly found themselves thousands of kilometers away, often in tiny hamlets that had never heard of them before. By exiling these popular figures, Mussolini was able to maintain an air of leniency while casting the voices of opposition into the winds of Italy's rugged coasts. And in doing so, he often brought educated, elite families into contact with the dirt-flecked, saltwater-drenched men and women who lived and worked in those seaside towns.

Such was the case with Alberto Procaccini. The son of a university professor and a leading intellectual in the east coast town of Porto Recanati, Alberto grew up in the company of scholars and activists, artists and politicians. Like his ancestors, Alberto was a fierce Republican, who saw Mussolini's rise as the undoing of all they had worked for during the Risorgimento. His eloquent railings against Fascism stirred revolutionary sentiment in Porto Recanati—so, unsurprisingly, he got a visit from the Blackshirts. When they tried to persuade him to sign their oath of fealty, he laughed in their faces. When they showed up again brandishing weapons, he laughed again.

By 1930, however, the pressure was becoming too great. Alberto had too much to lose: his wife, Rosa; his three daughters, Teresa (called "Betta"), Laura, and Gina; his son, Trento. By then the Fascists controlled everything, and their threats were becoming bolder. Every day, the thought of relocating seemed less like an act of cowardice than it had the day before. "Even Garibaldi had to flee for a few years," Alberto thought. So when the day came that he stumbled upon the Blackshirts force-feeding that man castor oil, the decision had already been made. The Fascists had picked out a new home for him—Porto Ercole, a sleepy fishing village on the Tyrrhenian coast—and his departure was only a matter of time. *One last chance*, Alberto may have thought as he charged at the men with the clubs. *One last moment to stand up to tyranny.* Bruised and bloodied, he returned home ready to build a new life out west.

The road into Porto Ercole must have been a strange one for the Procaccinis. Amid the ripped overalls, calloused hands and sunburned faces, the arrival of a well-dressed man and his family was sure to turn heads. It was not often that a new family moved into town, and a true rarity to see anyone even holding a book. The only school in town was an elementary school, and few students made it past fifth grade before leaving to work full-time on their family's boat. In short, it was no place for a learned man—that was the point, after all—and for the Procaccinis, it may have felt like stepping into a nightmare.

"How are we going to survive?" Alberto asked his wife that first night in town, lying wide awake in their too-cozy new apartment. "Imagine me working on a menaita, or packing sardines in the cannery."

Rosa laughed out loud at the thought, then patted Alberto's fleshy shoulder. "You'll find something," she promised.

And he did. It didn't take Alberto long to realize that his skills could be useful in Monte Argentario, reading letters and taking dication for the illiterate. So he offered up his services as the *scrivanno*, or scribe, for all of Porto Ercole and Le Grotte. Within weeks, people were lined up around the block, to ask for his help with everything from love letters to birth announcements. Soon, the former professor began consulting on legal matters with the *comune*, or regional government. In Alberto, the locals found a man they could trust, who took his duty seriously and never abused his position for personal gain. In fact, when people couldn't pay him, Alberto often accepted compensation in fish, fresh vegetables, and even a live farm animal or two. Soon, he was as revered in Porto Ercole as he had been in Porto Recanati, and at the townspeople's request began working as the *daziere*, or commercial tax collector, for all of Monte Argentario. By 1933, the Procaccinis moved from Porto Ercole to the municipal seat in Porto Santo Stefano, and established themselves as one of the most respected families on the promontory.

Alberto and Rosa's children enjoyed the fruits of their family's popularity. Within a few years of settling in Porto Santo Stefano, Betta, Gina, and Trento all married Monte Argentario natives. And one day, not long after the Procaccinis arrived in

Porto Ercole, Alberto's daughter Laura came upon a roguish young fisherman named Aldo Chegia. Though Aldo and Laura could not have been more different—he was an outspoken, boisterous ruffian with a soft spot for cards and liquor, while she was a shy, quiet redhead—opposites did what opposites do, and the two quickly fell in love. They were engaged by the time Aldo left for his two years of naval service, and married when the *Trento* came back for repairs. Nine months later, the life that had been growing inside La Rossa emerged, and the hot winds picked up in L'Ospizio.

CHAPTER THREE: SEA CHANGE

"A quei tempi, tutti paesani si conoscevano."[14]
- Cino Chegia

Spring, 1938. Cino totters around Doretta's small sitting room, babbling softly. Around him, the women whirl in the early morning light, effortlessly moving through the delicate choreography perfected through years of routine. Laura lights the wood stove for breakfast and heat, while Michelina sweeps past, clearing dust mites from the tiny kitchen. Faustina kneads the week's bread and whistles *La Donna è Mobile*—quietly, so as not to disturb her mother. Doretta, for her part, watches the proceedings like a pit boss stalking the floor. "More flour!" she barks to her youngest daughter. "More wood!" she barks to her daughter-in-law. "Now go sit down: you're too pregnant to be so near a fire."

"Mama," Michelina inquires, "isn't it time to get the eggs for the frittata?"

---

[14] "In those days, everyone in town knew each other."

Doretta looks at her wryly. "Why yes, my dear, yes it is."

Outside in the courtyard, Doretta pads past the rabbits nosing to the edge of their cages, pushing lettuce leaves through the bars. At the chicken coop, she clucks to the hens. "Which one of you will it be today, huh? Who wants to have some fun?"

One of the hens stops and looked up from her feed—big mistake. Quick as a fox, Doretta stoops down and snatches the hen into her arms, licking a finger and sticking it where the sun never shines. "About ten minutes, I'd give you!" she pronounces, releasing the violated hen from her clutches. It waddles away, splay-footed.

Ten minutes later, a fresh chicken egg sizzles in a skillet over a hot wood stove. Doretta tosses in potatoes, onions, zucchini from the family's small garden, whipping it expertly into the day's breakfast. "Make sure those loaves have time to rise," she calls over her shoulder to Faustina. "Our oven time is in two hours."

Just then, there is a stamping of feet at the door. Doretti and sons stagger in, carrying torn nets, cracked lamps, and a bag of fresh fish. As they haul their supplies to the courtyard out back, one peels off from the group, a smile dancing on his lips. His dark hair is swept back wildly, his mustache crystal with salt. He moves confidently, almost rakishly.

"Where is my son?" Aldo asks, kissing his wife and patting her belly. Laura nods toward the living room. Cino claps his hands and beams at his father.

"Wash your hands first!" Doretta scolds, but it is too late. Aldo swoops the boy up in his arms and parades him down the hall.

"I missed you—yes I did!" he says, poking Cino's nose and leaving a trace of grime behind. Cino grabs his finger and holds tight.

"Strong," Aldo smiles.

He has been home for almost two years, back on his father's menaita for nearly as long. The apartment he shares with Laura and Cino is truly a home, their second child less than six months away. But still, the whole family gathers in the old place in L'Ospizio nearly every day. And still, he has not tired of seeing the bright, happy face of his beautiful boy.

"Aldo!" Doretti calls from the courtyard, shattering the intimate stillness. "Get out here, son. Work ain't done yet." Aldo sighs and puts the boy down, tousling his hair on his way outside.

That's how life was in those days. Every night, the Chegia men—Doretti, Pietro, Aldo, Alcide, and Vittorio—rowed their lamp-fishing boat, *La Menaita della Domenica*,[15] out into open waters to scoop up anchovies and sardines. Every morning, they dropped their haul off at the cannery next to the port, where the local women packed them tight into tins. Then they clomped back to L'Ospizio, ate breakfast, fixed the equipment, and went home to sleep soundly until dinner was served. In the meantime, their wives and sisters cooked and cleaned, and once a week went down to the town square to do laundry and bake bread.

In Le Grotte circa 1940, there was no running water. If you wanted to boil pasta or mop the floor, you had to bring a bucket down to the fountain in the piazza and pump it yourself. Same thing if nature called. "In L'Ospizio there were four apartments and two bathrooms," Cino recalls. "A bathroom was a hole in the ground. But you had to bring your own water to flush it out!" For washing linens, the towns of Porto Ercole and Le Grotte built a

---

[15] The Sunday Menaita: a nickname Marietta gave the boat, because she claimed her brothers were so lazy that the boat was always the last one out and the first one in, like it was just going for a Sunday cruise.

communal laundry facility: three vats along a diverted stream where the women would gather and scrub. "The running water comes into the first vat, so that's the clean water," Cino continues. "The second vat, semi-clean. The third vat is dirty. You wash in the third vat, rinse in the second vat, rinse again in the upper vat."

And as they scrubbed, they chatted—especially Doretta, a big woman with a big mouth. "My grandmother was a bit of a *popolanna*, a gossip," Cino says, "[but] immensely generous." Still remembered in Porto Ercole as the heart and soul of the town, Doretta organized balls and bingo games for the town, and whenever anyone was sick would be the first person at their doorstep with a bowl of hot soup. But if you messed with her family, look out: "she'd be on you *come una vipera,*[16] as we say in Italy." Over the years, Cino saw plenty of the viper's fangs— sometimes lashing at him, sometimes in his defense.

So once a week there was laundry, and once a week there was bread. The small wooden stoves most *grottolani*[17] had at home did not get hot enough to bake the crusty *pane* that everyone loved, so a large bread oven sprang up near the 'laundromat' for the townspeople to use. To avoid baking frenzies, the comune government instituted a strict schedule: each family had one hour a week in which to cook all the bread they would need. When the Chegias' hour came, Doretta and her daughters would rush down to the oven, bringing their own wood for the fire and carefully balancing the seven lumps of dough that would feed them for the next seven days. One hour later, out would come seven golden-brown loaves, each scored in a cross at the top. "The first loaf of bread was always delicious, but by the time you got to day seven it was so hard you had to dip it in water just to be able to chew it!" Cino remembers.

---

[16] Like a viper
[17] Le Grotte residents

When the work was done, there was still time for play. "Nearly twelve families lived in our building," Cino recalls, "and we had many fun events there. My uncle Alcide played the accordion very well, and Vittorio sang beautifully; sometimes, we would get together in my grandmother's house or outside in the courtyard and play and sing together. On some calm nights, they would play there for the whole town: before the men left to fish by lamplight, they would come to L'Ospizio to hear my uncles play and sing." The strains of folk music followed the men down to the port and out onto the ocean—with Alcide and Vittorio scrambling behind it, trying to get *La Menaita della Domenica* into the water before it was too late.

The rhythm of the fisherman's life was broken only on Sundays. Sundays were the Lord's Day, and that meant Mass in the morning, followed by a family lunch that stretched well into the afternoon. (For the Chegias, as for many Italians, Mass meant socializing with their friends—gossiping in the back of the cathedral then gathering on the patio to smoke cigarettes and swap tales from the sea). After lunch, the men were released to the *cantina,*[18] to drink wine and play poker until the sun went down or they could no longer stand. "Those nights, Doretti would invariably return home drunk," Cino remembers, "sometimes so much so that other men would have to help him home. The moment these men would move to toss him into bed, Doretti would start to fight everyone in sight! The next day he would wake up and not remember a thing," and it would be right back to work.

———————

While Aldo fished and Laura cleaned house, Cino was beginning to come into his own. Blond-haired and blue-eyed, he had the angelic appearance of one morally bound to make

[18] Bar

mischief: he ran wild through the streets, chased chickens around the courtyard, always managed to be where you didn't want him to be, and never managed to come home without a dirty face or a torn shirt. And, as soon as he was old enough to realize it, Cino learned that he had a big chip on his shoulder: a chip the size of a country that he'd never even seen on a map.

"Chinaman, Chinaman!" children would call out on the streets, tugging at the corners of their eyelids. He and *Ciccia Nera*,[19] another boy with an irksome nickname, would ball their fists and go out in search of a fight—an excuse to sock somebody or grab a loose cobblestone and chuck it at some dim-witted bully. He still didn't fully understand what a Chinaman was, but he was sure it wasn't something that a young boy wanted to be.

To make matters worse, in 1938 La Rossa started to get fat, and then, right around Cino's third birthday (on October 24, as a matter of fact), this other little boy appeared, crying and wrinkly and soft...and now Mama spent all her time with him, and when Babbo came home he walked straight past Cino and picked up the little one, bopping him on the nose with his greasy finger like he used to do to Cino. Alberto Chegia, his new baby brother, whom they called "Albertino" to distinguish from his grandfather, who spent all his time pooping and puking but it was like he was Vittorio Emanuele incarnate or something, the way they adored him. Someday, Cino knew, he'd have to protect and love this little wrinkly thing, but for now the kid just got in the way.

Around those days, Cino started going to the *asilo*,[20] where they taught him his ABC's and 123's. He soon found that it didn't hold much for him either. Shapes and moo cows and singing songs with teacher—he didn't know how the other kids could stand it. So much adventure outside, so much foolishness within four walls.For

---

[19] "Black Meat," so-called because of his dark skin
[20] Nursery school

him it was like a nightmare, a dungeon with blocks. So he made his own adventures, with bugs and paste and little girls' pigtails— adventures that usually got him spanked and sent home early, where his mother would give him a look like, "What now?" then go back to feeding Alberto, so he'd just turn around again and head out looking for someone to fight.

But then—well, then the big fight came along, and things got bad fast, and suddenly little brothers and stupid nicknames and counting your tens didn't seem like such a raw deal anymore.

CHAPTER FOUR: WORLD AT WAR

"Credere, Obeddire, Combattere."[21]
- Italian Fascist motto

June 10, 1940. A crowd gathers in Piazza Venezia, Rome, watching and waiting. Two hundred and fifty thousand strong, they engulf the monument to Vittorio Emanuele II in their ranks. They stand shoulder-to-shoulder, carrying flags from every town and territory from Sicily to Piemonte. They crane their necks to peer up at the balcony high overhead. The silence of one-quarter million people is as deep as the Mediterranean Sea.

Finally he is revealed. Stock-still, in military dress as always. Regal, papal. *Sua Eccelenza, Il Duce.* The crowd roars. He grasps his belt with authority.

"The hour marked by Fate has struck in the heavens of our fatherland. The hour of irrevocable decisions," he intones. His words can barely be heard above the din of the faithful.

---

[21] "Believe, Obey, Fight."

In L'Ospizio, the radio sizzles and spits. The din of the faithful can barely be heard over the wails echoing throughout Le Grotte. Doretta grips the kitchen table so tightly that Cino worries she'll tear a chunk right out. "Bastardo." Vittorio, her youngest son, smiles triumphantly and smooths the front of his black shirt.

Aldo sits in the corner, swirling his wine. He leans back in his chair and smiles. "No surprise, right?" He turns to his wife, kisses her cheek. Kisses his mother and father and brothers. Turns last to his sons, kneeling and drawing them in. They can taste the salt from the sea, or perhaps from their tears. "Guess I'll go pack a bag, then," Aldo says.

By 1940, the Nazis were on the move. Less than a year after charging through Poland, they had taken Belgium and Holland, broken the French Maginot Line, and raised the Swastika over Paris. The war was about to be over, and Mussolini—for all his imperial ambition, for all his proclamations of a return to Roman glory—had done nothing at all. Not a single shot had been fired from an Italian rifle. Not a body had fallen on the field of battle. And without those, there would be no room for Italy at the peace table, no gains to be made from the violence that had raked its way across the continent.

On June 5, Il Duce told his advisors, "I only need a few thousand dead so that I can sit at the peace conference as a man who has fought." On June 10, he stood on the balcony of the Palazzo Venezia and looked out over the roaring crowd. By June 20, the first Italian forces crossed the border into France, and the first bodies began to fall. In the Alps, on the Riviera, in the waters of Libya and even at home on the mainland, the bodies fell.

Five days later, on June 25, 1940, France surrendered to the Axis Powers. Mussolini hailed it as a victory for Italy, but even then it was clear that the Italians were in for more than they had bargained for. The Alpine passes, where so many had died in the Great War, were proving no less treacherous; the defense was stauncher and the fighting fiercer than anything Italy had ever seen. Supply lines ran thin, old equipment stalled, the coast of Liguria smoldered from a French counterpunch early in the offensive. Italy simply was not ready for what was to come.

So Mussolini acted fast. All recent conscripts were reenlisted—including Aldo and Vittorio—and the military threw every resource it could muster into the war effort. Vittorio was sent to the Army, and would eventually receive a medical discharge after taking a piece of shrapnel from an American bomb in his arm. Aldo returned to fight in the Royal Navy: not on a battleship nor on a transport vessel, but on a *peschereccio*—a fishing trawler— with a machine gun welded to the foredeck and an Italian flag painted on the side. The hold still stank of its most recent catch.

The Navy sent Aldo to Greece, where Italy had launched its first solo offensive—the country's chance to prove that it belonged in this war, and Mussolini's chance to show Hitler that he could be trusted. They barely made it through Albania before the Greeks turned them back, setting up a drawn-out, bloody slugfest. Though Aldo assured his wife that he was safe guarding the coast, it did not look like he would be coming back home any time soon.

Laura, then, had a decision to make. Her house in Le Grotte was *her* house, and her sons' home, but without Aldo around it felt big and empty and too much to take. Back in Porto Santo Stefano were her parents: shelter, comfort, familiarity. Someone to help wrangle Cino—someone like her father, who might be able to teach him some manners.

Her father, for his part, urged her to move. "Come back, Laura, it's safer here. For the boys, for you. You know what your constitution is like." Laura tried to resist, for her husband's sake, but a few nights alone in that bed—in the dark—with the creaks in the house and the boys sleeping helplessly and thoughts of Aldo's fate running rampant through her mind—convinced her to pack up their things.

It *was* safer there, in the big city. Her father could protect her; her mother could help with the children. They had real schools and indoor plumbing, and it felt like you didn't have to worry there all the time. But, then again, it wasn't. Because while Le Grotte and Porto Ercole were tiny, wayward hamlets that nobody paid attention to, Porto Santo Stefano was a city of note. And in cities of note, you had Fascist Party organizations. These groups of everyday Italians held rallies and passed out pamphlets, and checked on their neighbors to make sure everyone was saying the right words at the right time. Even her father, respected though he was, had to keep his head down. So when October, 1940 rolled around and Cino turned five, Alberto could only watch as they tried to turn his grandson into his worst nightmare.

"They made me a '*Figlio della Lupa*',"[22] Cino says, "part of a Fascist organization for boys 5-8 years old." Along with his enrollment in Porto Santo Stefano's *asilo*, Cino received free, mandatory admission into the *Gioventù Italiana del Littorio* (GIL), the Italian Fascist Youth Organization. Mussolini's answer to the Hitler Youth, the GIL's sole purpose was to entrench children from an early age in the ways, the words and the will of the Fascist Party. From Figlio della Lupa, nine-year-old boys would graduate to the rank of Balilla, and then Avanguardisto after that. The next step was *Squadristo*—Blackshirt.

The GIL was the Fascist indoctrination machine working at peak capacity. Figlii della Lupa sang songs to Il Duce, did group calisthenics, and chanted *Credere, Obeddire, Combattere* until it rang through their heads. Even the name "Figlio della Lupa" was

---

[22] Son of the She-Wolf

pure propaganda: the *Lupa* was the great mother figure of Italian folklore, the She-Wolf who raised Romulus and Remus to be the founders of Rome. To be her son was to be a great man, a great warrior, a great Italian. And, of course, in those days, to be her son was to be the son of Il Duce—the son of Fascism—the son of the Master Race.

But the most potent form of mind control that Mussolini practiced on his Figlii della Lupa was the *colonia*, or colony. "For us kids," Cino reports, "going to the Figlio della Lupa colony was a kind of vacation. Those who lived by the sea got sent to the mountains, and children from the mountains were sent to the coast. We loved it!" These "vacations" were opportunities for the Fascist Party to further mold the minds of the GIL's children. Away from the influence of their homes and their families, the Figlii della Lupa could be taught that the only family they truly needed was the Party. By the time a Figlio della Lupa came back from the colony, he was hooked; if he advanced to the rank of Balilla or Avanguardisto, he was usually a Fascist for life.

At the time, however, Cino saw none of that future stretched out before him. All he knew was that every day after school he got to put on his special outfit—"a little black cap, a black shirt with two white bands across the chest, and black shorts,"—go with all his friends to the GIL center in Santo Stefano, and march. "They gave us wooden rifles, you know, and we marched just like in the military." Cino's uncles Pietro and Vittorio were card-carrying Fascists, and would sometimes come by the parade grounds and watch their nephew march. Their black shirts consumed the sunlight.

Imagine the frightful visage it made: hundreds of boys marching with toy guns, cheeks rosy and steps delightfully random, squeaky voices piping words they hardly understood. Soon to be men, in lockstep: steel in their eyes, steel in their guns, carrying cartridges of copper and powder, carrying death to democracy in Europe. After just one year, just one trip to the *colonia*, just one time hearing his grandson Cino say, "The Fascists will bring glory back to our country," Alberto Procaccini knew he had made a mistake.

"You have to get them out of here," he told Laura. "Go back to Le Grotte, before it's too late."

She nodded; she was a mother; she knew. Besides, a father commanded and a daughter obeyed. She packed up their things once again and moved back to the home that had stood empty without them.

Spring, 1941. The Greeks have pushed the Italian Army back into Albania, and an angry Adolf is forced to send Nazi troops to do what Mussolini's men cannot. Scrambling to assert Italy's potency before the Germans arrive, Mussolini organizes an all-out assault, which he himself personally oversees. The Spring Offensive lasts for two weeks, and ends in devastation. Italy gains no ground, and loses thousands of soldiers. The Mussolini propaganda machine paints a picture of glorious victory, but word from the front says otherwise. Through coded letters and hushed whispers, the people hear the truth: death tolls ticking higher; artillery cannons blackened and twisted; fighter planes spiraling out of the sky.

For Laura, every day is a torment. She wonders by the hour where her husband is—if they're shooting at him, if he has enough food or warm clothes. Every morning she opens the newspaper to the page where they list the dead soldiers, skimming her finger down the rows looking for *Chegia, Aldo*. Every night she lies awake, wondering what happens to bodies at the bottom of the sea. Something persistent and lingering throbs in her chest; sometimes her heart beats so fast she has to clutch it just to keep it inside.

Then, late one night, a surprise knock at the door. A startle, a shock—a *paura.*[23] Laura leaps from bed, her head woozy with the sudden rush of blood.

"Who is it?" she calls. No response.

Cino, awoken by her call, stumbles out. "Mamma, what is it?"

"Nothing, honey. Now be quiet. Go back to bed."

"But Mom—"

"Shhh, Cino! Now!"

He retreats to his room. She steps toward the door. Her feet fall heavy, heavier. Her breath is ragged and short. She wracks her mind: *who could it be? A robber, a killer? The Navy, come to tell me he's gone?* Holding her heart, she throws open the door—nothing. Nobody. Just the night and the wind.

The next day, Cino rises and wanders the house. It's quiet, empty, cold. Mamma should be up by now, lighting the stove for breakfast. Where's Mamma? He peeks through her door.

"Mamma? You there?"

"…Cino," croaks the reply. "Cino, come here."

She's in bed, covers drawn to her chin. Her face is pale, almost green. Her hand shakes as she holds it out to him.

"Cino. Go…next door. Tell her to fetch *Zia*[24] Gina…tell her I need…" and she closes her eyes, and she falls back to sleep.

Cino turns on his heel and dashes next door, pounding like whoever it was last night. A middle-aged woman flings it open.

"What?"

"Zia Arduina! I—my mom…she's sick. She's in bed and she's all green. She says you need to get Zia Gina now. Hurry, please!"

---

[23] Fright
[24] Aunt

Arduina gasps and runs down the stairs. A few minutes later she and Gina return, running at top speed into Laura's bedroom. Gina grabs a glass of water and splashes it on her sister's face— Laura comes to with heaves and sobs.

"Hospital…" she mutters. Gina and Arduina each throw one of her arms around their shoulders and hoist her off the bed.

Cino stands in the doorway, watching, saying nothing. From his bedroom, he can hear Alberto crying and rattling the bars of his crib, frightened by all the commotion.

Gina looks down at her nephew. "We're taking your mother to Grosseto. You stay here and look after your brother until I get back. Don't you *dare* leave, and don't you think about opening the door unless it's for me or your grandparents. Understand?"

Cino nods, his eyes like bowls of shimmering water. Above him, his mother mumbles, half-conscious. They stagger out the door. Cino watches them all the way down the steps, around the corner, and to the *carrozza*[25] stop at the top of the hill before he loses them out of sight.

Hours later, Zia Gina returns with her parents by her side. Their eyes are red and puffy, and they cling to each other like sailors on a sinking ship.

"Cino, Alberto," says Alberto Procaccini. "There's something I have to tell you."

"It was the biggest and saddest event of my life," Cino reflects. What else could it have been? The silence afterwards. The emptiness. The shaking of heads, the wringing of hands. His grandfather, proud, strong, sobbing like a child for his beloved baby girl, lost at age 26. They would never learn what killed her; in those days, they had no way of knowing. "A *paura,* a fright."

---

[25] Carriage. *La Carrozza* was a horse-drawn carriage that took passengers to the Orbetello train station from Porto Ercole and Porto Santo Stefano.

That's all they could say. Just a *malaccio*[26]—one of so many things that could not be named back then, that no one could even see until they rose up and revealed themselves, fully formed. Memories of times when she could not keep up with her sons, when she had to sit down and catch her breath to stop the dizziness. Road signs to a destination no one knew they were reaching, beyond whose borders lay a pain and a confusion none could even yet fathom.

They held the funeral at Zia Gina's house, the boys sitting apart from the mourners, holding hands. "I remember…crying in a corner without knowing the reason why," Cino notes.

Alberto, pushing three years old, fidgeted in his oversized, hand-me-down suit. "I want to go home," he whispered. "Where's Mommy?"

Cino just stared down at the floor and wiped his eyes.

After the service, the townspeople passed by and caressed the boys' faces. "What poor darlings," they said. "It would have been better if the Lord had taken these two children as well."

"I understood what they meant and, tucking one hand under my other arm, made the sign of the Devil's horns at these people," Cino continues. When Alberto asked what he was doing, "I said— when the people do like that…say the heck with you! Curse them." That day, Cino made a vow: no one would ever wish him or his little brother any harm without facing the consequences. Not friend nor foe, not young nor old—no one. He was the man of the house now, and he would look after his brother no matter what.

But Cino, all of five years old, couldn't take care of Alberto— that was obvious. He couldn't even take care of himself. And there was no way the Navy let Aldo go home just because his wife had died; they hadn't even let him come back for the funeral. So, then, the question: where are these boys going to live? Both families

---

[26] Grave illness

were stretched thin already—times were tight and there was a war on. And it was one thing to take in one growing boy, but two?

"Look at our house!" Doretti yelled to Alberto Procaccini. "Look how many people are in this tiny little shoebox already. You want me to take on two more? We'll all starve!"

"It's not like we're much better off!" Alberto retorted. "You think anyone pays the daziere when it's all gone to crap? I've got kids of my own moving back in, and bills I can't afford, and—" and here he would stop, and swallow, and swallow, and clench his jaw—"I don't know if I can. Not both of them. It's too soon."

So there was only one way to go after that—only one way that made any sense. "The boys will see each other on weekends," they reasoned. "It's just down the road." Then they turned to the brothers, still entwined and bewildered. "Come with me, Cino," said Doretti. "Come with me, Albertino," said Alberto.

There was likely no audible tear. The sound of two lives diverging is usually more of a murky silence, sheepish glances and cleared throats. But Cino could still feel the way they pried Albertino from his arms, and he could see the look on his brother's face as they carried him out the door, and he could smell the focaccia burning in the oven and he could taste something bitter and elusive. As he watched the Procaccini clan lead Alberto out of the house and along the road to Porto Santo Stefano, he felt that this was the worst possible thing they could have done in the whole world, because he had just started to understand what's so important about brothers—why you hold onto them and how they can be taken from you just like that, just like everything else. And he guessed he knew something about having things taken from him now, too, because it seemed like all he had left was his anger.

Cino wasn't the only one nursing the embers of rage in his belly, though. Walking home with his grandson in his arms, Alberto Procaccini held onto something else, as well. Everyone said it was a fright that took his beloved Laura from him, but Alberto knew better. It was that cad, Aldo. He had never been the right match for her. Too mischievous, too fickle. A gambler, a drinker, a womanizer in his younger days—a womanizer still, he suspected. At any rate, an impermanent sort of man, who came and went with the tide. Not the sort to take care of his beautiful, fair, innocent daughter—the sort to leave her in her grave while he played Navy man hundreds of miles away. Never mind that it was his duty. Never mind that he had been told, not asked. For the first time in his life, Alberto Procaccini found himself bereft of logic— or, perhaps, outside it, beyond it. He wrapped this torment, this unreasoning hate, around himself and his grandson like a blanket.

Cino watched until he couldn't see them anymore, then turned back to his new home. The Chegia family looked at him with tender compassion: Doretti and Doretta; Alcide (unmarried and unfit for the war); Faustina and her two children, Santina and Giulio. Cino tried to swallow the anger, for their sakes. They meant well; he would try. It would be hard, but he would try.

At first, things didn't go well. Cino was still only five years old, and after the funeral found himself with little to do and a lot on his mind. He raised hell in L'Ospizio, until Doretta got so fed up that she sent him outside to raise hell somewhere else. He stole food from markets, stuck out his tongue and used his fists when his words would do fine. It was then that he first discovered the whip of Doretta's *vipera* tongue, the sound her wooden clog made when she flung it at his head. In Le Grotte in 1941, there was no time to mourn and no patience for acting out.

What saved Cino in those days was soccer. Like all Italians, he was born with the sport in his blood, but it wasn't until then that he found it in his legs, his lungs, his eyes. Hungry for the ball like a hawk for a mouse. Watching, waiting, ready to strike. Moving fast, seeking the goal. Thinking of nothing else. Just the goal: something real and definitive, with a beginning and an end. Not like a war. Constant, not like life—just one point, every time. No surprises. They played in a small field by the marina, where the statue of a World War I soldier now stands. They played barefoot, with a balled-up sock or some newspaper wrapped in tape or whatever they could find that would roll on the ground. All that mattered was the game.

In those days, too, Cino started to work. His quick temper wasn't the only reason that he went with the Chegia family while Alberto went with the Procaccini: the other was that Doretti desperately needed help on the boat, and Cino was old enough to lend a hand. He wasn't big enough to cast the net or sort fish on the deck of the boat, but he could certainly learn a thing or two about the trade. So most days, in the waning afternoon light, Doretti would call Cino into the courtyard and teach him how to clean a lantern or darn a net, pinching the weave between his chubby child's fingers and threading through the hole so that the fish couldn't escape. "You let one out, all the rest will follow," Doretti advised.

In that way, the days passed. School let out for the summer of 1941 and resumed again in the fall. The war raged on with no sign of stopping. Cino turned six and there was a party, but it was not a happy one and he didn't think much of it. He saw his brother on weekends, as they had promised, and every time it seemed like Alberto was a little bit bigger and a little bit different. He talked more like a Procaccini, pronouncing every consonant and syllable. His hair was combed and neat. But, still, they raced each other down the *lungomare*, cracked jokes, played jacks, threw sticks at the Egg Man who zipped his scooter through Porto Santo Stefano every day. They were still brothers, still kids, despite it all.

One of the best parts of Cino's trips to Santo Stefano was the ride there. In those days, there was a steam train that ran from Orbetello to Porto Santo Stefano. Cino would pick it up on the outskirts of town and ride it through a tunnel dug right out of the hillside, whooping and hollering in the inky darkness. The smoke from the coal engine hung thick in the tunnel—so if you were a boy of five or six and you stuck your head out of the train just then, you'd come out the other side with your face and hair all covered with soot. Then, when you arrived at the station, you could shake it off like a dog and spray it all over your brother or uncle or grandmother. Eventually, Nonna Rosa started greeting him there him with a towel held out in front of her like a shield.

In December of 1941, word got around about some big surprise bombing on the other side of the world. Folks in town said that the Japs had hit a Navy base on some islands, and that these guys called *Americani* were sure to declare war soon. Many seemed scared, but Doretti rubbed his hands together in glee. "The sleeping bear has awoken," he said. Cino wondered for a moment who these Americani were and why Nonno was so excited about a bear, but then his friends came by with a real-life soccer ball they had found, and he was out the door and onto the field in a flash.

CHAPTER FIVE: THE WAR COMES HOME

"Testa di cavolo!"[27]
- Italian insult

Spring, 1943. A hand clamps down on Cino's prone body, leather-brown and strong as a vise. He struggles against it but it grips him harder, shaking violently. The soft, beautiful world slips from his grasp.

"Why?" he whispers.

"Why? Somebody's got to get your lazy butt out of bed, don't they? Or are you just going to lay there like a potato, until you grow roots out of your eyes and someone comes along and eats you for dinner? Huh?"

"Not now, Nonna…"

"Not now! Not now! Every day it's, 'Not now, I don't wanna, just give me a few more minutes!' Did you know that your cousins

---

[27] "Cabbage head!"

have already been up for an hour, helping their mother in the yard?" Cino did know that, in fact—they all slept in the same bed. It's just that he was better at it than they were.

"Fine. I'm up." Cino putters to the bathroom, Doretta right on his heels.

"Did you know that Santina is getting top marks in asilo? *Maestra*[28] says she's ahead of everyone else. Do you know what Maestra says about you?"

Suddenly, Doretta stops short. Cino springs awake. A high-pitched wail from the kitchen pierces them both like a lightning bolt. Grandmother and grandson race down the hall, praying that it isn't what they think it is. But somehow they already knew.

Faustina sits at the table, children on her knees, newspaper laid out before her. She curls around them, shivering tears. "No, no, no, *amore mio...*"

Doretta rushes to her side. "Show me the paper—where is it? Show me. Faustina, show me!"

Faustina points. There, among the hundreds of names printed every day, of Italian servicemen killed in action. *Scotto, Giovanni.* Faustina's husband; Cino's uncle; Santina and Giulio's father. A Navy man like Aldo, conscripted by Mussolini, ripped from his family to fight and die for the good of the Fascist state. Doretta studies the page for typos, smudges—any flaw, any mistake. Nothing. *Scotto, Giovanni.* There it is.

"I am so, so sorry," Doretta mutters, "my beautiful daughter, my beloved grandchildren...I am so, so sorry." She hugs Faustina, Santina, and Giulio tightly, and they sob into her shirtsleeves.

---

[28] Teacher

In town, the attack was all you heard about. The horror of it, the wretchedness. A convoy set upon by Allied planes, sunk to the bottom of the sea. Hundreds of good men were gone—husbands and fathers, fishermen and sailors, who were just trying to do right by their country. Monte Argentario men, too, not just Giovanni Scotto. Nearly everybody lost someone that day. People kicked up the dust in the streets, hoping it would take the shape of the one who had died.

"The Americans," said the Fascists. "They dropped the bombs that killed our boys. Could have even been some Italians in those planes, immigrants they brainwashed into returning home and killing their own people. Remember this day, *paesani.*[29] Remember what they've done to us. *Ave Maria, piena di grazia...*"

That name again, that word that seemed to stir so much anger and sadness and awe. *Americani.* What did it mean? Why did people look so heavy when they said it? Cino felt something mythic hovering about these bears of men, and though he still wasn't sure whether to curse them or cheer them, he wouldn't soon forget the sound of that name.

On that day, it all became real. The fighting and the destruction and the death, it wasn't just the stuff of newsreels anymore—this was war, real war, with real people who walked and talked. People like Cino's own uncle, whose face he knew but would never see again. Father to the boy and girl who shared his bed, who now had only their mother left to guide and protect them. And now Cino was thinking of his own babbo, hoping that he was safe wherever he was, wondering what sound Nonna would make if *Chegia, Aldo* ever turned up in those papers. Americans, Nazis, Il Duce, La Lupa; bombs and ships and guns and fire; the deep-sea cold, the ambulance's keen; Faustina curled around her babies, like a rose unblooming. This was the world now.

---

[29] Countrymen

From that day on, everything changed. Word spread like the sound of jackboots, the squeal of treads: the Allies were on the move, and the Germans were coming. Mussolini could no longer hold his own line, defend his own country against the enemy. Hitler's ally had become his burden, and he sent his stormtroopers into Italy to shoulder the load. They swept down from the north, digging out batteries on the rapturous cliffs of Le Cinqueterre and stocking ammunition in fortresses that hadn't seen war since people fought it on horseback. The soldiers seized what they needed and told the ragged farmers to put it on Il Duce's bill—which, they assured, would come due soon. Few mourned the thought.

As the Wehrmacht inched down the Boot leaving a sap-like residue behind, the laces tightened in Monte Argentario. The Allies were building up in North Africa, preparing to cross the Mediterranean and invade Italy. And all signs were pointing to La Feniglia as a landing site.

"The Americans love landing on beaches," folks said. "You see what they did in the Far East, you see what they did in North Africa. Where is there more beach than La Feniglia? Besides, landing here gives them a straight shot to Rome. They'll bring their battleships and launch their little landing craft, and the Krauts will set up in Forte Filippo and rain fire down on them, machine guns and artillery like you've never seen. So many fish dead, and so many men. We just better be damn well sure we get out of the way when they come."

Before they could begin preparations, however, an unexpected skirmish broke out. For years, Fascists and Republicans in Monte Argentario had maintained an uneasy détente, squaring off on street corners but falling short of an all-out clash. The impending invasion brought with it an ultimatum: choose a side and live with the consequences. It was just the spark that the powder keg needed.

One day, it erupted. Fascist forces charged up the steep cliff behind Le Grotte and stormed fully armed into Forte Filippo. They ran their flag up the pole to announce their arrival: the *fasces* standing starkly out from the black background, with an axe blade sticking out at a sharp ninety-degree angle, like a man flexing violently. Cino watched from below, wondering exactly whom the Blackshirts planned to fight from their vaunted position overlooking the sea.

He didn't have to wait long to find out. Cino awoke that night to the crackle of gunfire: small arms mostly, and far off, but enough to make a seven-year-old leap from his bed and dive under the covers between his nonno and nonna.

"Who are they?" he asked from down by their knees.

"*Partigiane*," said Doretti.

"Partigiane?"

"Partisan fighters: bands of rebels fighting for Italy's freedom. They've been gathering in the woods, raiding Nazi convoys and the like, making things hard on Hitler. Getting ready for what's to come, I guess. Tell ya what, I'd go out there and fight with them if I weren't such an old man."

Outside, the crackle intensified into a flurry of bursts and short, muffled explosions. Cino curled up even tighter.

By morning, the fascists had fended off the partisans, and the rebels defiantly but prudently settled into La Rocca. For months after that, the two sides stared each other down from across the cove, lofting stray bullets and the occasional mortar round from one fort to the other. Neither side had the manpower nor the weaponry to take the other's position, and neither had much interest in dying before the real fighting began. So they rattled their sabers through the stalemate, each on high alert—not so much for the other as for which army would arrive first. If the Nazis crossed from the mainland before the Allies arrived, Forte Filippo would erupt and La Rocca would burn. If the Allied armada appeared on the horizon, the fascists would be advised to get out of Filippo while they still had a chance.

"We have to be ready to leave here," said Doretti one day. "Once they come, whoever comes, it won't be safe. Keep a bag packed, and when I say so, we'll go to Pietro and Jenny's farmhouse. I've already talked to them—they said we can stay in their barn."

"When will they come, Nonno?" asked Cino, breathless.

"Nobody knows, *nipote.*[30] When they come, they come, and that will be that."

He was right. They came when they came, and that was that. Cino stood by the road with his eyes wide as saucers, the whole town stretched out behind him, huddled together like strange tufts of wheat. It was the Germans, in tanks and trucks. They brought with them guns as big as houses, that looked like they could tear a hole right out of the sky. The shells alone were as long as his arm. Behind the trucks, a long line of men, with green helmets and buttons that gleamed, and black epaulettes on their drab green-gray uniforms. They carried their rifles against their shoulders; the barrels cut slivers into the hillside behind them. Cino wondered if they had once learned on wooden sticks, as he had.

At the fork in the road, the commander directed his men. The main force went north, to Porto Santo Stefano—Cino said a quick Hail Mary for his brother and grandparents. The rest turned south, to Porto Ercole and Le Grotte, preparing for the Allied invasion. There was a pine grove on the edge of La Feniglia, and there the men pulled out shovels and dug holes in the sand. The big guns—

---

[30] Grandson/daughter (also means nephew/niece)

Ottantotti,[31] people called them—went into an empty field higher up the hillside, where the fair used to set up when it came into town. The SS set up its headquarters in Forte Filippo; the partigiane got the hell out of La Rocca. The Nazis shut down the train and dumped ammo in the tunnel, rebuilt a dormant torpedo factory in Santo Stefano, and started landing seaplanes on Lake Orbetello. They set up curfews, posted men on the docks, and eyed the young ladies like caged tigers. Then they waited. They all waited.

On July 10, 1943, the battle for Italy began. The Allies landed—in Sicily, not Tuscany—and pushed north like Garibaldi had 100 years earlier. The Italian and German armies retreated to the sole of the Boot, while the Sicilians hung American flags from their windows and sang lusty songs of liberation.

Meanwhile, in Rome, the Mussolini government fell apart. With the Allies at the door and the Wehrmacht occupying more and more of the country, the Fascist Party had had enough of Italy's Supreme Leader. On July 25, the Grand Council of Fascism voted to remove Il Duce from power and restore full constitutional authority to King Vittorio Emanuele III. The next day, King Emanuele dismissed Mussolini as Prime Minister of Italy—just like that, the reign of Benito Mussolini was over. Across the country, the cheers and the cries both deafened.

From then, it was only a matter of time before Italy bowed out of the war completely. For about a month the government maintained that the country still fought for the Axis, but secretly plotted a separate peace with the Allies. Finally, on September 3, 1943, a secret envoy from new Prime Minister Badoglio met with General Dwight D. Eisenhower in Sicily and offered him the full, unconditional surrender of the combined Italian Armed Forces.

---

[31] Eighty-eights

They made the announcement on September 8, and Italy went wild. Flags flew, confetti fell, and from Naples to Venice there was dancing in the streets. Even Cino, approaching his eighth birthday at the time, remembers it well. "All over town people laughed, shouted, and kissed one another. Everyone was happy and said that the war was finally over."

They were wrong. On September 9, the gunfire began. Across Europe, German soldiers turned their guns on their Italian allies, taking over one million prisoners in a matter of days—including a Navy patrolman named Aldo Chegia. On the Greek island of Cephalonia, the twelve thousand men of the Italian *Acqui* Division fought back against the Wehrmacht, banding together with local Greeks against a German siege. Fifteen hundred Italian soldiers were killed in the fighting; the German Army executed over five thousand more.

At home, the black shirts came out, shoulder to shoulder with Nazi gray and green. From the hills, from the woods, from the countryside poured the partisan fighters: Communists and Socialists and Catholic Democrats, all united in their hatred for anything reeking of Il Duce. Skirmishes broke out on the hills of Tuscany, on the beaches of Liguria, in the mountain crags of Le Apennine. Eisenhower and Badoglio called for Italian citizens to stand up against their German oppressors and occupiers. German broadcasters railed against the "treacherous intrigue which for weeks had been enacted by an Italian clique, serfs to Jews and alien to their own people." Ordinary people drew back from open windows, and mothers rushed children to their homes. The streets fell abandoned once more, silent in the pregnant hush of joy quickly deserted.

The Nazis, as it turned out, were prepared for Italy's "open treason." Since July 25, Hitler had begun laying the groundwork for an immediate German/Italian Fascist takeover, moving five more infantry divisions into the country. Despite strong opposition from partisan forces, the Nazis sprang Mussolini from prison, and in October of that year declared Northern Italy—including Monte Argentario—a new Fascist nation called the *Repubblica Sociale Italiana*[32]. The RSI's first order of business: declare war on Southern Italy and its allies. The Italian Civil War had begun.

---

[32] Social Republic of Italy

CHAPTER SIX: FIRE ON THE MOUNTAIN

"Dopo il primo bombardamento, al paese non ci voleva stare nessuno."[33]
- Cino Chegia

November, 1943. When that first blast hits you—whoa. It'll knock you right out of your shoes. You could be running at it full speed, you know, and it'll just fling you right back the way you came. Like a doll or something; like a leaf in the breeze.

Cino huddles against the wall of Giulia's store, watching the nightmare unfold. His head pounds, his heart charges; his eyes are blurry and his nose stung with smoke. Everywhere there is running, and screaming, and crying, and blood—is that blood?— on the cracked cobblestone of the piazza, where those boys had been playing just minutes ago… He claws to his feet, rubs his eyes, looks around. A deep gouge in the stone piazza, like the first scoop out of a tub of gelato. Bricks and shattered wood cast about, among

---

[33] "After the first bombardment, no one wanted to stay in town."

the bodies, among the groaning. Men and women stumbling about, gasping, calling out in ragged voices. The groaning below, the groaning above…the bombers trundle along in their slow loop, as if they hadn't even noticed. Morning sunlight glints off the American flag.

"Run, boy, run! May be more coming!" yells a man galloping by. His hat is all askew on his head, twisted around as if to get one last look at the wreckage. His eyebrows are gone, and a chunk from his cheek. *Yes*, Cino thinks. *It's time to run.*

November, 1943. Ten minutes earlier. Cino trips and trots down to Giulia's store, whistling to friends and neighbors. He has just turned eight years old—not much of a celebration this year, but still, he's young and the day is fine and he has grown used to the sight of guns, so he takes his time picking up the whatever it was Nonna asked him to pick up, and he pets a dog ambling by and he kicks a soccer ball back to some boys playing in the piazza, and he listens to the sound of the birds in the trees.

Suddenly, the birds take to wing. In a tumult, all at once. The sirens blare from Forte Filippo: wwWWWOOOOOOOOOO AAAAAAAAAAHHHH-AAAAAOOOOooooo. People stop, look up, and laugh. How long has this been going on now? How many days, how many weeks, all sirens and no planes? The first time it happened they had fled for the hills: grabbed their bags, hunkered down in the olive groves, and waited. Nothing. The planes never came, and the planes never came—and who could blame them, because what was there to bomb in Porto Ercole, anyway? Just a few Germans with some really big artillery. So eventually, people stopped listening to the air-raid siren, or at best wrinkled their noses at its bray while they went about their business. On the piazza that day, the boys don't even look up from their match.

The roar of the propellers changes everything. Two props—no, four—no, eight—thundering down from Corsica, around the curve of the coastline, giant hawks with wings outstretched. Traced in their arc by hundreds of eyes, and the sights of anti-aircraft guns caught by surprise—still spooling, still training, too late. Their bellies open; people scream and scatter for cover. They drop their loads tenderly, silent from such a distance—tumbling down like weights on a line, like a net cast to trap *pesce*[34] in the deep.

The first bomb hits just north of the cliff walls, in Cala Galera. Dirt and rock spew out in a plume; the ground shakes beneath Cino's feet. He plugs his ears and inches toward the wall of the store, feeling suddenly like a very young, very small boy. The second smacks dead-center in the piazza, less than a hundred meters away. An arm's reach from where the other boys had just been playing. The blast hurls Cino back into the wall, and all is screams, and blood, and smoke.

———————

Cino ran to the olive grove, where he knew the townspeople would gather. He cast about frantically for a familiar face: his grandfather's bald head or his uncle Alcide's hunched back, or even Pietro's *camicia nera*.[35] He heard his name, saw a tall woman barrel toward him and snatch him into her arms. "Oh, my grandson, I thought I lost you."

They arranged to leave town immediately, to take shelter in Pietro and Jenny's farmhouse nearby. They would wait out the fighting there, they said. Probably wouldn't be more than a few weeks before the Americans took Rome. Soon after that, they would storm across Lake Orbetello and force the Germans off La Feniglia—or just blow them all sky-high, for all anyone cared.

———————

[34] Fish
[35] Black shirt

Pietro and Jenny put them up in the barn, because there wasn't room for them all in the house. Doretta clucked at the piled hay and lowing cows, but she said nothing: better here than out in the trees, where a lot of their friends were forced to wait out the fighting. They settled into the hayloft as best they could, ready to weather the storm. It wouldn't be long now.

One month later, reality set in. Once the bombs started falling, they didn't stop: day after day, night after night, until the air raid warning became as regular as the tolling of the church clock. The Allied army had been stopped in its advance, and was still a long way from Rome—meanwhile, German ships had begun taking shelter in Porto Ercole's cove whenever the seas got too rough. "While the Germans were docked, nobody in the town was safe," Cino remembers. The partisans—now backed by the Allies and known as the Italian Co-Belligerent Army—would send word to the base on Corsica, and soon the sirens would sound and the engines would rumble. American planes during the day, English bombers at night. Bringing the dull thuds that paced out those days, the only reliable thing left.

Between one bombing and the next, life continued as best it could. The adults organized a system to distribute food, and when the coast was clear Doretti and others would go fishing, tentatively and with one eye cast out at the horizon. People salvaged whatever they could from the rubble, finding old pots and pans caked in the dust of their former walls. Cino and his cousins picked wood for the fire and herbs for the rabbits; Doretta made bread whenever she could rustle up a little flour. "There was never much, but there was always enough," Cino says.

After a while, the Fascist government stepped in and built *cappanne* for the displaced townspeople: little canvas huts just big enough for an Italian family, which they nestled in a nearby olive grove to protect from bombings. The Chegias moved out of the barn and into a cappanna of their own, gathering what they could from the remains of L'Ospizio. Cino found a nook he could call his own, set a photo of his mother by his bedroll and took stock of their surroundings. It wasn't much, but it would have to do.

One night in the cappanna, Cino asked his uncle Vittorio about the Americans. Vittorio had fought in the War, and been injured by shrapnel from an American bomb, so Cino figured he knew better than anyone what those guys were all about.

"Why does everyone talk about them so funny, like they're our own people or something?" he asked.

"A lot of them are our people," Vittorio replied. "America's a country of immigrants. You know what an immigrant is?" Cino shook his head no. "It's someone who moves far away to start a new life somewhere else. A lot of people in America moved there from all over the world, including from here, from Italy. Most of the folks in town know someone who moved there, some not even too long ago. So in a way, it feels like there's a little bit of Italy over there."

"So then why are they bombing us?" Cino asked.

Vittorio bristled. "Well…because they don't like us very much, I guess. And we don't like them very much either, now do we? Do we, Cino?"

Cino shrugged. One minute everyone said the Americans were the Devil, the next they were coming to save the day. Now, it seemed like they fought for the good guys—the guys his nonni thought were good, at least—but every day they dropped death on innocent people. Were these the heroes he was looking for, or the enemy Vittorio wanted them to be? The more he thought about it, the more it confused him, and no one seemed able to give him a straight answer.

No one, that is, except the *Americani* themselves. "The Americans…didn't only drop bombs, but also pamphlets," he recalls. These fluttering scraps of paper, falling to Earth like Vesuvian ash, told him everything he needed to know. *Stand strong, brothers and sisters*, it read, *all this will be over soon. We will rid your land of the Fascist scourge and you will be free. Viva la libertà.*

"They had me convinced," says Cino. "Every time there was a bombing we would run up a hill and watch the bombs that fell on our town and in the water. …I asked myself time and again where these planes came from, and who the people were who flew them. From that moment on, I began to dream of a faraway land I had never seen."

While Cino watched the sky clamor with wings and flak and tracer rounds, Doretta kept her eyes on the horizon. She never said why, really, but she was always looking, around, beyond and behind everyone, as if expecting something or someone to materialize there. And then someone did.

They were sipping *brodo* outside the cappanna, enjoying the stillness that sometimes punctuated the terror, when they saw him coming up from the road. His skin was creased by the sun, plastered with dirt; his beard was long and ragged like a hermit's. That roguish half-grin he always wore, that mercenary sneer that at times melted into playful mischief, was nowhere to be found. In its place was a thin red line.

But still, it was him. Cino dropped his bowl. "Babbo!" he cried as he dashed. The thin red line widened and broke, bowing into a toothy smile. Aldo knelt down and wrapped his son into his arms, stroking his hair, crying as he laughed.

"My son," he said. "How much you've grown."

Cino led his father to the cappanna, where the rest of the family stood waiting. Doretta, who had seen him coming before any of the others, held her back straight, her chin high and dignified. When she reached for him, though, her hands shook like Cino had never seen before.

"Sit!" she ushered. "*Mangia.*"

She ladled broth and broke bread and the Chegias gathered around Aldo, yearning for the wandering knight's tale. For a moment, he just sat and slurped. Then he looked at them as if from a lifting fog, as if from a great, calamitous distance.

"I suppose you want to know where I've been all this time," he said.

The Tale of Aldo Chegia

"They tooks us prisoner in August, after the surrender. Sure you heard about that. Tens of thousands, maybe millions of us, all at once. Nobody knew what the hell was going on. One day we're at war with the Americans, next day the Nazi dogs are boarding our ships, guns in our faces, ordering us to go with them or they'd shoot us where we stood." He paused; no one spoke.

"We went with them, you know? What else could we do? The war was over for us at that point. Nobody wanted to fight anymore. So they chain us up, one to the other, and make us walk, kilometer after kilometer, until we get to a train station. They put us on these trains—crammed in there like cattle, stinking to high heaven—and take us all the way up to Germany. Somewhere outside Munich, I think. Then they say, 'Okay boys, get to work!'

"We were working in a munitions factory, making bullets we knew would go straight to the front. Hundreds, thousands of men, working like slaves: hot, cramped, no food, no water…" he shuddered without knowing he had.

"After a while, they come back around and say, 'Had enough yet? Come fight with us and you can leave here right now!' Few of them guys went with 'em, said their Heil Hitlers and all that, but I told 'em I'd break rocks a million years before I linked up with scum like them."

Vittorio coughed, but Aldo didn't notice. Doretti handed him a wineskin and he took a deep, grateful pull.

"So this whole time we're living in this little village not far from the factory. Stone houses and all, not too different from...well..." he gestured out over the smoldering town. "And they have us camped out in these tents out in the field and, well, one day when no one's looking, me an' some other guys just made a run for it! They tracked down a few of us—shot 'em right there—but me and the rest made it across this little creek and then into the woods, and eventually we lost 'em. Hid out there for a few days watching the camp, watching the roads, waiting for 'em to come for us, but they just didn't. Guess they had too much else going on to worry about a few sad sacks like us.

"So we started walking. Hitched rides when we could, once we got on friendlier ground. Worked our way down here sleeping in ditches, finding food where we could, stealing it when we needed to...not proud of that, but we did what we had to do. Made it to Italy a few days ago, took the train to Grosseto and here I am!" He scratched his beard, cracked a half-hearted smile and held his hand out for the wine.

No one knew quite what to say, for once. Then Vittorio leaned forward, elbows on his knees.

"He had no choice, you know? Hitler. What else was he going to do? Mussolini can't hold his own, and then here comes the Grand Council to stab him in the back...that Pietro Badoglio, if I ever lay eyes on him...they betrayed him, you know? Our Great Leader, after all he's done for us! Turn around and make peace with the Americans, let them onto our soil…it's betrayal, plain and simple."

Aldo wheeled on his little brother. "Betrayal? The only person I know betrayed anyone is Mussolini, when he convinced all us suckers that he knew how to get anything done. Whose side are you on, anyway?"

"*My* side!" roared Pietro, rising. Their matching black shirts drank in the fading light. "The side of Italy, of glory, of *Mare Nostrum*! Mussolini was a fool, sure. Couldn't win a battle if the other guys had rocks and sticks. But Fascism can still save us, brother. We can still hold strong if we pledge our fealty. Show Hitler that Italy still stands…still stands for something. Join us, Aldo. Fight for your country now—for the first time, perhaps."

Aldo stared at his brothers, wild and wide. His beard sucked up the last drops of broth in his bowl. Then he started to laugh: slow at first, a low growl, that built up speed and strength until the dirt lines cracked and his browning teeth showed, and his eyes bulged from their sockets like a *commedia dell'arte* mask.

"What am I, an idiot?" he shouted. "What did I just tell you? Once was more than enough for me. You boys can throw lives away with that bunch of psychopaths, fine. I won't try to stop you. March in the streets, sing your songs, threaten your own neighbors—do whatever it is you people like to do." His tone darkened. "But if you *ever* try to get me, or one of my sons, to become a drone like you again, you will pay a very dear price."

"Watch yourselves, brothers," he said, and he walked out onto the twilit hillside.

———————

With the turn of 1944, the bombings only got worse. Waves of planes like clockwork, dropping their payloads, watching the flumes of water and earth spout back up at them. More and bigger ships, for the Germans—more and bigger guns in the grove, more and bigger roars from the belching barrels. No one laughed at the air-raid sirens now—they just ran as fast as they could. Once the coast was clear, though, they turned right back around, returning to the marina to finish whatever they had started. They were brave in their steadfastness, in the small ways they kept hold of their lives, and Cino was proud to be among them.

That's why it was so hard for him to watch his father, in those first few weeks and months. After that first argument with his brothers, he seemed to fold in on himself, like a sail that no longer caught the wind. He started getting up early in the morning to go sit by a nearby haystack, waiting for his friends to arrive. Soon they would—Siro, Adulio, Attillo, and Settimo—and they'd pull out cards and wine and bags of rolling tobacco, and for hours the men would sit and play poker. They spoke little, like old friends, like men who would rather not say what's on their mind. They just played cards by the haystack until it was too dark to see, and then Aldo would come home, sip his *brodo* and gaze at his son.

The people who passed by them cursed them, hauling their lives on their backs. "Get up, lazy bums!" they called out, but the men paid them no mind. Eventually, the townspeople gave them a nickname: *Gli Uccelli del Pagliaio*—The Birds of the Haystack.

One day, when there wasn't much else to do—and there usually wasn't much else to do in those days—Cino sat down by the haystack and watched the men play cards. He admired his father's subtle, sure movements, betraying nothing. He watched how his eyes beckoned his opponents to make the first move, to slip and fall into his trap. Playing cards brought out a certain mischief in Aldo, a sense of recklessness and cunning, that both entranced Cino and frightened him at the same time.

As Aldo was about to lure Settimo into a losing bet, however, the siren blared. All around them, people dropped their things and ran to the tent city, not looking back. The Birds, too, rose and set their shoulders, then took off—not to the cappanne, but down toward the marina!

"Babbo, where are you going?" Cino shouted. But Aldo was already gone. As the moan of the bombers rose in the distance, Cino retreated to the cappanna, wondering what his crafty father was up to now.

The next time the siren went off, Cino dashed out to the haystack. The men were rising once again, dusting themselves off.

Cino clung to his father. "Babbo, can I come with you, please? Wherever you're going, I can help. Please let me come.".

Aldo laughed and peeled Cino off. "Not a chance, son. Stay up here with your nonna." Then he and the Birds trotted down to the water, just as they had done before.

Cino didn't stay with his nonna: he raced to a low hillock overlooking the cove, where the other boys gathered to watch the battles unfold. They were already there, pointing north.

"They're coming in close!" the boys shouted.

And they were—closer than Cino had ever seen them before."They were flying so low that we could read the numbers on the planes and see the pilots' faces!" he remembers. Nearby, the German anti-aircraft guns spun in their sandbag dugouts, unleashing a chug-chug cacophony of shells streaking into the sky. The fighter pilots nimbly wove in and out, and Cino could have sworn that one of them nodded at him as he passed. He waved and whistled, thinking once again of the far-off land of stars and stripes.

Suddenly, Ciccia Nera jolted them all. "Over there!" He

pointed in the opposite direction: two German fighters, flying low, flying fast. Straight at the American pilots.

"They began to shoot at my beloved Americans, and a dogfight developed," Cino continues. "We kids watched it all. One of the bombers started trailing smoke behind it, and began to fall into the sea. Seconds later, four dots exited the plane, and we could see above them what looked like four white balls. It was the pilots of the bomber, who had ejected from the plane—we watched as the wind pushed them out to sea."

Cino and his friends raced home, screaming to their families to send help, to call in the partisans—to do something, anything, before it was too late. Their families just hugged them and told them to stay in the cappanne until the all-clear sounded.

That day, Aldo came home later than usual. Cino stood by the cappanna until he saw his father approach, stooped and walking slowly. It seemed like something hung on his shoulders, weighing him down...something that trailed behind him, sopping wet. Cino watched, bewildered, as Aldo pulled up to the hut and dropped his load in a heap.

"Babbo, what are these? What did you do?" He bent over to pull at the material, like bundled white sheets...white sheets but heavy, canvas-like, strung with firm ropes of braided nylon. White like the balls Cino had seen float out to sea, carrying men's lives in their grasp...

"Wait, are these the—from the four—what's going *on* here, Babbo? You have to tell me!"

Aldo looked down at his son blankly, like he had just noticed him. "Okay," he said. "But you can't tell a soul, not even your friends. And definitely not your uncles."

The Tale of Gli Uccelli del Pagliaio

"Those guys from the haystack and I, we go way back. Grew up around here, running these hills like you and your friends. Figured we'd live a quiet life just like our parents and grandparents and so on. All did our time in the military, came back, and got shipped back out when the War broke out. We had a hell of a time of it, you know? Taken prisoner, treated bad, wounded, everything. We came back wanting to kill some Fascists for putting us through it all.

"We get back and we're talking about the resistance, about joining the partisans, and Settimo says, 'Listen. I got this boat I've been keeping hidden away—a speedboat. My friend in the ICBA[36] told me the Allies are desperate to rescue their pilots, that every one who gets shot down either winds up captured or killed…they're losing too many men to keep this up.'

"'So what does that have to do with us?' we all said.

"'I want to take my boat down to the water, hide it out in this little spot I know. When they come fly the runs, we can go down there, and if anyone has to bail out we go try to rescue him. See if we can get there before the Krauts do. If we can get them back to shore, the partisans can get them to Corsica. So, you guys in?'

"We all thought about it for, oh, a minute or so, then said, 'Yeah, let's go, let's do this.' We knew it would be dangerous, sure, but we had to try. If we could only save one pilot, it'd be worth it. So we stashed the boat in a grotto down by La Rocca where no one could see it. The partisans gave us guns, ammo, blankets, binoculars. Now, every time the siren goes off we run down there and watch the skies. If a plane goes down, like today, we wait for the parachutes to pop—then we hop in, scoot out to where the pilots are landing, and haul them out of the water. One

---

[36] The Italian Co-Belligerent Army

spots, one drives, two grab the pilots and one stands guard in the back. When we fill up we take them back to the grotto, hide them out til nightfall, and then get them into the woods where the partisans can take them back to Corsica."

Cino's mouth hung open as he processed the news. Aldo sat down on the pile of parachutes.

"We can usually get about half the ones that go down. The other half: most don't make it out of the plane. Others get tangled up in their 'chutes, and it pulls 'em down too deep for us to grab 'em. Few times, Nazi boats have made it out there before we could get there...who knows where those guys are now."

He unwound a set of dog tags from the pocket of his shirt. The tags clinked together like a small, tuneless windchime. "When we find them and they're already...gone...we weigh them down with rocks and take these from around their necks. Someday, when this thing's over, I'm going to give these to their commander, so their families back home can know that they died like men."

He held them out to Cino. Cino ran his fingers over the embossed metal, trying to absorb their memories. All these men, coming from across the sea...giving up everything to fight, to die. For what? For him? He prayed for their wives, for their children.

"I don't want you to worry about me," Aldo said. "I'll be all right. This is just something that I have to do."

Cino nodded, wiped his eyes, and hugged his father harder than he ever had in his life.

CHAPTER SEVEN: THE BEGINNING OF THE END

"Keep Calm and Carry On."
- British World War II motivational poster

June 6, 1944. Adolf Hitler's Nazi army controls much of mainland Europe. In Italy, the Allied advance is slow and arduous, deadlocked with the Wehrmacht and the army of the Italian Social Republic. From Monte Argentario to Moscow, innocent people hold their breath, praying that someone can defeat the forces of Fascism before it's too late.

On H-Hour of D-Day, 155,000 American, British and Canadian infantrymen land on the beaches of Normandy, France, storming the German fortifications. Over 10,000 men die on those shores. Within six days, the Allies have seized a sixty-mile-long stretch of northern France, a front that will allow them to stage attacks across Western Europe and even into the heart of Germany. It is the beginning of the end of the Second World War.

"We're not leaving here," Alberto Procaccini said firmly. "Not until the Nazis bang down our door, stick guns in our faces and make us. I let them scare me off once—I won't do it again."

"Alberto, be reasonable," said his Rosa. "We have the little one to look after. Besides, in Porto Recanati there weren't bombs falling on our heads."

"Not here either! They're just falling...nearby, that's all. They're on our side, Rosa."

"You think I don't know that? But guess what, Alberto: bombs can't tell the difference between a partisan and a paratrooper. Or a child, for that matter."

Alberto spat into his spittoon with a clink. "Still, we're safer here than anywhere else. For now."

Alberto took stock of their house. They had barely stepped outside for months, except to go to the market and to Sunday Mass, which Rosa insisted on attending. It was simply too dangerous— the bombs came too often, and too unpredictably, to brave the outside world for very long. Even when there were no German ships in port, they went after the artillery guns, the supplies in the tunnel, the torpedo factory on the edge of town. It seemed like for every bombing run over Porto Ercole or Orbetello, there were three over Santo Stefano. (In fact, of the 140 sorties the Allies flew over Monte Argentario from 1943-1945, 108 targeted Porto Santo Stefano. An unexploded bomb still stands next to the city's main port, enshrined in concrete—an eternal reminder of the desolation of war.) He wasn't a fool; he knew they couldn't hold out much longer. All their friends had already fled, and it was a miracle that they had so far escaped harm. They would hold out as long as they could, but they all knew that one day even the powerful arms of Nonno Alberto would not be enough to protect them.

That day, when it came, came without warning. It started the way most important days start: just like any other. Alberto and Rosa woke early to tend to their affairs; Zio Trento, a ship's mechanic, went to town to scrounge up work; Alberto Chegia, age five, sat on the floor playing with wood figurines.

"Nonna, I wanna go to market with you," Little Alberto said.

"No, sweetheart, you can't—it's too dangerous," she replied. The look in his blue eyes tore her apart: brimming with tears, crestfallen, yet still full of an exuberance yearning to burst forth. She swallowed, gave his grandfather a look, and relented. "But you have to stay *right* by my side."

"Thank you, Nonna!" he beamed. He raced to get his hat and put on his shoes, then stood before her like an anxious puppy.

Hand in hand, grandmother and grandson walked down to the harbor. The cobblestones, jarred loose by the blasts, wiggled under their feet. Piles of concrete and plaster dotted the side of the road. To Alberto, the place looked like a playground: mountains just big enough to climb, holes just small enough to jump over. He pulled and twisted to free himself, but his Nonna held tightly to his hand.

"Stay with me, *nipote*. You can't just go running off around here."

"I know," he said. He snagged a small piece of rubble with his foot and started dribbling it like a soccer ball.

The market was crowded that day. People filled their bags in a hurry, one eye always on the sky. Something ominous hung in the air, something that made her pace quicken. She knew right away that she should not have brought Alberto: he was too small and too slippery to let out of her sight for a moment. She reached out for a tomato, her grip on his hand loosened, and he was gone.

Rosa turned around desperately: now on her tiptoes to see over people's heads, now on her hands and knees looking for her grandson through a sea of legs. "Alberto, where are you?" she called. Half the men in the town turned around, but none was the Alberto she was after.

Just then, the siren—loud and immediate, crying out. The market turned to melee, people dashing this way and that to get out of the open. The vendors hurriedly gathered their wares. Rosa stood rooted to the spot. "Alberto, where are you?" she cried out, as the crowd thinned into nothing around her.

She should have known where he was going. Free from her grasp, Alberto made his way right back to the piles of rubble, which he could now freely explore without his nonna holding him back. When the siren sounded, he was deep into the examination of a strange bug traversing a mound of broken windowpanes. He raised his head, knew that noise. Knew what it meant: the scary, shaky time was coming, the time when people curled up small and hugged each other and prayed. The time when you run and hide, get indoors, find your family, NOW.

He looked around. No Nonna. Where was Nonna? Nonno at home, yes, zios and zias and cousins off somewhere else—but Nonna, Nonna was supposed to be right there. Why did he run from her, when she told him not to? How could she have let him go? The siren so loud he couldn't think. The bug scurried back into the rubble pile. Didn't she know where he was? Didn't she know it wasn't safe? She was probably on her way now. She would want him to wait there fore her. But then the drone of the engines started to grow louder, and he could see people hurrying into their homes, and he thought that maybe it was better to move, to run, to find a pile of his own with a hole big enough for a little boy.

He took off back toward home, as fast as his legs could take him. It wouldn't be fast enough, he knew. The drone grew to a roar. Hearing someone call out, he turned to see a group of people standing in the doorway of an apartment building. They shouted and beckoned to him, glancing hurriedly up at the sky. He started their way, but something told him to turn around. Instead, he found shelter in a nook dug out of the hillside, tucking his knees to his chest and quaking with fear.

The first bomb whistled down right before his eyes, seeming almost suspended in flight before it rushed to the street and erupted, right at the rubble pile where he had been playing moments before. The next one hit the apartment building where those people had called to him, gouging a hole out of the wall near the door. Alberto peered through his fingers and prayed that they had all made it down to the basement. The door dangled limply on one hinge. "If I had stayed where I was I wouldn't be here today," he reflects now—an old man with grandchildren, an old man very much alive.

By the time he made it home, Nonna Rosa had already arrived. She swept him into her arms, cradling him against a chest still heaving with sobs. "My darling, my darling," she murmured. His grandfather wrapped his arms around both of them, silently kissing Alberto's smudged cheek. Then he slung a bulging burlap sack over his shoulder.

"Let's go," he said, and they walked out and didn't look back.

When Cino saw them approaching, he did somersaults down the hill. "What are you doing here?" he exclaimed, kissing his brother, his grandma and his grandpa in turn.

"We're on an adventure," said Alberto brightly. Nonno Procaccini nodded a sort of caution to the elder brother.

"I'll bet you are," Cino said, grabbing Alberto by the hand. "Come on, I have so much to show you. You have to see our cappanna, and the hill where the planes fly, and the haystack...oh, Albertino, we have to go see Babbo right away!"

Alberto stayed where he was. "Babbo?" he asked timidly, looking up at his grandfather as if for confirmation.

"Yeah, Babbo!" said Cino. "He's back from the war, don't you know that? Didn't he come visit you?"

Just then, a voice rang out from nearby. "A-HEM," it said, reedy but with authority. Alberto jumped. Cino just smiled.

"Cino, is your reunion over?" called the voice. "May we get back to our studies now?"

"Yes, Maestro Camerini, you may get back to your studies...I will join you in a few minutes," Cino said. A wave of young voices burst out laughing. Maestro Camerini blushed and cleaned his spectacles.

Albertino peered through his grandfather's legs at the scene before him. Thirty or forty kids sat in the shade of a large cypress tree. Some were as young as his age, others as old as thirteen. He recognized faces from Porto Ercole, Le Grotte, Santo Stefano: they looked up and waved from their chalkboard tablets. Nestled under the tree, at the top of a rise, was the man Cino had been talking to: Maestro Camerini, the only working schoolteacher on Monte Argentario.

He was a very fat man, Alberto first noticed—one of those types whose cheeks were always rosy from the effort of getting into and out of chairs. He wore a friendly, almost unwavering, smile, and constantly dabbed at his brow with a handkerchief. His desk was a low stool on which he half-sat, half-squatted, and a broken chalkboard almost white with eraser marks. *Cino has to be making mincemeat out of this guy*, Alberto thought.

And, in fact, he was. "We...often made fun of our poor teacher," Cino recalls later. "One time...one of my friends looked up in the branches and said, 'Maestro, there are two small birds making love in the tree!' Maestro Camerini stood up, and while he looked for the birds my friend Robert and I moved his chair off to the side. When he went to sit down again the chair wasn't there, and he barrel-rolled almost five meters down the hill! Imagine a man that big tumbling to the ground...I got a big fat zero on my report card for that stunt."

That day, however, Alberto Procaccini was around—and when Alberto Procaccini was around, he made the rules. "Cino," he said, "why doesn't your little brother join you for the rest of school time today? I have some...business to attend to."

Alberto nodded vigorously and grabbed Cino's hand, tugging him toward the tree. Cino stumbled to keep pace, glancing balefully back at his grandfather. Nonno Procaccini just smiled. It was only later that Cino would find out what business Nonno Alberto had to attend to—later, on the day when everything flipped upside-down again, and one little boy wondered where he had left to turn.

It was supposed to be a treat, damn it. Take the boys to Grosseto, get them out of the cappanne for a while, let them see what life is like in a real big city. Buy them pizza and gelato like a grandpa is supposed to do for his grandsons. Who knew it would end up like that.

A few months after the Procaccinis arrived on the hillside, Nonno Alberto got a call from *comune*[37] headquarters in Grosseto. Ninety kilometers north of Monte Argentario, on the mainland, Grosseto is the seat of the province that encompasses Monte Argentario, Orbetello, and more. Dating back to 803, the old city lies fifteen kilometers from the Tyrrhenian Sea, cloistered inside its own pentagonal walls. Beyond it, modern-day Grosseto stretches

---

[37] Basic administrative division in Italy, roughly equivalent to a township or municipality.

all the way to the water. With Romanesque cathedrals and wide piazzas, Grosseto dwarfed Porto Santo Stefano—the only major city in the region. You even had to take a bus and a train to get there!

So when Cino found out that Nonno Alberto wanted to bring him and Bertino along, he just couldn't wipe the smile off. Nonno had said that he needed Babbo's permission, so Cino scampered off to find him.

"No," Aldo said firmly. Cino's jaw dropped.

"But *why*, Babbo? Nonno said it was all right!"

"It's not safe, Cino. The bombs are falling everywhere these days."

"There, here—what does it matter? Bombs are bombs. Besides, we'll be kilometers from the sea. Grosseto's safer than here, Nonno says. And we'll be extra careful and we'll be back before sundown, I promise. Anyway, Albertino's going, and he's only five. Why can't I?"

"Albertino's going?" Aldo's voice caught in his throat. "How is he? Never mind. Well, if he's going, then I suppose it's all right if you go, too. But be back by supper or there'll be hell to pay!" Cino wrapped his father in a hug and ran out to share the good news.

They left the next morning bright and early. Alberto hung on his grandfather's hand; Cino danced all the way to the bus stop. When the bus came, the boys darted in and plastered themselves against a window, gazing with delight as the bus wound through Orbetello. Their grandfather wondered, as he often did, at the kind of world these boys were growing up in, that they could pass through smoldering cities without blinking an eye.

On the train from Orbetello to Grosseto, the chatter was nonstop.

"Are we almost there, Nonno?

"What are we gonna do when we get there?"

"Do we have to walk? My feet are tired."

"I'm getting pizza!"

"I'm getting gelato!"

"I'm gonna throw your gelato on the ground and make you lick it up like a dog!"

"Nonno, Cino said—"

The doors hissed open and the boys leapt out, slurping in the city air. It was mustier than back home, more flavorful: smoke from the engine mingling with the distant scent of brick ovens and bakeries. "Grosseto!" called the train conductor. They were already halfway off the platform.

Inside Old Grosseto it was warm and the pigeons clucked hungrily. Cino scooped mouthfuls of water from the fountain in the piazza, as the Albertos gazed placidly on the zebra-striped marble of the *Cattedrale di San Lorenzo.*[38] Here, they did not feel the constant strain of occupation, the constant weight of fear—but still, the city was heavy with Nazis, and people hurried about as if they didn't want to be around to see what might happen next.

Alberto the Elder turned to Alberto the Younger, who was eating the second half of his pizza like a watermelon slice.

"Bertino," he said, "Procaccini men use a knife and fork."

Just then, the clock struck noon. Nonno Alberto cleared his throat, gathered his things and left some *lire*[39] on the table.

"Okay boys, I have one more surprise for you, then I have to go to work. You ready?"

---

[38] Cathedral of San Lorenzo, the main cathedral in Grosseto.
[39] Plural of *lira*, the Italian currency before the Euro.

"Yeah!" they sang in unison.

"There's a little amusement park nearby, with a carousel and fun little games. If I take you two there, do you promise you'll be good when you come to Nonno's office with him?"

"Ye-yeah!" they sang again, faltering a bit on the reprise.

"Then let's go!"

They were less than halfway across the piazza when the sirens sounded—loud and fast, like the roiling sea. Alberto Procaccini froze, and something hardened in his eyes.

"Run, kids," he urged, corralling them toward a nearby archway. Around them, people screamed and scattered. Engines roared and three shadows approached behind them, low and fast in the sky.

Alberto shoved the boys under cover just in time to see three American fighters screaming over the piazza, diving down at attack speeds to unleash their fury on a spot just out of sight. The sound was thunderous: machine guns spitting, loud reports of concrete and gunpowder; the shriek of metal twisted as if on the rack. The wails of women and children, growing louder and more anguished. A brief pause, like a break in a storm—then another wave came, and another, and another. "The strafing and bombs went on for thirty minutes," says Cino, "then there was the smell of something burning and an eerie silence over the whole area."

The sirens sounded the all-clear, and the aging man and his grandsons emerged from the archway. People stumbled in from where the bombs had just fallen, crying and cradling bloodied limbs. Around a bend, began to rise from the wreckage. *My God*, Alberto thought, *that's right where…*

"Stay here," he told his grandsons. They sat down and stared. He pushed his way through the aimless crowd, striding right into the heart of the confusion.

It was worse than he could have imagined: the amusement park, in tatters. Popcorn stands blackened, ferris wheel cars dangling from their harnesses...and the children, dear God, the children everywhere. Mangled, sobbing, wandering lost—or, worse, lying motionless on the ground. *If we had been five minutes earlier...* He reeled back with anger and fear, then ran to take his grandchildren to safety.

They were right where he left them. "Let's go," he said.

"Nonno, what happened?" begged Cino. "People are saying it was the Americans. The amusement park? Did they—did they?"

"Let's go," he said.

On the train, on the bus, all the way back to Le Grotte, the three travelers stared down at their hands. Every once in a while Cino looked up at his grandfather, eyes pleading for answers, but for once Nonno Procaccini had no wisdom to give. All they had—all anyone had—were questions to ponder. *What was that? Why did they do it What kind of people could have done such a horrible thing?* There had to be an explanation...there simply had to, or all would be lost.

When they got off the bus, they were mobbed. Harried women pawed at the boys' faces looking for their own sons; men called to each other across the platform; and everyone wanted to know if it was really the Americans who had done such a horrible thing. Alberto felt every minute of his age as he dragged his weary grandsons through the station.

Suddenly, Cino was swept into strong arms, and Nonno Procaccini found himself looking straight into the fiery eyes of Babbo Chegia. "I should never have let you take the boys," Aldo sneered. "Put them in danger again, and..."

"Save it, Aldo," sighed Alberto. "Just be thankful that they're safe." He turned to guide his grandson away, then stopped.

"I'm sorry," he said, without turning around. Albertino waved goodbye to his brother, and looked up wide-eyed at the tall man he hardly knew.

As they trudged home, Cino asked his father a question he'd asked many times before. "Why can't Alberto come with us? Why don't you talk to him?"

"Because...because he just can't," Aldo answered, as he'd answered many times before. "I can't."

That night, Cino's dreams were filled with sound and light: the horrible crush of death, the helplessness of being a small boy in a world tumbling into madness. *How could something like this happen?* he wondered. *My American heroes? Impossible.*

The next morning, they told him fifty people had been killed, mostly women and children. "A mistake," they said. "German tanks parked nearby. Bad intel, the wrong target. What a shame." Tears slipped down their faces. Cino, though, was relieved. They had not killed those innocent people on purpose. America still fought for good. The world flipped right side-up again.

February, 1945. When they captured that boy, it was clear that the tides had turned. The Allies were closing in, and the fighting was fierce: the sky "covered in airplanes," bombs falling in fours and fives. Fighters deafened overhead; anti-aircraft guns harrumphed from La Feniglia and the field on the hillside. The sea spouted salt water, leaving schools of fish belly-up on the surface. Cino watched it all from his favorite spot, crouched in an imaginary cockpit with the Stars and Stripes on the wing. In his mind, he lined the Krauts up in his sights, sending them caterwauling to their maker. He thought of his father in the boat in the grotto, watching the German planes fall, letting them fall...he dropped the Nazis into the water for Babbo.

But, outside, the real fight went the other way. The Luftwaffe drew the Americans into intense dogfights, flying low and fast through the shoals. This left the Yankee bombers wide open, fat bellies exposed to the big guns on shore. They paid the price.

The first plane tore apart almost brilliantly: an artillery shell hit its mark and sent pieces of the Flying Fortress screaming out in all directions. Cino and his friends flinched and shuddered. As he always did now, Cino watched for the black dots that would float down from the wreckage, that would send the Birds zipping through flaming flotsam to haul bedraggled men back to shore. But there were no dots, no 'chutes. The nose of the plane hit the water and sank softly, silently beneath the surface. Cino said a prayer for the brave souls onboard. His salt tears tasted like the ocean waters.

But there was no time to dwell—a second bomber was going down. Trailing smoke, pinwheeling toward the Tyrrhenian. This time, the pilots ejected: four black balls, four lives drifting through the air. Cino felt his father drop the binoculars, heard him give his friends the signal and hop in the boat. "Go, Babbo," he said. The engine revved, the throttle shifted, weapons cocked—the Birds darted out into open water.

When the fighting was over, the men of the town slipped down to the seashore and scooped the dead fish straight from the sea. Cino sat in his grandparents' cappanna and waited for Aldo to return, waited for him to sling parachutes from his shoulder and speak proudly of the lives he had saved. But that day, his father came back empty-handed. Not a parachute to be seen, not a heroic rescue to be recounted. Just a few sets of dog tags, jangling hollowly.

"They were all dead, save for one," he said. "We couldn't get there in time for him. The water was choppy—we were going as fast as we could—there he was, in the water, flapping like a bird— but the Nazis got there first. He's just a boy…God. Just a boy."

Aldo fell silent and looked down at his hands—sheepishly, almost. As if he expected Doretta to smack him, to scream at him for failing his mission. Instead, she rose slowly and took her son's face in her hands.

"You are the bravest man I know," she said.

They had him on display down by the port, like triumphant fishermen showing off a prized bluefin. Seated in the bed of a truck, surrounded by Nazis and Italian Fascists, blood flowing freely from a wound on his ankle. Head bowed, eyes slitted, face pock-marked but youthful. The first American Cino had ever seen in the flesh. *Just a boy*, he thought.

They took him to Forte Filippo—SS headquarters—for questioning, and one by one the port'ercolesi returned to the pressing needs of their lives. At dinner, no one spoke. Cino kneaded his polenta into the shape of a plane and sliced it in half with his fork. Night fell and only the crickets took notice.

Then, suddenly, a flash of blinding light. The air raid sirens howled. People poured from their cappanne to see the sky lit up like a fireworks display.

"What's going on?" Cino shouted out.

His father's voice in his ear, his father's strong hand on his shoulder. "Flares," he said. "From the Americans. They're coming to get their man."

The crackle of weapons echoed up from Forte Filippo. In the light from the flares, Cino could see partisan fighters charging the hill, taking the Fascists by surprise. They stormed the fort and a few minutes later appeared again, carrying the wounded man in their arms. A low cheer rose through the clusters of villagers: slowly growing, swelling and cresting, gaining strength and audacity—tumbling down to the Nazi encampment, flecked with laughter like foam. *Viva Italia! Viva America! Viva la libertà!* Cino stood with his father and yelled into the coming of the dawn.

CHAPTER EIGHT: AFTERMATH

"Dopo la guerra, al paese era una barca a torsa."[40]
- Cino Chegia

Spring, 1945. Elvira screams and swings her broom at the heavy brow of the man in front of her. It connects with desperate force—long, brittle twigs, sharpened on concrete floors, rake across his face. Droplets of blood arc behind her follow-through. The man yelps and stumbles back; Elvira snarls with grim satisfaction. Outside, the crowd gasps. "Stay away from him!" she shouts. "You'll pay for this—I swear you will!"

They had come for her son, her little boy. They had come to take him away with them, to carry their food and ammo as they beat a hasty retreat across the Gothic Line. The Allies were knocking on the door to Monte Argentario, and the Nazis needed bodies to help them make their escape. So the SS turned to local Fascists like Pietro and made a gut-wrenching request: *Show us*

---

[40] "After the war, the town was a complete mess."

where the young men live. Point them out to us and we will "enlist" them. The Fascists complied. Within a few days, dozens of boys had been wrested from the arms of their mothers and thrust into action.

Elvira swings her broom again. The SS officer grabs it, wrenches it away from her and flings it to the ground. Elvira backs against the wall of the cappanna, pressing her son behind her into the canvas.

"Enough," the officer says. He grabs her shoulder and shoves her aside; she falls to the hard ground, weeping.

"Mamma!" shouts her son. But the officer has already grabbed him by the collar, and frogmarches him quickly away as he strains to get back to her side.

One by one, the townspeople outside dissipate, wearing and whispering. Elvira wipes her tears and looks up, just in time to see Pietro shrink, shame-faced, back into the olivetto.

After the Americans rescued that pilot, Monte Argentario began counting down. Word was coming in from all over: the Allies had taken Naples. The Allies had taken Rome. The Fascists were fighting back bitterly, but it was only a matter of time. Soon, the Social Republic would fall, and the Italian Civil War—a war that was never supposed to begin, brought about by a war Italy had no business being in—would be over. The people prepared for freedom, hanging Italian flags from their cappanne and making plans to start rebuilding their lives.

But outside, from La Feniglia to Santo Stefano, the Wehrmacht prepared for an invasion as well. Minelayers buried explosives under thin layers of sand, while boats too small to draw Allied attention scattered magnetic mines into the Tyrrhenian Sea.

The tunnel between Porto Ercole and Porto Santo Stefano, where Cino had once hung out of soot-covered train windows, was wired to blow at the push of a button, destroying the German munitions within it. Every piece of equipment the Fascists couldn't take with them, they planned to destroy. Every piece of infrastructure they could afford to cripple, they prepared to cripple. When the Nazis went, they wouldn't just take Monte Argentario's sons with them—the docks, the roads, the only bridge from the promontory to the mainland would go, too.

Meanwhile, desperation crept upon Monte Argentario. The winter had been hard: cold and unforgiving. Food and fuel were running scarce. Soon, life would resume again, but what kind of life would it be? For the sister cities, salvation lay in only one place—out there on the water—and, mines or no mines, it had to be sought. So as soon as the Nazi gunboats moved off, those whose menaite could still make the trip set out for sea. They knew the waters; they charted safe routes through the minefields. But, really, it was only a matter of time.

Sometimes, in a small town, you can feel the thing that's happening before you know there's a thing happening at all. One morning that spring, Cino awoke to find the tent city shrouded in melancholy. People huddled in small groups, staring down at the village; below them, Cino could see a river of port'ercolesi surging toward Porto Vecchio.

"What's going on?" he asked the first person he saw.

"They're dead," she said. "All of them. Boom, poof."

"Who?" he asked, but the woman was already gone.

Cino took off for the port. There, the mob chattered in wild-eyed confusion. A menaita was docked nearby, and her crew stood by her, smoking and shuffling their feet.

"Tell me what happened," Cino, eight and a quarter years old, demanded of them.

One glanced at him with red-rimmed eyes. "We was out there on the water last night," he said. "They was just beyond, not far off, dropping their net. Then they just…went! Blown sky-high. There one minute, then gone. Mine musta clung to 'em. We got over there as fast as we could, but there was…nothing we could do. Nobody to save. Nothing left."

Cino tried to count the menaita on the water to see which one was missing. *Whose fathers, whose sons died last night?* he wondered. He closed his eyes and thanked God that Doretti's boat had been damaged months before.

Suddenly, the roar of the crowd rose and shifted, molded into a sonic shape Cino recognized: violent and fearful, tumultuous and threatening.

"*Achtung!*"[41] came a voice from behind him. Cino spun to see the local SS commander flanked by a row of soldiers, brandishing a megaphone. "You are violating a militarized zone. Leave now or you will be arrested. There is nothing more to see here."

The crowd railed against him, demanding to know who had been killed. He nodded to the soldiers, who shouldered their rifles and drew back the bolts with an ominous click. They took aim at the gaunt, weary faces in front of them. An electric chill ran down Cino's spine—a chill he had come to know well. It was the feeling of walking a tightrope between two cliffs, knowing that one wrong move—one curse flung too hard, one soldier with his finger too hot on the trigger—could send everything tumbling down.

The crowd stood firm. The guns stayed leveled, trained to tear holes through flesh. On the front lines, fifteen women linked arms, pledging not to move until the Germans told them exactly which boat lay in pieces at the bottom of the sea. A tense heartbeat, then another, then a third.

---

[41] Attention! [German]

Finally, the commander raised his bullhorn. "Fine. If you must stay, then stay. There's nothing left to be done anyway." He nodded again and the men lowered their guns, trotting off with unnerving precision. Like machines, programmed only to kill.

Seven hard-working men died that day, two of whom were the Chegia family's cousins. When the rest of the menaite returned, the whole town gathered in the bomb-scarred graveyard for the biggest funeral any of them could remember. Two bodies had been found, and those men were buried next to their kin. Of the other five, all that remained was a marker in the ground. Nobody went out on the water for weeks after that—no food, no market was worth that price. They would just have to sit tight until the Americans arrived.

Throughout the slow Nazi retreat, the bombs continued to fall. Zia Marietta, who lived in Old Porto Ercole beneath the stone walls of La Rocca, lost most of her house in a blast. She and her family spent the remainder of the occupation living in Doretti's drydocked boat. And, in Orbetello, the waning days of the war claimed one more life from the Chegia family.

Zia Michelina, Aldo's sister, lived in Orbetello: she had moved there years ago, when she married Gennaro Ricci and had the first of their four children. Though no German warships docked there, the town still was not safe from Allied air assault: the Nazis used to land seaplanes on Lake Orbetello, and when planes bobbed on the water, the bombs fell just as hideously.

One day, late in the spring of 1945, Michelina stood in her kitchen, stirring pasta for the family lunch. Her son, Divo, studied at the table. Blessedly, the rest of the family was out of the house.

Just like that, the sirens blared urgently. There was no time to run, nowhere to go. Divo looked up from his book, petrified. The bombs pounded nearby, shaking the house to its foundations.

"Under the table, NOW," Michelina demanded. Mother and son dove for safety, holding each other tightly. They could hear faint screams from outside.

The next bomb came down right on top on them, caving the ceiling in. Chunks of stone fell like ice in an avalanche, crushing the table beneath them. Michelina was thrown from Divo's side, trapped beneath rubble an arm's length from her boy. Unable to reach him, unable to move. Dust and smoke swirled in a low fog. She couldn't see Divo anymore.

"Are you all right, son?" she called out.

"I think so," came the reply.

"Can you move?"

A grunt. "No."

"Neither can I. We'll just have to wait for help to come."

Michelina tried not to despair. The bombardment was over, the sirens subsiding, and rescue teams should be coming soon. Gennaro and the others were surely on their way back, too. She and Divo were broken but alive—they would make it out of this together. They just had to be patient.

But, then, there was the dust. Damp and starchy on the lower palate, tasting of plaster and sand. It coated the tongue, coated the throat, coated the lungs—building a wall to stop air from flowing. After long enough, it blocked the breath entirely and you suffocated behind the mortar.

Minutes passed, then hours. Michelina managed to free one hand from the rubble and clamped it over her mouth and nose.

"Can you move your arm?" she shouted to Divo. "Cover your mouth with your hand or your shirt—you have to keep from breathing the dust."

"I…can't…" he moaned.

"Try, son! I need you to try. I need you to try hard for Mommy now. Please."

Divo did not make a sound.

By the time the rescuers arrived, the smoke had all drifted away. Michelina could just make out her son's face, caked in white, flat and unmoving on the cold ground. The puffs of dust that once danced in his breath drifted slowly downward. He looked scared—scared, and utterly alone. She had not been there for him when he needed her most. When the fire brigade pulled her from the rubble, she screamed and clawed until they released her, then curled up next to her son. His body was already beginning to cool. She closed his eyes and wept bitterly, leaving chalk white trails on his skin like dried riverbeds.

Today, Divo Ricci stands in Orbetello's Piazza Cavour: one name next to a dozen others just like it, on a monument just like the one in Porto Ercole, like the one in Santo Stefano, like the one in nearly every city and town in the great, gorgeous nation of Italy. One more life snuffed out by the reckless desolation of war.

Finally, the Fascists withdrew: Nazi soldiers followed by Blackshirts, followed by the young men forced into action. As the last of them crossed the bridge to Orbetello, they flipped a switch, a chorus of explosions rose up around the promontory. The bridge tumbled into the lake; the tunnel caved in on itself, sending artillery shells pinging into the sky like fireworks. Smoke issued from the barrels of the FLaK guns in the meadow, and from the rubble of the torpedo factory in Santo Stefano. The only sound louder than the blasts was the steady cheer of the Italians—men, women, and children who stood tall for years in the face of unfathomable danger.

Freedom! Joy! Open air! Cino dashed through the cappanne and out of the olive grove, through the streets and the fields, past rusting boats and overgrown farms; arms outstretched and head flung back, howling at the sky. Everywhere, people pulled accordions from their hiding places, tuned fiddles and strung bows—unleashed robust strains that they may have thought they'd never hear again. Their stomping feet turned the soil for seeding.

Across the lake, another dust plume rolled steadily their way: Yankee Doodle and Union Jack, come to save the day. They crossed the Giannella tombola to waving flags and lusty songs, skins of wine and wine-soaked kisses. Just outside the town, a young boy snaked through a forest of limbs to the front of the line. How long he had waited for this, how many hours he had spent on that hillside...how many dreams he had dreamed of these men in their screaming planes, their Plexiglas bubbles, so far from the land of their birth. Nothing would stop him from being the first to salute them. When the Americans crested the hill into Porto Ercole, Cino Chegia would be there, strewing rose petals in their path.

They arrived even grander than he could have imagined: sun-tanned and scarred, waving to the crowd from truck windows and tank turrets. Every now and again they jumped from the caravan, passing out chocolate and cigarettes to the grateful onlookers. Old women kissed their cheeks; young men shook their hands. Elvira thrust a photo of her son into their hands, asking if anyone had seen him on the road. Alberto appeared by Cino's side, hugging his leg, not sure whether to be afraid or enraptured. Cino, for his part, wasn't sure either. They were men, he could see that—men just like his father, with stained teeth and rough hands—but still, somehow, they weren't. They were something more than that. If he squinted his eyes just right, it was almost like they shone with a kind of light he had never seen before.

The caravan passed through town and settled in right where

the Germans had left—on La Feniglia, amid smoldering artillery and cookfire ash. Their job was to protect and rebuild, to rid the land of war's leftovers, and to leave when their number was called. Monte Argentario slept well that night. The next day, the adults rose at dawn and marched straight down the hill, determined to rebuild their ports and patch up their boats. Determined to restore what the Fascists had destroyed, and thus to win, in the end, the only war that really mattered.

Meanwhile, the kids ran down to the beach and hovered on the outskirts of the American camp. Nobody knew what to do, what to say. It was like an invisible forcefield separated them from the soldiers: they knew there was nothing to fear, but something still held them back. Just the sight of strange men on that beach, sweating and laughing in unfamiliar tongues, gave them all a strange sense of dread.

All, of course, except Cino. He pushed past his friends and instantly shattered the barrier, marching right up to a man digging out spadefuls of sand. The man looked at him curiously—his dirty feet, his bright smile, his intelligent eyes—and handed him the shovel. Cino got down to work as the rest of the kids streamed past him into camp.

From then on, Cino Chegia was a constant fixture in the American camp. Eager to please his idols, he offered to help in any way he could. He and his gang were the soldiers' go-fers, their field workers, their freight loaders. They refilled canteens, cleared brush from the encampment, led the men around town—tiny feet in wooden clogs, scampering ahead of the long strides of ground infantry in combat boots and faded fatigues. To their surprise and delight, the boys found that many of the soldiers spoke Italian; they were from Italian families, and still spoke the old tongue around the dinner table back home. Cino thought back to what his uncle had said, about people from their country moving across the ocean to be part of that new world. He wondered what his life might look like there.

One day, a young woman—buxom, with a painted face—gave Cino a new mission. "You know the soldiers, right? Tell them my friend and I just set up a little 'shop' near Porto Vecchio…they can come see us if they're looking for some 'quality time.' Okay?"

Cino nodded, not at all sure what she meant. What kind of "quality time" was she talking about? Picnics? Card games? But he relayed the message, and soon he found himself leading bands of nervous soldiers there every night. The men paid him and his friends handsomely, in real American dollars and Army-issue Lucky Strikes. Cigarettes were like gold back in those days—the kids had no use for them, of course, but they fetched a hefty price on the black market.

When Cino wasn't working with the troops, he was trooping around the town he could once again call his own. There was so much to explore there in those days: fortresses, ruins, minefields, ammo dumps—everything a boy could want, everything he shouldn't be touching. And Cino found it all.

Like one time when Beppino Bertocchini, Zia Betta Procaccini's son, came by L'Ospizio and said, "Hey, you wanna go blow some stuff up?" And Cino looked around for Doretta, and not seeing her nearby, nodded quickly and then they were off. Up the steep slope to Forte Filippo, past American soldiers sitting on the anti-aircraft guns that surrounded the fort, drinking wine. They made no move to stop the boys—they didn't seem much to care.

They should have cared, Cino thought when he and Beppino got inside. The storage room was full of things to kill people with: guns with real bullets, grenades, mean-looking things he couldn't even name. Even Cino felt that he shouldn't be there, and he hesitated for nearly a full second before running in after his cousin.

It felt like being in a museum, where everything was yours to touch. The rows of machine guns and artillery shells glinted with a steely ferocity, a definitiveness that Cino found strangely alluring. He picked a Luger up off a shelf—it was heavier than he expected. It made his arms shake to hold it out in front of him.

"Cino," Beppino called. "Come here."

He was back at the far end of the room, reaching into a dusty corner. From the shadows, he pulled out a long, thin tube with a rope sticking out of one end.

"What do you think it is?" he asked.

"I don't know, and I don't think I want to."

"Aw, come on, not just a little bit? Take it outside with me and pull the cord. Or are you too chicken?"

"I'm not chicken. I'm not a dummy, either."

"Oh, is that it? You're not a dummy? You must just be a wussy Chinaman then. Is that what you are?"

Cino ground his teeth and turned red. He cursed his cousin for playing to his weakness. No, that's not what he was—not that at all. He knew that. Beppino knew that. He knew that Beppino knew that. He could have just walked away and it would have been fine. But that was never going to happen now. No one called Cino Chegia a wussy Chinaman.

"Gimme that thing," he said.

Outside, the sky had turned a touch gray. There was a breeze blowing through that tickled the tip of your nose. The boys glanced around, but they couldn't see any soldiers. They walked up to the battlements and stood facing the water. Beppino grabbed the front of the tube and pointed it out over the cliff.

"Pull it," he said.

"What do you think it's going to do?"

"Shoot confetti, dummy. How should I know? Just pull it."

"If you insist!" Cino held his breath, counted to three and pulled the cord. The blast knocked him on his ass worse than that first bomb did, sending him skidding back against the battlement wall. The tube flew out of his hand. Unseen by either of them, a signal flare shot out over the water, exploded like a firework and cascaded down into the sea.

Cino's ears rang. He couldn't see or feel much, but he heard the screams—and through the thinning smoke he looked up and saw Beppino clutching his arm, leaking blood.

"Oh, no, no, God no," Cino muttered, rising to his feet. Beppino howled and writhed like a fox in a trap. "Are you okay?" Beppino managed to nod. Cino took off his shirt and wrapped it around the older boy's arm. "We have to get you home."

They ran as fast as they were willing down the hill and back to town. The blast had set Porto Ercole on alert, and people peered suspiciously from their windows. Beppino's father was waiting at the door when they arrived.

"Something told me that might have been you," he said. Then Beppino showed him his arm, and he paled and hustled the boys inside.

It turned out to be no more than a flesh wound: just a graze by the shoulder, a bandage and a scar. Beppino's father cleaned them up, kissed their heads and sent Cino on his way to Doretta. The butt-whoopings came later, of course, but Cino didn't much mind those. It was good to feel alive.

Then there was this other time, with the artillery shells. In preparation for the Allied invasion, the Germans had set up an encampment of *Ottantotti*—88-millimeter FLaK guns—In a field not far from town. The "Eighty-eight" was the Wehrmacht's favorite method of blowing things up: a 16,000-pound, spindly steel behemoth that resembled a praying mantis craning its neck toward the sky. Its barrel alone was 16 feet long, and spit out shells at speeds of up to 60 miles a minute. The shells were grooved on the inside, designed to explode on impact into fist-sized hunks of shrapnel. A single direct hit could take down an entire Flying Fortress. When the Nazis left Monte Argentario, they blew up the guns along with everything else, but left the shells scattered across the field, like seeds of death sown on the hard dirt. Soon, they would be pecked up by the birds—and, every so often, they would peck back.

There was a man in town buying up as much copper as he could. Monte Argentario was rebuilding bigger and better, and modern high-rises meant pipes and electrical wiring, which meant lots and lots of copper. There was no copper in the mountain (just as there was no silver), but there was copper in the fields—inside the casings of the Ottantotti shells. Spend a day collecting casings and you could make enough to feed your family for a week. As 1945 stretched on and work at the American camp waned, more and more boys found their way out to the artillery field, pecking for copper.

Cino was slow to hop on the copper-casing bandwagon, and did so only reluctantly. After the incident with the flare, he wasn't in a hurry to handle live ammunition again. Besides, the giant shells were the size of his forearm, and weighed upward of twenty pounds. Removing the casing from the live round was no easy task, and was an extremely dangerous operation: one wrong move and boom, you're done. He had seen what these cartridges did to airplanes at long range, and he had seen what even a small signal flare will do to a boy's body close up. He shuddered to think of the forces of power and proximity in one.

The only reason he went out there that day, in fact, is because he felt so secure in his method. It had worked for him dozens of times already, and by that point he was so fluid in his motions that he didn't worry much about the danger. He would bring an empty casing with him and lay it on the ground, then pile the live cartridges nearby. One by one, he would unscrew the top from the projectile and gently—GENTLY—tip it over, using the spent casing as a fulcrum. When done correctly, the live round would slide out of the casing and land safely on the ground, leaving you with an armful of precious—and harmless—copper. The trick, Cino found, was to be cautious yet confident: to handle the devices deftly and without fear, but never to forget that they wielded all the power. If only all the boys treated them with the same respect.

It was late spring, and the yellow Tuscan sun warmed the back of his neck. Cino sifted through the field with his friends Erasmo and Angiolino, each of them experts in casing removal. They breathed steadily and spoke only when necessary, like minesweepers, focused on the task at hand. Everything was going fine, as it had before. But then another threesome appeared: two brothers that Cino knew and a friend of theirs, laughing loudly and kicking rocks along the path. They hailed Cino and his friends, stopped to chat for a bit and then moved off to another trench to begin their own search.

Nearly an hour passed, mostly in silence. The boys worked deliberately, slowly piling up enough casings to wire a whole building. Snatches of conversation and clinking metal drifted over from the nearby trench. Rounds slipped cleanly from their sheaths. Then, a blast—the ground shook—a roar ripped across the field, terrifying yet familiar. Smoke and dust billowed up from the trench where the other boys had been working. Their cries drifted out on the wind: strangled, helpless, full of mourning. Cino and his friends ran full-tilt to the trench.

It was like nothing he had ever seen before—not during the bombing, not during the partisan fighting, never. The dirt was scorched black and studded with bits of twisted metal. The two brothers sat a dozen feet from the blast center, clutching at their arms, their legs, their chests. Their skin bubbled black hot tar. At the center of it all lay their friend, splayed spread-eagle on the ground. His stomach was blown completely to shreds, intestines lolling out of the cavity where his body once was. It looked like a clock with the faceplate removed. There was no more turning of the gears, no more ticking of the dial. His chest neither rose nor fell. Blood pooled on the ground beneath him. There was nothing to be done. Cino staggered backwards, holding down the bile. Erasmo and Angiolino fell to their knees, weeping.

"Stay here," Cino said. "Look after them. I'll go get help." And he was off.

Running back to town, he felt every beat of his heart. The rocks bit sharply through the soles of his shoes, and as before he welcomed the pain. To think that it could be taken from you so quickly, that the motor could run and then suddenly stop—like there was a power switch somewhere, and no one ever really knew when and how it would be flipped. He thought of the soldiers, of his father, who had to face that thought every day. His heart swelled for them.

Cino dashed through the streets of Porto Ercole, past women walking to market and under improvised scaffolds where men raised masonry up to the second and third stories of apartment buildings missing their walls. Through the piazza where the first bombs fell, skirting the laundry and the bread oven, and into the office of the *Carabinieri*.[42] Breathless, he told them what had happened. The office burst into a torrent of activity: officers rounded up first aid supplies and shouldered out of the station,

---

[42] Italian military/civil police

radioing the volunteer ambulance corps to meet them at the field. Sirens wailed then faded out of tune as they raced off down the road, toward the dead and wounded boys in the ruins of the trench.

Suddenly, Cino was all alone. The stillness of the afternoon rang in his ears, and he shivered as the adrenaline ebbed from his limbs. He walked slowly home and folded himself into his grandmother's arms, finally allowing the sobs to take him over. She didn't even ask what had happened.

In the late spring of 1945, the long war came to a close. The Italian Co-Belligerent Army broke through the Social Republic's last line of defense, and on April 27 captured Mussolini in the village of Dongo, Lombardy. On April 28, they shot him twice in the chest and dumped his body in a piazza in Milan. There, average Italian citizens took turns kicking and spitting on his corpse, then hung their former Supreme Leader upside-down from a meathook at an Esso gas station. Two days later, Adolf Hitler holed up in a bunker below Berlin, bit down on a cyanide capsule and shot himself in the head for good measure. By May 8, V-E Day, the war in Europe was over.

It was the biggest party Cino had ever seen. Bands struck up, pigs were slaughtered; horns honked, flags waved; fathers offered drinks to their sons. The Americans built bonfires on the beach and danced around them with every woman they could find. From the hillside, he could see similar fires burning in Orbetello, Albegna, even—if he strained—as far off as Grosseto. He felt sure that those same fires burned from Palermo to Venezia to Paris to London to New York, and in every free city, town, village and hamlet in between. That's what made it so special: it was so much larger than he was, so much larger than his town and his world. Cino felt his joy radiate outward, bolstered by every new joy it encountered, building a warm web that stretched across the sea to the land he had only seen in his dreams.

A few days later, his father turned to him over breakfast. "Want to go somewhere with me today?" he asked.

"Of course!" said Cino. He was not in the habit of saying no when Aldo invited him to do something. The two men cleaned up their plates, and as they walked out the door Aldo swung a white linen sack over his shoulder.

They went first to the famous haystack, where the Birds had sat day in and day out during the bombings. Siro, Adulio, Attilio, and Settimo were already waiting. Together, the five men and one boy tramped down to the American camp at La Feniglia. The troop's commander met them outside the large, drab tent that served as their headquarters.

"Thank you for coming," the commander said in passable Italian. He smiled in recognition at Cino, then held open the flap and ushered all six of them inside.

The cheer almost knocked Cino off his feet. It seemed like half the United States Army was crammed into that tent, clapping and hollering for the Birds of the Haystack. Aldo and his four friends stepped into the scrum, while Cino hung back near the entrance to watch it all unfold. One by one, the burly, crew-cut men came up to embrace the Birds, wrapping them into bear hugs and whispering into their ears. Many of them had tears in their eyes. They passed around glasses of champagne—a delicacy usually reserved for Santo Stefano shop windows—and raised them in a toast to the men.

"We are here today to celebrate five men who risked their lives over and over again for our cause," said the commander. "They didn't have to, but they did it. Out there with just a speedboat and a few guns, they put their necks on the line to save our boys and get them back to where they belong. Each of them once fought for the enemy—not because they wanted to, but because their country demanded it. Each of them *chose* to fight for us—not because we demanded it, but because it was the right thing to do. These are men of true character, and they deserve all the honor we can give them."

He turned to face the Birds. "Siro, Attilio, Adulio, Settimo, Aldo: thanks to you, dozens of good men can go back home to their wives and families. Thanks to you, we were able to keep taking the fight to Jerry, no matter how many of *our* birds he shot down. On behalf of all the men in this room, all those who can't be here today, and the whole United States Military, I salute you." He clicked his heels together, straightened into full martial posture, and raised his hand slowly to his forehead. The Birds of the Haystack returned the salute proudly.

"Cheers!" said the commander, and the tent broke into loud thanks and swigs of bubbly. Cino hopped up and down, overflowing with pride for his father.

After the hubbub subsided, Aldo stepped forward, clutching the sack. He cleared space around a table in the center of the tent, then dumped the contents of the sack onto the table. Dozens of sets of dog tags spilled out, silencing the crowd with their all-too-familiar clink. The men looked somberly at the pile.

Aldo beckoned the troop's translator to his side. "These are the dog tags we pulled from the pilots we could not save," he said. "The ones we couldn't get to in time, or who were already gone by the time they hit the water. Their bodies are with the sea now, but we want to make sure these get home to their families. Maybe they will bring them some…solace, at least."

The commander held out his hand. "We will see to it that these get where they belong," he said. "Thank you, Aldo." The two men shook, then embraced.

As the Birds of the Haystack walked off with Cino in tow, the soldiers gathered by the tent entrance and shouted their final thanks. Over sixty years later, Cino still remembers that day as one of the proudest and happiest of his life.

The war's end did not bring only joy to Porto Ercole, however—it also reminded the townspeople of all they had lost. Cino saw the anger everywhere he went: sizzling in the eyes of every person he passed, crackling through every curse shouted in the street or muttered into the hull of a broken-down peschereccio. It was the Fascists who brought this war upon them, who tore their lives apart and forced them to rebuild piece by piece. The people had never wanted to enter the war, never wanted to join the Germans, never even wanted Mussolini to proclaim himself Il Duce. Only the Fascists wanted it, and they took it without permission. They took it because they were stronger, had better guns, were more prepared to kill—because, while everyday Italians were busy working, they were busy plotting. In what felt like the blink of an eye, they stole the power from the people: but now, finally, it was back where it belonged. And now the Fascists were going to pay for what they had done.

Elvira led the charge. Months had passed since they took her son, and she still had not heard a word from him since. Every day she grew more and more restive, seething with hatred for the men who had ripped him from her. Men who had once been her friends, her neighbors. Men who had played with her son when they were teens and he just a boy, who had gone swimming with him and invited him to join their soccer games. Try as she might, Elvira could not comprehend how human beings of real flesh and blood—Italians, no less—could consign their own people to slavery, send them away from their families to starve in a foreign land.

She felt no compassion for them; not a drip of compassion.

She felt only pity and hate. At night, she saw their faces in front of her: leading the Nazi scum to her cappanna, holding back the crowd so that the man could tear her son from her, falling in line as they dragged him away into the darkness. She saw *his* face clearest of all, slipping away into the trees. His cowardice, his fear, the ugliness that seeped from his pores. If *he* didn't bring her son back, alive and happy, Pietro Chegia was a dead man.

He didn't bring her son back, alive and happy. He didn't bring her son back at all. Pietro and the rest of the Fascists snaked their way back from Germany alone and in secret, hoping for a place to hide out from the murderous rage to come. But word got around: the Fascists were back, but the boys weren't with them. Most, they learned, would never see Italian soil again. Many were dead, executed once the retreat was over and they were no longer of use to the Nazis. The rest the Germans sent running through the snow-capped hills; running to God knows where. Hitler's Nazis were thieves of life, and the Fascists had handed them Monte Argentario's finest young men.

When Elvira found out, she went on a rampage. She rounded up the women in the town—many of whom had lost sons of their own—and rallied them to the cause.

"They took our sons from us, our lives, and for what? To carry some guns across the border? To be slaughtered like cattle where they stood? We cannot let these evil men get away with it—these murderers, who hid behind 'orders from the Fürher' and tore our families apart! They can all go straight to Hell."

"Straight to Hell!" yelled the women—from strangled lungs at first, slowly crystallizing into a war cry.

"Well? Let's go send them there! Now who knows where Pietro Chegia is hiding?"

They found him in a hut in the woods, weary and waiting.

They stormed him like a Mongolian horde, battering him with sticks, rocks, rolling pins, and anything else they found lying around. Elvira shoved him down in the corner, pinning him to the floor and pouring her revenge out through her fists.

"Somebody get a rope," she spat. "We're stringing this murderer up."

"Leave him be," called a voice from the doorway. The women turned to see several policemen gathered outside. "You've made your point, now let us bring him to justice."

Elvira snarled, but climbed off Pietro's slumped and broken body. As they walked off, the women dropped their sticks and rocks behind them, scattering his blood throughout the forest. Their faces shone with vengeance.

CHAPTER NINE: HUMAN MOVEMENTS

"Faccia dura, cuore tenero."[43]
- Italian saying

June 2, 1945. The goat shudders and stamps on the cliff above Porto Ercole. The wind whips by. The men finish stuffing the base of the platform with hay, test the connection and nod to each other. The man holding the rope pats the goat on the rear, as if to say, *It's all right, just stand firm. It will all work out as God wills it.* He guides the goat to the platform, looping the rope around a hook suspended above it. Another gust blows through; the goat rears back, tries to run. There is hardly enough rope to move a step.

Down by the buoy, the men in the boat flash the signal—they are ready. The crowd tenses on the half-finished boardwalk. The goat brays. The torch-bearer kneels at the goat's feet, offering up a prayer in soft Latin. His robes are those of a priest. He crosses himself, kisses the goat and wedges the torch into the hay.

---

[43] "Hard face, soft heart."

The platform erupts into flames. A cheer rises from the boardwalk. The goat bleats, frantic and fearful.

"Uno, due, tre!" shout the men, then they grab poles and shove goat, wood, and fire off the cliff.

The connection holds. The platform zips down the cable from the cliff to the buoy. Hurtling, picking up speed. Engulfed in flames, like their own shooting star. Seconds tick by, then the whole contraption slams into the buoy at top speed, exploding into shards of fiery wreckage. The goat catapults out into the water, soaring through the air, somehow still alive after its ordeal. The crowd roars its approval. Then men in the boat haul the goat out of the water, take it to shore, and slit its throat on the dock. This will be a good fishing season.

After *Il Volo Della Capra*,[44] as hunks of goat are passed out among the townsfolk, old people tell stories about Santo Erasmo, patron saint of sailors and Porto Ercole.

"He was tortured by Emperor Diocletian," say the historians. "They wound his intestines around a windlass. That's why he's the patron saint of sailors—and of intestinal pain."

"I heard an angel brought him to Formia to perform miracles," say the good Catholics.

"Once, during a real bad storm, I saw sparks like lightning coming from the top of the mast," say the sailors. "They told me it was Santo Erasmo, looking over us."

The Americans nod along. "Back home, they call that 'St. Elmo's Fire.'"

Cino watches it all, awestruck. The last time the town celebrated the Festival of Santo Erasmo, he was just a little boy. He can remember walking hand-in-hand with Mama under the

---

[44] The Flight of the Goat

ribbons and banners, squirming in his Sunday best as the town gathered for morning Mass. He can remember her next to him, waving flags as the parade wound by; laughing at the blindfolded men racing in their rowboats; cheering for the ones trying to paddle around in wine barrels. She lives for him still, in every cobblestone of the street, in every word of congratulations and comfort passed between friends.

Alberto never got to know her like I did, he reflects. He worries that his brother will forget what she looked like, what she smelled like. He wishes Alberto were there with him, so he could tell him about her: how she would kiss her rosary and mutter prayers of safe passage as they blessed the menaite. But this is the Festival of Santo Erasmo, not Santo Stefano, and Alberto is not there.

The Festival feels different after so long. To see what it means to the town after all they've been through, to understand that it's not just pretty lights and bright colors. To realize that it's life and death: an offering to the high seas. It's his first experience of metaphor, perhaps. The foundation held firm, the connection held strong. Even as the winds blew and the fire raged, the goat stayed on his feet, all the way to the bitter end. And now it was something that they could all share—port'ercolesi and grottolani, together. There was no turning back now. *It's all right, just stand firm. It will all work out as God wills it.*

———————

As the Second World War came to a close, the people of Porto Ercole and Le Grotte bent their backs to the work of rebuilding. Most of their homes had been destroyed, including L'Ospizio: months passed before Cino and his family could move in again. While Doretti and Alcide worked on fixing up *La Menaita della Domenica*, the rest of the Chegias hauled bricks and laid mortar, side by side with their friends and neighbors. They set to the task not with resignation, nor with anger, but with hope and ambition: for all its destruction, the war had provided them with an opportunity to reshape their home in a new vision of solidarity.

"What are we doing here?" asked the elders of Porto Ercole and Le Grotte, sitting down for a meeting not long after the Fascists departed. "Our villages are sisters, tiny clusters separated by no more than a few football pitches. So we are from the South and you are from the North. So what? If this war has shown us anything, it is that we must stand together."

They shook hands, and it was decided: they would rebuild as one city, united. Porto Ercole, bigger and stronger than it could ever have been as two towns. They would extend the port from one side of the cove to the other; they would repave the road from La Rocca to Forte Filippo. Eventually, they would build shops and cafes along the waterfront, where tourists and townspeople could sip espresso and watch the sun scamper on the sea.

Not long after, Doretti sat his family down. "The boat has been fixed," he announced. "It's time to get *La Menaita della Domenica* back on the water."

Afterwards, Cino ran up to him. "Nonno, Nonno, can I work on the boat with you? I'm old enough now, I'm strong. Strong enough to dig ditches for the Americans!"

Doretti looked over Cino's head at Aldo, who nodded. He bent down and winked at his grandson. "Okay, you can come with us. I know you're strong, my boy, but soon we'll find out: can you be still?"

That night around 10 PM, they took the menaita down to the dock and dropped it in the water. Ten meters long, the wooden vessel was specially equipped for its unique purpose: lamp-fishing.

Unlike *pescherecci*—large fishing trawlers that simply drag a net through a fishery and catch whatever they catch—menaite use lamplight to draw schools of anchovies and sardines to them, then encircle the entire horde and scoop all the fish at once. This delicate, night-time operation requires great communication, concentration and stealth—perhaps another reason why *La Menaita della Domenica* never won any awards for best catch.

Doretti sat down in the bow of the boat, poring over charts and maps to plan their night's journey. Mid-deck, near the fish hold, his sons locked oars in place and checked the floating anchor. Aft, the Nieto brothers attached a large, tightly-woven net to a two-armed post protruding up and out from the back of the boat.

Lastly, the men gathered to lower two small wooden dinghies into the water behind the menaita, affixing each to a ring at the back of the larger boat. Each dinghy had its own small set of oars. Into the base of the dinghies, they screwed two tall, curved lamps, each with a glass bulb at the tip and a small receptacle just above it. While Cino watched, Aldo scooped seawater into the receptacles, then dropped a small, porous rock into each one. The water began to fizz like *acqua frizzante*,[45] and a steam-like vapor rose from its roiling surface. Aldo capped the receptacles, trapping the gas inside.

He turned to Cino. "You ready for this, son? *Menaita* fishing is like a ballet: you gotta know all the steps. We only have one chance to get it right, and it all comes down to you and your cousin. You know what to do?"

Cino nodded, jaw set.

"Good," said his father. "Then let's catch some fish."

Cino climbed into one of the dinghies, Anteo Nieto into the other. Once they were settled, Aldo knelt down, unscrewed Cino's

---

[45] Carbonated water

lamp bulb and held a lit match to the mesh "sock" affixed to the end of a pipe running down from the receptacle. The sock lit up brightly, burning the gas produced by the chemical reaction of the rock in the water. Aldo screwed the bulb back into place and did the same to the lamp in Anteo's boat.

The lamps lit, the Chegia men climbed into the menaita and rowed out to a spot Doretti had selected. Cino and Anteo trailed behind them, using their oars to steady their boats so that the lamps did not go out. They arrived at their location and bobbed silently on the water. The bright, white light of the lamp cast a pale glow, like a small and luminous star. All around the cove, Cino could see dozens of other similar stars, hovering eerily a couple meters above the water.

Suddenly, Cino caught a silver flash from the surface of the ocean next to him—then another, then another. He looked down and saw that the Tyrrhenian was teeming with tiny fish, circling furiously around the two points of light. Cino caught Anteo's eye—he saw. Anteo flicked his hand back and forth in front of the lamp, signaling to the menaita that the fish were ready to harvest.

On the menaita, the men dropped the net into the water so that it sunk to the sea floor, and threw a floating weight toward Cino and Anteo's lamp boats. The boys dug their oars into the water, holding their dinghies as steady as they could so that the light would not flicker and scare the fish away. Slowly but surely, the men rowed *La Menaita della Domenica* in a wide circle around the lamp boats, trailing the net behind them so that it enclosed the school that swarmed to the light. Cino and Anteo tensed their muscles, holding the oars firm as the menaita circled around them.

The menaita returned to the spot where it began, closing the loop beneath the two boys, and the men prepared to haul in the net. On the count of three, they pulled ferociously, cinching the net up and in until it was level with the surface of the water. Beneath

Cino, the feeding frenzy became a frantic tumult, as anchovies, sardines and bluefins struggled to free themselves from capture. Some flung themselves into the air, a few even landing in Cino's boat!

"Let's go, said Anteo, and the two boys rowed out of the roiling mass. With them gone, the men on the boat cinched the net shut and dragged it in, bulging like *Babbo Natale*'s[46] sack. By the time the boys rowed back to the menaita, the hold was full of flopping.

"You did it!" Aldo exclaimed, pride shining from his face. "Good job, boys." He extinguished the lamps, scooped the fish out of the dinghies and kissed his son on the top of the head. Cino's face flushed.

The men rowed home, packed the fish up to go off to the cannery, reeled int the dinghies and trooped home, exhausted but overjoyed. Cino sighed with contentment and looked east over the water, as the first gray fingers of dawn crept over the horizon.

Two years of late nights and early mornings later, Cino sat on his bed in the room he grew up in, staring down at a battered leather suitcase. One by one, he pulled his few belongings from a drawer, cradling them thoughtfully before packing them away. Each piece of clothing held a memory: the shirt with the oil stain, from when the American ship sank outside Civitavecchia, and they waded out to scoop K rations from the black water. The shorts he had worn when he stepped on that nail on La Feniglia, and Doretta had made him lie on a bed in the kitchen until the swelling died down. The cloth shoes that Babbo and Attilio used to make, before that all fell apart. Cino sniffed back a tear, buckled the suitcase, and prepared to leave Le Grotte for good.

---

[46] Father Christmas (Santa Claus)

It all started with those pen nibs, he thought. After the sweet summer of 1945—a summer blooming with *barroccini*[47] races and makeshift soccer games—the old routine had settled back over Porto Ercole, and things started creeping toward normal. The menaite drew circles on the water; the cannery wafted its sickly, salt smell over the docks; men heaved and hoed as new buildings stretched like infant fingers between the two sister villages. Cino kept working on *La Menaita della Domenica* while his father made his way to Civitavecchia, seeking more lucrative work on one of the larger town's pescherecci. The Procaccini settled back into Santo Stefano, and most weekends Cino hitched a ride over and sat by the seaside with his brother.

When the fall came around, another old routine picked up again: Cino went back to school. He tried to protest, but Doretta insisted. "You waste your mind thinking about fishing, and fighting, and America," she said. "You want to be something someday? Go to school, listen to your teacher, and learn how to be a good boy."

Cino wasn't so sure that was going to happen, but you had to finish fifth grade to qualify for a *libretto di navigazione*[48] and he was still stuck back in third, so he figured it couldn't hurt.

Crammed around a single, long table in a too-small classroom, Cino and his friends debated about who their teacher would be.

"I hope we get Maestro Cammerini again," one said. "He's soft like a marshmallow."

"Nah," said another, "he won't be back. Not after Cino here sent him tumbling on down that hill like—what's his name?—Humpty Dumpty!"

---

[47] Soapbox carts
[48] Seaman's license – the document needed to work on a peschereccio or shipping liner

The class laughed and struck up the rhyme that the soldiers had taught them: *"Humpty Dumpty sat on a wall / Humpty Dumpty had a great fa—"*

The door flew open. In its frame stood a large woman, silhouetted by the sun. The children shielded their eyes as she strode in the room.

"Good morning class," she announced briskly. "My name is Signorina Carbone, and I will be your teacher this year." She wrote her name on the chalkboard and turned to face her students, picking them over like a farmer seeking out rotten apples. Cino gulped.

She was a good teacher; there was no doubt of that. Smart, stern, and strong-willed, Sig.na[49] Carbone reigned over the classroom like the Roman Emperors she spoke of in her long history lessons. She lived in Orbetello, and every day rode her bicycle across the bridge to the promontory—come rain or come shine, come hell or high water. Nothing could stop Sig.na Carbone.

Not that Cino didn't try. Ten years on Earth hadn't softened his sharp edges—more like refined them into a subtler blade—and he was still one of the "liveliest" kids in the class. It wasn't that he sought to make trouble: just that there was only so much room in his brain for dates and names, the tedious regurgitation of verses written by thousand-year-old men wrapped in sheets. Math was the only subject that could hold his attention: he found a certain beauty in the regular dance of numbers and figures, like waves in the ocean. How to chart a course, how to bake bread, how to chip the goalkeeper—it all came down to a sequence of inputs and outputs that worked every time, for everyone, everywhere. *I'm learning the same math here that they learn in America*, he found himself thinking. That was something he could take with him.

---

[49] Abbreviation of "Signorina"

The other stuff, though, just felt useless, so while Sig.na Carbone prattled on, Cino's mind wandered, and his hands fiddled, and soon enough he would look up to see her glaring eyes boring into him, and her meaty finger pointing to the timeout spot in the corner. He spent so much time kneeling in that corner with his nose to the wall, he wondered if eventually they would become one. So he understood why he took the fall for the pen nibs, though that didn't make it hurt any less.

She was talking about the Renaissance that day, or something. Something about a painter, or a sculptor, or one of those foofy de Medicis who bankrolled everything back then. It didn't matter. All Cino could focus on was the winter briskness in the air, the bird singing just outside the window. They called to him to run, to bound, to breathe deeply. So he was as surprised as everyone else when time came to copy down Signorina's lecture, and they all discovered that the pen nibs had disappeared from the inkwells!

(In 1945, see, pens were no good without nibs. Mechanical pencils and ballpoints hadn't yet reached Porto Ercole, so people wrote with yellow No. 2's and fountain pens. The pens had detachable metal nibs that you dipped in small tubs of ink, then scrawled across the paper like those old men in their sheets. Without nibs, fountain pens were pretty much just sticks, only good for sword fights when Signorina Carbone's back was turned.)

A hand shot up. It was Teresa, Cino's neighbor in L'Ospizio. They were friends—he may even have had a bit of a crush on her—but she was a no-doubt, A+ teacher's pet: *capoclasse*[50] of the third grade, a smart aleck and a goody two-shoes.

"Signorina Carbone?" she said. "Somebody stole all the nibs."

---

[50] Head of the class: the student in charge of collecting homework, stocking supplies and helping the teacher.

"What do you mean, stole?" Sig.na Carbone asked.

"Well, they were all here this morning—I put them out myself—and now they're gone. So I think someone took them."

"Is that so? Okay class, who here stole all the pen nibs?"

Thirty pairs of eyes turned toward Cino—not including Carbone's, which had never strayed from his face. They did not accuse so much as assume: nobody had seen him take the nibs, and few would care if he had. But they were students of history, in their own way, and history told them that if someone played a trick right under the teacher's nose, it was probably Cino. Even if it weren't, he was the perfect scapegoat: always in trouble and usually guilty. He had made his own bed, now he got to lie in it.

"What?" Cino exclaimed. "Why are you looking at me? I had nothing to do with it." His classmates shook their heads disapprovingly, while shooting him thumbs-ups under the table. He looked down at his chest to see if there was a bulls-eye painted there.

Evidently Teresa saw one, because she drew an arrow from her quiver, notched it and took aim. "I saw him do it!" she squealed. "He took them all and hid them somewhere."

Cino shot her a wounded look. *Et tu, Teresa?*

"Is this true, Cino?" blazed Sig.na Carbone.

"What? No! I've just been sitting here listening to…to all that Renaissance stuff you said! That was really great stuff…"

"That's IT!" she shouted. "I've had enough of you disrupting my class. Go to your corner and I won't hear another word out of you!"

There was nothing he could do. The inquisition was over, and he had been found guilty without a trial. He assumed his familiar spot in the corner, flinging daggers over his shoulder at Teresa's triumphant face. Sig.na Carbone, however, was not satisfied. Enraged, she grabbed his bookbag and swung it about, Goliath with a sling of his own. Taking aim at the kneeling, saintly David, she hurled the bag at the back of his head. Direct hit! Cino pitched forward from the blow, almost breaking his nose against the classroom wall. After that came books, papers, anything she could get her hands on. *What is it with big, angry women and throwing things at my head?* he wondered.

Eventually, Sig.na Carbone settled down, the nibs were located and the class bent their heads to the task. Cino kneeled and seethed—he had been framed! Here he was, just a young boy trying not to pay attention in class, and they had all made him the bad guy. Especially that *bimba,*[51] Teresa. Some friend she was. She probably forgot to put the nibs out in the first place, then blamed it on him to cover her own butt. So much for love: this was war.

Cino stole a glance behind him and realized, to his delight, that he had been forgotten. The kids scribbled studiously while Sig.na Carbone sifted through paperwork on her desk. Now was his chance. As quietly as a churchmouse, he gathered up his possessions and packed them into his bookbag. He breathed deeply, counted to three, then stood up and scampered out the door. Nobody moved to stop him.

Cino ran out of the school and didn't stop until he reached Porto Vecchio. He didn't dream of going home yet: if he came back too early, Doretta would know he had run away from school, and would send one or two of her wooden clogs flying his way. So, instead, he sat by the sea and plotted revenge on his new nemesis.

Eventually, school let out and Cino made his way back. Doretta greeted him warmly and made him a snack; clearly, she had no idea. Cino offered up a silent prayer to the god of small

---

[51] Child, infant

favors. The next day, he went straight down to the marina—there was no way he would go back to school until this wrong had been righted. Looking out over the sparkling sea, he let his mind drift to a place where no one could hurt him: America. *In America*, he thought, *no one puts you in a corner.* Not for the first time, nor for the last, he wondered how and when he would make it to the great nation of his dreams.

Several days passed this way. Cino spent his mornings refining his plan—or just daydreaming—and his afternoons hoping that Doretta did not find reason to come to the harbor. Then, one long-awaited morning, he decided to carry out his attack. Telling Doretta that he had to be at school early to meet with Sig.na Carbone, he rushed from L'Ospizio and hid in a bush near the school. Minutes later, as children streamed from their homes, he spotted Teresa. Closer and closer she came—as she passed the bush, Cino leapt from his hiding spot and was on her before she knew what was happening. "I managed to slap her three or four times before they pulled me off her," he recalls, with only mild embarrassment.

As he wreaked his vengeance, Cino screamed at Teresa to take it back. "Tell them it's not true! Tell them you didn't see me steal those nibs! Tell them!"

Teresa sobbed out the truth. "Fine, Cino, I didn't see you take them. Are you happy now?" She turned and ran back to L'Ospizio, face in her hands and blood on her nose.

When Cino realized that she was going to tell her parents, he sped off in pursuit. By the time he got back, three stern faces and one tear-stained girl were waiting for him.

"What in the world world has gotten into you?" Doretta exclaimed. "Hurting this sweet little girl? Skipping school? Who do you think you are?" Cino had nothing to say. Teresa's parents just shook their heads, like the kids in class that day.

"Get inside," Doretta said. "You are not going to like what's coming to you."

A few minutes later, she came inside and silently stared him down. Then she snorted a bit, and a smile she couldn't contain spread over her lips.

"Teresa told us what happened. Said you were just paying her back for falsely accusing you. Don't think you're off the hook for skipping school, but as for this? Maybe your Nonna will just let this one slide. After all, sounds like she got what she deserved!" Doretta winked and walked out the door, as Cino collapsed in a heap of relief.

The next day, Doretta walked him all the way to the door of the schoolhouse. Sig.na Carbone and Teresa's family were already there. Teresa admitted to lying, Cino to hitting, and the two sides made peace. "After that," Cino remembers, "Teresa and I became friends, and would always defend each other."

Cino finished out the rest of the school year without incident, and even made it through the fourth grade in 1947, but he knew that his time in a classroom was nearly over. He took no pleasure in lessons and homework: he wanted to be out on the menaita with his grandfather, take long peschereccio trips like his father, and start figuring out how he was going to get to America. Though Porto Ercole was growing, he was growing faster—and soon, he thought, he would leave its shores for good. He just didn't yet know how soon that would be.

Babbo made a big mistake. Cino knew it—Aldo knew it— Doretti and Doretta knew it—Attilio sure knew it—hell, everyone in town knew it. That was the whole problem.

After a few months in Civitavecchia, work dried up for Aldo.

So he came home, and teamed up with Attilio, his haystack *amico,*[52] to make and sell shoes. The shoes they made were of fine quality, made of braided rope encased in cloth. They were stylish, comfortable, and much more lightweight than the wooden clogs that most port'ercolesi wore. They also cost about twice as much as anyone in town could afford—but, in those days, the tourism industry was starting to pick up, and visitors were looking for a hand-crafted, "artisan" piece they could take home as a souvenir. Aldo had the vision; Attilio had the know-how, and an extra room in his house they could use as a workshop.

So the old friends got to work, churning out shoes day and night. They cut cloth, braided rope, stitched the pieces together so they flexed but held firm. Eventually, Attilio's wife began lending a hand: her dark, beautiful eyes staring intently at the cloth, her nimble fingers tracing the lines before she cut deftly and without restraint. Sometimes Attilio would go out to pick up more materials, and then it would just be Aldo and the wife, alone, together, in that dark and cramped room. Sometimes, too, her eyes would dart up from work at hand; her hands would steal across the table; her foot would run up the leg of her husband's rakish partner. Those times, his fingers would clutch back; his eyes would lock with hers; cloth and rope would go flying to the floor.

One day, Aldo showed up at Attilio's front door and found his friend waiting there, shoulders heaving.

"Let's have a little talk," Attilio said.

"About what?" Aldo asked.

"You know what, you sonofabitch."

"What are you talking about?"

"Haven't I been good to you? Haven't I given you my home,

---

[52] Friend

my work, my… Does that mean nothing to you? Does our friendship mean nothing to you at all?"

"Attilio, I—"

"She's pregnant!" he exploded. "And you are nothing but a scoundrel."

Aldo's eyes widened. "Congratu—" the world spun and he hit the ground.

Attilio shook out his hand and spat. "Don't ever come back," he said as he slammed the door shut.

Eight months later, the poor woman pushed and pushed, dark eyes watering in pain. Her husband stood beside her, jaw clenched. The boy emerged—they spanked him and he cried. His mother held him tenderly; Attilio walked out of the room. Aldo was already long gone.

He left just a few days after Attilio's accusation, back to the mainland for more fishing work. A spot on a peschereccio out of Santa Marinella opened up, and Aldo jumped at the chance to leave town. For the next two years he spent most of his time on the water, living with a port'ercolesi family in Santa Marinella between trips. He ventured home only rarely, and then just for long enough to eat his mamma's cooking and give his son a kiss. Then it was back to the mainland before anyone could find out he was around. It reminded Cino of when his uncle Pietro hid from the angry women, and he flushed with shame.

In early 1948, Aldo materialized again. It was a Saturday: his boat had just come in that morning. Cino came back from playing to find him sitting in Doretti and Doretta's living room, sipping wine.

"Come here, son," he beckoned. Cino hesitated—something didn't feel right.

"Come here," said Aldo. "I have something to tell you."

Cino sat down.

Aldo leaned toward him, toying with his hands in his lap. "I'm moving to Santa Marinella, permanently," he said. "I met a woman there, and we fell in love. I'm going to move in and then we'll be married soon."

"What!" Cino almost fell out of his chair. "Why?"

Aldo looked puzzled. "I—because I love her? Because it will be good for our children?"

"Who? Who is she?"

"Her name is Anna D'Andrea. Her husband died in the War, now she lives with her grandmother and father and son. They're making ends meet, but it's hard. Think about it, Cino—we can be a family again! We don't have to be alone anymore!"

"What do you mean, *we*?"

"You and me, of course. Cino, I want you to come with me. Not now, but in the summer, when school's over. I want you to come be part of our family."

"Why should I?"

"Because you're my son."

"So is Alberto."

There was a pause. Aldo cleared his throat uneasily. "You know he can't come. You know how this works."

"Not really," Cino said, honestly. "How long would we be there for, anyway?

"In Santa Marinella? Forever, of course! Or at least until you're old enough to get your libretto. Then you can go wherever you want."

Cino thought for a moment. "No thanks."

"What?"

"I mean no thanks—I'll just stay here with Nonno and Nonna."

"I don't think you understand, Cino. This isn't a choice. I've already discussed it with your grandparents. When the school year ends, I'll come get you and you'll live with me."

So now, in the summer of 1948, twelve-year-old Cino buckled shut his battered suitcase and ventured one last look at the life he was leaving behind. He wondered what his bed would smell like next time he was back, what doily things would take over the shelf where he kept his rocks and bits of metal. They probably didn't have barrocini races in Santa Marinella, or places where you could watch the pescherecci do their *scocciatura*[53] as they came in. He certainly couldn't just hitch a quick ride to see Albertino...Cino sighed, a deep sigh, and met his family at the door. He kissed each one in turn and hugged his nonno and nonna extra tightly, thinking that maybe if he took a bit of them with him, he wouldn't be so lonely when he got there.

Sullenly, and without a word, Cino lugged his battered suitcase into the strange apartment. When he straightened up, there she was: his Wicked Stepmother. Average build, curly brown hair, bright, lively eyes. She smiled at him sweetly and bent down to kiss his cheeks. He ducked away from her, right into a smack upside the head from his father.

"It's nice to meet you, Cino," she said. "Your father's told me so much about you."

---

[53] Coming in from a fishing trip, peschereccio fishermen toss excess fish and scraps overboard, resulting in seagull feeding frenzies that writhe behind every returning peschereccio.

Cino scowled like he had just stumbled upon a rotting anchovy on the beach. He allowed himself to be subjected to her kisses, unmoving like the stone walls of Forte Filippo. *You're going to regret asking my father to bring me here*, he thought, as Aldo ushered him off toward his room.

From then on, Cino made it his mission to torment Anna as much as he could. If he saw her mopping, he would run outside, get dirty and track mud over the spot she had just mopped. If she arranged glasses or trinkets on the shelf, he would make sure to rearrange them—or, perhaps, *de*-arrange them—as quickly as possible. His plan was simple: make Anna's life so miserable that she would march right back to Aldo and say, "I changed my mind—that child is a nightmare. Get him out of here before he drives me mad."

But Anna didn't crack. She kept smiling that sweet smile at Cino and saying things like, "You must be hungry after all that running around in the mud!" or, "What a clever arrangement! I never would have thought of that myself." Her resolve was strong, and the longer it took to break her the less Cino could remember the smell of his nonna's kitchen, or the music tinkling in from across the L'Ospizio courtyard. He searched his pockets for the traces of his grandparents he had brought along, but he couldn't find them anywhere.

One day, he stepped it up a notch. It was almost dinnertime, and Anna was boiling pasta for the family. Aldo was at work and Mario, her five year-old son, was coloring in another room. The only other person around was Maria, Anna's half-sister, who was four years *younger* than Cino. Anna was alone, defenseless, with her back to the doorway. Cino crept up behind her and in one swift motion darted to the left, reached out and dropped a live toad into the pot. It flopped frantically in the hot water, and she let out the kind of scream that curdles milk—the kind of scream he'd been hoping to hear. Cino stood triumphantly in the middle of the kitchen while she steadied her breathing. Then she turned to him.

"Well?" she demanded.

"Well what?"

"Well, aren't you going to go sit down? Dinner's almost ready!"

Cino hesitated.

"We're having frog linguine!" she scoffed. Her laughter followed Cino back to his room.

Cino spent most of that summer out of the house, avoiding his new fake family. He could barely even tell them all apart: Anna's grandmother, Adele, lived with her and Anna's father, Alfredo, in the house; Anna's mother, Ernesta, lived down the road with her *compagno,*[54] Vincenzo, and their two children, Angelo and Maria—the half-sister younger than Cino. Anna's full sisters, Lorenza, Mirella, and Anigella, lived elsewhere in town with families of their own. On Sundays, they gathered for Mass and a meal—a large, boisterous, and not always friendly dinner that lasted for hours. In this way, at least, Cino felt right at home.

It's not like Aldo made things much easier for Cino, either. As much as he hated to admit it, his father was a *farfallino*: a little butterfly, flitting from place to place like he had no responsibilities at all. That summer of 1948, he spent his days working as a lifeguard on a private beach, and his nights leaving half his paycheck behind at the poker table. When he was at home, he would do magic tricks for the kids and dance his wife around the

---

[54] Companion. In Catholic Italy, where divorce was illegal until 1974, it was common for unhappily married couples to separate and live with other people, while remaining married to each other. Often, as was the case with Ernesta, *acompagnati* even started their own families.

apartment, but when the time came to do chores or discipline his son, he would vanish like Harry Houdini. For the life of him, Cino couldn't understand why his father had gone to the trouble of bringing him to Santa Marinella if he was just going to ignore him like he always had.

So Cino started exploring the city, and found that it was not altogether so bad. Built on a steep hillside rising up from the Tyrrhenian, Santa Marinella had breathtaking views of the sea and plenty of nooks and crannies to explore along the shoreline. The kids didn't hold barroccini races, but they did ride bikes: Cino and the neighborhood boys would take turns racing down the switchbacked streets, pretending they were Italian hero Gino Bartali taking the yellow jersey in the Tour de France. Sometimes, Cino would stroll past the shops on the *lungomare*, gazing at their wares and counting the few coins in his pocket. Other times he would sub in for his father at the private beach, sitting in his lifeguard chair and gazing hawk-eyed at the vacationers splashing around in the water, primed to dive in and save the day. Still, the days dragged along, and every night he wondered what his friends were doing back home, and how tall Alberto was, and if he still spoke like a Procaccini, like their grandfather, like a learned man.

Finally, the summer ended. Anna urged Cino to enroll in school for one more year, but he would hear nothing of it.

"I hated that place in my own town—you really think I'll go here?" he asked.

"Fine, then. You don't want to go to school, you'd better find yourself a job."

He started work a month before his thirteenth birthday. The local switchboard office needed a runner—someone fast, with a lot of energy to burn—and he was just the young man for the job.

"When a call comes through, you take this note to the client," they told him. "Then you bring them down here and we will patch the call through."

In 1948 on the Tuscan coast, there was no such thing as a home phone. The telephone company had the only phones in town, so when someone got a call they had to go all the way to the company office to answer it. Most people made appointments to speak to their loved ones, but even then, the fact remained: if you wanted to make a call in those days, you were going to be on hold for a very long time.

After a few months at the switchboard company, Cino found new work: delivering coal for the Simone Brothers, the richest men in Santa Marinella. The Simone Brothers owned two hardware stores, a bakery, and a gas station, but the core of their business was coal. Coal was the premier fuel source in those days—more efficient than wood but cheaper than propane—and the Simone Brothers had the Santa Marinella coal market cornered. Every day, women would stop by the Simone Brothers' shop during their grocery runs and order a bag or two of coal. Cino would then load as many of the three-pound bags as he could into the basket of a special tricycle, and would pump his way haltingly up the switchbacked streets to deliver them to their doorsteps.

The job was agony, a Sisyphean trial of up and down, up and down, endlessly looping. In the winter, the rain made the roads slick, and his heavy-laden tricycle slid back down the hill as often as it went up. In the summer, the Mediterranean sun sizzled, and Cino wondered why anyone would need to burn coal when they could just heat things on the sidewalk. Somehow, the ride back down was worse than the ride up. Freed of his burden, Cino would glide down the hill, letting gravity take him and whooping into the whipping wind. But in just a few short minutes, he would be back at the bottom again, and a new stack of bags would be waiting for him to start all over again.

The only thing that made the job worthwhile was the money—
and Cino made a lot of it. Between his hourly wage from the
Simone Brothers and the tips from the old ladies, the teenager soon
found himself flush with cash. So he stopped into the shops that he
had browsed past during the summer, and suddenly the
port'ercolesi boy who ran the streets in tattered jeans and bare feet
was strolling the Santa Marinella strip wearing clothes that fit and
shoes that squeaked. He kept his hair slicked back like the men in
the movies, and even bought himself cologne, though he wasn't
quite sure yet what the point of it was.

One day, on his way to work, Cino noticed a glint in a shop
window. He turned and gasped. It was a sleek, shiny racing bike,
just like the one Cino imagined that Gino Bartali rode in the Tour.
He had to have it—and, after saving up for a few weeks, he did.
Riding home, Cino could hardly believe how his life had changed.
Six months ago, he would not have been able to imagine owning a
bike—or anything else, for that matter. He was suffused with pride
in his hard work, in the dedication he had shown to his job. For the
first time, he felt, he had truly earned something—and he would
cherish the bike the way he cherished that feeling.

"Even with all this though, I still wasn't happy," Cino reports
now. Outside the house, he had everything he wanted: the respect
of his bosses, the affection of his clients, even a few good friends
he could crack wise with. But once he crossed that threshold, he
felt himself grow cold and distant, stray far from the boy he knew
he was. He had to go home.

Finally, he couldn't take it any longer. In the spring of 1949,
Cino told his friends Pietro and Silvestro that he was going to run
away—to escape his wicked *matrinia*,[55] he said. "That was a
complete lie, but I believed it at the time."

---

[55] Stepmother

Perhaps, instead, Cino was running from an even more threatening presence: his half-brother Giuseppe (called Pino), Aldo and Anna's son, born in 1948. The baby couldn't even talk, and Cino already found himself avoiding it—walking into other rooms when he heard it coo, or just pretending like it wasn't there. The anger, the guilt, the frustration, it was all too much to bear. This precious baby boy, tearing his family apart.

Cino may have been lying to himself about the reason, but he made good on his plan. One day, he left home as usual, but instead of going to work he walked to the train station and hopped on a train bound for Orbetello. He wasn't exactly a paying customer, but the way he figured it, fair was fair—there weren't any seats on the train, either. All the passenger cars had been seized by the government during the war, and now riders were forced to sit or stand in cattle cars, holding onto the slats as the train rattled along. Still, you were supposed to have a ticket, so when the ticket collector came around, Cino just hopped to the next car, then back to the first when the guy wasn't looking.

It was a straight shot back to Monte Argentario, sixty kilometers as the crow flies. To pass the time, people sang the old Italian songs. It transported Cino back to those perfect nights in L'Ospizio, when the sky was clear and the moon was high, and the people crammed into the courtyard to dance beneath the warble of Vittorio's voice and Alcide's accordion. It felt like his heart filled up more and more the closer they got to home. That was where he belonged—and when his nonni heard how awful Anna was, they would surely agree to keep him there.

"We can't keep you here," said Doretta. Her voice was firm but her eyes were soft.

"Please, Nonna!" Cino begged. "She treats me like a dog on the street."

"Oh does she now? And how would that be?"

"Well, you know…"

"Does she kick you?"

"No, but—"

"Does she feed you scraps?"

Cino sighed. "She's just…she's not you."

"I know, dear. It's hard, starting over. And we miss you, we do. But you can't just run away from your life. You're a man now—you wanted to be one. And a man handles his responsibilities."

"Not some men I know," Cino mumbled.

Doretta ignored him. "You can stay with us through the weekend, but I'm calling your father to pick you up after Mass."

The next time Cino ran away, he made sure he was better prepared. If playing the sympathy card wasn't going to work, he would have to convince his grandparents he could make it on his own. So he gathered up his nice new shoes and clean new clothes, withdrew all his money from the post office—which is where people kept it in those days—and rode his bike to the station. Gleefully, he imagined the looks on their faces when they saw how well he had done for himself.

That's when he realized his mistake. There's no way he could get on the train with all that stuff, not even with a ticket. He cursed Mussolini's stupid war for getting him in that mess. He gazed west down the tracks: if he peered hard enough, he thought he could see Orbetello just over the horizon. There was only one thing to do. He mounted his bike, balanced his suitcase on the handlebars, and started to ride.

Sixty kilometers he rode, following the tracks. Trains hurtled past, shaking the suitcase loose and caking him in exhaust—like the boy who leaned out the window on the train to Santo Stefano, only with none of the wild-eyed freedom. It took him all day to get to L'Ospizio, and he arrived drenched in sweat. His grandmother eyeballed him at the doorway.

"I'm not letting you in like that," she said.

Cino reached into his pocket and pulled out a jumbled wad of bills, damp from the ride. Doretta looked down at his hand then back up at his dirty *faccia,*[56] then back down again at his hand. She moved aside to let him into the house.

Three days later, Aldo came for him. Cino sat where he could see the bus stop and waited for the inevitable. When his father's wavy brown mop ducked out from *La Carrozza* into the sunlight, Cino ran. He hadn't been meaning to, but he did. His feet took him to the outskirts of town, back up the hill he had known so well. His hands took off his nice shoes and his toes gripped the grass, and his body sank down until he was on his back listening to the bombers thunder over the cliffs, seeing their steel bellies glint as they waggled their wings. *What are you doing now?* he wondered. He imagined a shiny steel plane dropping him off at Lady Liberty's front door; he imagined her smiling to greet him. *Someday,* he thought.

Hunger is what finally brought him back home. He figured if he was going to go back with his father, he might as well get a nice meal first. But when he got to L'Ospizio, Aldo was already gone. In his place was Doretti, beaming.

"You can stay!" Doretti said—cried out, really. Then he did something Cino hadn't seen him do since before the war: he started to laugh! Like a parched desert floor his face cracked open, the

---

[56] Face

sound bubbling forth like spring water. Cino gaped in disbelief. He looked at his nonna, who was seeing to the *sugo*.

"But one mistake and you're out," she said, smiling slightly.

Cino could have jumped for joy. He kissed his grandparents on the cheeks and, while Doretti's laughter still frothed about, ran and dove onto the bed next to the now-doily-covered nightstand.

The next day, Cino polished his bike to a silvery sheen and whipped it through the hills of Monte Argentario. Down from Monte Filippo he flashed, past the convent that looked out over the lake and around the water's edge to Santo Stefano. He felt like a rider on his home course, following his intuition through every curve and crest—like he could simply close his eyes and let the road guide him there. When he swung to a stop in front of the Procaccini house, he felt that the eyes of the whole town were upon him. He rang the doorbell.

A tall boy answered the door—almost as tall as Cino, and lean like their father. Cino enveloped Alberto in a hug. "I can't believe how you've grown!" he exclaimed. "You wanna take a ride?"

"You know it!" Albertino said, as he climbed on the handlebars.

Cino steadied the rig, pumped his foot and they were off. The cobblestones rattled beneath them. Old ladies jumped aside and glared. The wind whipped Alberto's hair back, and he closed his eyes to feel what the birds must feel: the tip of danger, the weightlessness of being surrounded by nothing, but held in place by a force that could only be experienced, never seen.

Down at the *bar*[57], Cino bought his brother a Coke. A few of Albertino's friends walked by, and called out to him.

[57] Café

"Hey, Procaccini Alberto,[58] who's the new guy?" they said.

"Who's this Procaccini Alberto?" he called back. "You looking for my nonno? I'm Chegia Alberto. And this here is my big brother, Chegia Cino. He's been gone for a while, but we're back together again."

Cino patted Alberto and raised his glass. *"Cin cin."*[59]

---

[58] In Italian, it is common for people to call you by your family name first, then your given name.
[59] Cheers

CHAPTER TEN: THE PLUNGE

"Vagabondo sporco!"[60]
- Italian insult

Summer, 1949. Cino stands on Lo Scoglione, a small rock platform on the cliff just below Forte Filippo. Fifteen meters below him, on the water, the tourists cluster in the bow of the boat, pointing and cheering. The tide washes out, revealing sharp rocks like teeth directly beneath him.

"Now!" he shouts. The tourists throw coins into the shallow tidepool between the rocks. The tide washes back in. "Three, two, one!"

Cino flings himself off the cliff, golden and alive in the sun, then dives down headfirst just as the rocks disappear beneath the rising water.

---

[60] "Dirty tramp!"

By the summer of 1949, Monte Argentario was beginning to take a new shape. The rebuilding was almost done, and across the promontory buildings sprouted up bigger and shinier than they had been before. In Porto Ercole, the twin towns grew closer together, touching fingertips like God and Adam in the Sistine Chapel. In Porto Santo Stefano, hotels and villas loomed high up the hillside, lighthouses beckoning in yachting Europeans and adventure-hungry Americans.

That year, for the first time, they came. And when they arrived, with their foreign tongues and expensive jewelry, Cino Chegia came to life.

"The tourists were my favorite people in the world," he says—especially the Americans, of course. When Cino wasn't working as an olive picker or unloading pescherecci on the docks, he took *La Menaita della Domenica* out and ferried wealthy New Yorkers around the promontory, swapping tales of bombing raids for stories from the streets of Manhattan. The more adventurous types he would anchor near Lo Scoglione, then dazzle and delight with the death-defying dives of the Magnificent Cino.

"Many of my friends…cracked their heads open on the sea floor," he says, "but never me." When he emerged with the tourists' coins, the applause would echo through the enclosure. They always let him keep the change, too.

All in all, everything was going great until the incident with the peaches. Cino was making money, spending time with his family, even staying out of trouble—mostly. But then the peaches thing happened, and suddenly it was all turned around again and his father was at the door and he was packing that damn suitcase again.

It started with carob seeds, actually. One of the farmers in town had a carob grove on the property he was tending, and he used to let the neighborhood kids climb into the trees and snack on the seeds. Cino and his friends would often stop there on their way to the swimming hole in Cala Galera, to fuel up before splashing around. One day, as they sat among the branches, dropping empty pods onto the dry grass below, a man approached them. They thought it was the farmer, but it wasn't—it was the landowner himself, a "mean and miserly man" who hated the kids he accused of stealing from him.

"Get down from there!" the landowner shouted, picking up rocks and heaving them at the boys. Under a hail of stones, Cino and his friends dropped from their perches and raced off.

They didn't stop until they reached Cala Galera, and it was only there that Cino realized his stomach was still growling. After a few hours of swimming, he decided to head home, still angry with the landowner for throwing rocks and angry with himself for getting into trouble. Doretta's leash was tight, and he knew that any more ruckus could earn him a one-way ticket back to Santa Marinella.

But still, his hunger churned, and it was hours yet until dinner. Trekking home, he battled his appetite with every step.

"Come on, just a quick snack," it said. "You're a growing boy—you need it!"

"Quiet," Cino snapped. "Haven't you caused enough problems already today?"

"Think about it: you get home hungry, what are you gonna do? Pester Nonna till she hits you with her clog. Go home full, everybody's happy!"

Cino had to admit that his stomach had a point. "Yeah, but it's not like food just magically appears—"

"PEACHES!" it shouted. "Right there! On that tree!"

"That's somebody's farm."

"So? Do you see anybody there? He's probably at home back in Le Grotte. Besides, it's just a couple peaches. The longer you wait, the more likely you are to get caught. Just do it!"

Cino sighed, powerless as any 13 year-old against his own body. He scampered to the peach tree and plucked the ripe fruit from its branches.

Heading home sated, he licked the juice from his fingers and congratulated himself on a wise choice. That's when he saw the man running right at him, eyes burning with anger. Cino knew him right away: it was the farmer who owned the peach orchard!

"You little punk!" the farmer shouted. "*Vagabondo sporco!*"

Cino found himself rooted to the spot, as if terror and guilt were conspiring to hold him there awaiting his punishment. *How on Earth did he find out?* he wondered. But there was no time to solve that puzzle: the farmer was upon him, and his big, calloused hands were flying. The blows came from everywhere, all at once— slaps and kicks, punches, elbows. Cino fell to the ground, nose spurting blood. In the fetal position, he felt like an infant: all sense and no cognition. He could hear the man's shouts, taste the blood and the dirt, feel the pain course from his head to his toes. Finally, the farmer slowed his savagery; the sight of pooling blood pulled him from his violent reverie. He stepped back in shock and dismay, and Cino did not waste the opportunity. Prying himself off the ground, he staggered toward L'Ospizio as fast as he could.

By the time he got home, he was covered in blood. Doretta gasped and clamped a rag down hard on his nose.

"Damn it, Cino! What now?"

"The farmer, from down the street...I took a couple of his peaches. He hit me, Nonna!"

"Well I can see that…sounds like you deserved it, too. How many times have I told you—?"

"A lot. A lot."

"Yeah, a lot. Maybe you'll remember this time. Now go get yourself cleaned up. I'm going to pay a visit to the rotten scumbag who beat up my grandson."

Cino watched from the bathroom window as his grandmother stomped straight over to the farmer's house, just a few doors down. Her hair was gray and thinning—even pulled back into a bun, he could see her scalp through the wisps. She walked with a stoop now, but she was still an imposing woman, and as she strode to the farmer's door he felt almost bad for what was to come. The man opened the door like he had been waiting for her, and the battle began. Hands and spit flew as Doretta mimed beating an invisible but helpless boy. The farmer pointed in retort: up to Cino's window, out to his farm, right in Doretta's face. Slowly he curled his fingers into a fist, waggling it as if to say, "Go home now, or this thing is coming after you next."

"Well," Cino recalls, "that is not something you want to say to Doretta." Turning on her heel, she stepped off the porch and disappeared from view. Cino craned his neck to see where she had gone, but didn't have to wait for long: seconds later she came back into view, twirling a stick like a policeman's baton. The farmer's eyes widened, but it was too late—she launched herself at him, whipping the stick across his arms, his chest, his cheeks and temples until he went down in a heap. He held his hands up in submission, and she dropped the stick by his side.

"*Come una vipera*," Cino muttered, stifling a smile.

That night, Zio Vittorio invited a few friends over to L'Ospizio for dinner. Conversation at the table was drawn taut like skin, and blue-black tension welled up under the surface: the farmer had two sons, and there was no way they would stand for what had happened. It was only a matter of time before—

BANG BANG BANG. Three knocks, loud and demanding. Vittorio nodded to his friends. "You'd better let us get this one," he said solemnly. BANG BANG BANG.

"Yes?"

"Let us in, Vittorio."

"Now why would I do that?"

"You know how this works. Your mother disrespected our father, and now it's time she gets her due!"

"How about this: why don't you give *us* her due, and we'll make sure to pass it along to her?" Vittorio's friends sniggered behind him.

"Don't make this harder on yourselves."

"Let's do some counting, shall we? I count one-two-three-four of us, and only one-two of you! So maybe it's you who shouldn't make this harder on yourselves."

"Our issue is not with you, Vittorio—just let us see your mother and we'll settle this!"

"Your issue *is* with me, actually! You really came here to beat up on an old woman? After your father punched a little boy? Well come on then, let's have some fun!"

Vittorio and company bristled. The two sons glanced at each other. The air hung heavy between them. Then: "This is not over, Chegia. Our family does not forget such disrespect. We'll be back, don't you worry." Their footsteps echoed down the road.

The next day was Sunday. Cino skipped Mass, saying he didn't want the whole town to see his swollen face, and his grandparents didn't argue. He spent the morning filled with foreboding; no one had said anything, but he knew what was coming. After Mass, everyone in town gathered around the field where the bombs first fell, watching the local boys square off in a furious game of *calcio*.[61] Cino watched from afar, hiding from view. Soon enough, he saw him—that familiar wavy mop wending its way through the crowd. Once again, his feet took him to his favorite spot on the hill.

He didn't come back home for hours. He hoped that his father might have a boat to catch, that if he waited long enough Aldo would be forced to go back home empty-handed. His stomach voiced its displeasure, but this time he was dead set on ignoring it. Still, when the moon rose and the night turned cold, Cino picked his way back to L'Ospizio ready to face his fate.

Aldo was sitting at the kitchen table, leafing through a newspaper as if he had nowhere else to be. He looked nonchalantly up at him.

"Oh, hi there son," he said. "You about ready to go?"

Cino shrugged.

"Great! Your bag's already packed. Go get your bike and we can make it to the station in time for the last train."

The next time Cino left would be his last; they all knew that. Aldo had given up on trying to convince him to stay, to work, to build a life in Santa Marinella. Anna still smiled at him sweetly, and little Pino laughed when he saw his brother again, but it was no use. Everyone was simply counting down to the inevitable.

It pained Cino to know that he couldn't go back to L'Ospizio. Aside from those few magical years with his father and mother, it

---

[61] Soccer

was the only home he had ever known. After Laura died, after Aldo and Alberto were taken away, L'Ospizio was there. Even as the bombs fell, gouging holes in its beloved walls, L'Ospizio was still there. But now it was closed to him, battened down against the trouble he had brought upon it. Doretta's warning rang out in his head, and he knew that it was one he would have to heed.

Which really only left one place to go: Cino's ace in the hole, the card he'd been saving for the decisive hand. The only place he could think of that could still be a home to him, but where his father would not dare to go. A few months after his return to Santa Marinella, Cino packed up his clothes again, got on his bike and rode straight to Nonno Procaccini's house.

His grandfather answered the door. Age had thinned Alberto out in every way—his hair was thinner, his body thinner, his voice and even somehow his eyes seemed thinner—but he still loomed inside the doorway. With one glance, he sized up the situation: the bike, the suitcase, the hope and resolve.

"It's about time you showed up," he said. "Rosa! Alberto! Trento! Dirce! I have a surprise for you!"

CHAPTER ELEVEN: SALT OF THE SEA

"Tutto a posto."[62]
- Italian saying

Fall, 1949. Cino shivers in the frigid waters of the Tyrrhenian, wiggling his toes to make sure they still work. Daybreak paints the sky pale yellow, teasing him with its feeble light. He bends over the water, scraping fish scales from a weathered wooden crate labeled *Ala*. Dozens more just like it lie in a pile on the beach behind him. They await his ministrations, the renewal of a bitter cold baptism. He dunks the crate one more time and watches the salt water carry the grit out to sea.

Nearby, two young boys laugh and dash about on the jetty. He watches them for a while. In his mind they have risen early to watch the *pescherecci* leave and the *menaite* return, and now the day is theirs to author. In his heart he remembers their game—not by its name, but by the pure expanse of freedom it inhabits. When

---

[62] "It's all good." (Literally, "Everything is in its place.")

he was their age, on the wharves of Le Grotte, he played sailor or soldier or airman. Now, he just works and watches.

Lost in thought, he almost doesn't notice when the boyish shouts cease, when the morning grows eerily still around the creak of the boxes. The silence reverberates, though, and he looks sharply to the jetty. The two boys have become one: just one, small and frightened, waving his arms over the gloomy water. Cino drops the crate and races to the boy's side.

"What's going on?" he demands.

The boy grabs his hand, looks up at him through tear-filled eyes. "Help us, help us! My friend fell in and he doesn't know how to swim!"

If the boy says any more, Cino doesn't hear it, because he has already flung himself into the water. He spies the other boy quickly, floating limply below the surface. Ushering all his strength, Cino grabs him and flings him back up on the jetty.

"He's not breathing!" cries his friend.

Cino pushes him aside and leans over the boy's body. His father's words, the lessons he learned as a lifeguard in Santa Marinella, resound in his head. *Open the airway. Five quick pumps. Pinch the nose and breathe into the mouth. Don't give up.* He tilts the boy's head back and pumps: One. Two. Three. Four. Five. He squeezes and breathes. Again. One. Two. Three—

The boy coughs, retches, rolls to the side. Seawater spews onto the jetty. His friend cries out and cradles his head as he slowly opens his eyes. Cino laughs loud then sits back, suddenly exhausted and freezing.

"Take him home," he says. As they boys hurry off, he drags himself to his feet and stumbles home, leaving the crates piled on the beach.

Nonna Rosa is the only one home when he arrives: Nonno Alberto, Zio Trento and Albertino are all working, and Zia Dirce has taken her young son Roberto to market. At the sight of him, Rosa throws down her ladle and wraps him in a towel.

"Go sit by the fire," she instructs him, without even asking what happened.

Hours later, the towel has become a blanket and there is a cup of tea between Cino's knees. The doorbell rings. Cino heaves himself up in his best impression of his grandfather, hawking one into Alberto's spittoon for good measure. The woman at the door is all arms and bosoms and cheeks, that envelope Cino before he can even think to protest. He tries to dodge her kisses and tears, but only manages to tangle himself up in his blanket.

"You brave, brave boy," she murmurs. "That was my grandson you pulled from the water, you brave boy."

She draws two dusty bottles from a bag at her side. "The best vintage from my cantina. Usually, we save this stuff for the tourists—no one here can afford it—but it's my gift to you. I know it's not much compared to what you gave me, but it's the best I can do."

With that, the woman turns on her heel and walks off, giving him one last twinkling look as she rounds the corner. Cino smiles down at the bottles—he knows just what to do with them.

The next day was Sunday, and like any Sunday you could follow your nose all the way down to the Ala Company warehouse. The delicious aroma of simmering sugo wafted up on the salt breeze, carrying heavy notes of fish and the smell—almost a feeling—of softening bread, like the earth after a thaw. It was *cacciucco*[63] day at Ala, and the fishermen sang as they stirred the mammoth pot with a wooden spoon nearly as tall as Cino.

They looked up as he rounded the corner of the warehouse, and the heckling started almost immediately.

"Well, well, would you look who it is! It's the hero himself. You hear he saved a baby from drowning yesterday?"

"I heard it was two. Or was it twelve?"

"I hear that after he saved that boy he dove back in, rescued five baby ducklings from the mouth of a shark, then helped a crippled man on his way home!"

"Strange how after all that good work, somehow he couldn't get around to cleaning out the rest of them crates over there!"

The men laughed uproariously, and Cino laughed right along with them. Suddenly, he whipped the two bottles out from behind his back and waggled them before their eyes.

"I mean—what a good lad that Cino is, isn't he?!" they said suddenly.

"Wasn't I just saying to you how good a lad that Cino is?"

"Listen, son, why don't you come pull up a chair around the cacciucco pot and pass around that wine, and you can tell us all about your great heroism!"

Cino sat down and popped the cork, and their faces grew ruddy as toasts were raised to the boy of the hour.

After Cino arrived in Santo Stefano, his first order of business was to find a job. Fortunately, that wasn't too hard: his uncle Trento, Laura's brother, was a mechanic with the Ala Fishing

---

[63] Fish stew

Company, which owned a few pescherecci, and set Cino up doing odd jobs around the warehouse. Albertino, 11 years old at the time, also worked for Ala: he was apprenticed to Trento, and spent his days in Ala's machine shop, running for spare parts and watching his uncle cut out gears for engines and winches. Every morning, the three men trooped down from the home they all shared with Nonno and Nonna Procaccini—Trento and Alberto headed toward the shop, and Cino circled around back to clean out crates of fish.

The work was brutal from start to finish: crates would come in from the markets where Ala sold its wares, and Cino would scrape off the gunk to get them ready for the next hauls. With that done, he would carry the crates to the warehouse and start chopping ice from a large block, wielding an icepick with numb, clumsy hands. When the pescherecci came in and dumped their catches, he packed them all into the crates, layered each with ice, and loaded them onto a truck to head back out onto the mainland. If peddling coal was a Sisyphean task, working in Ala's warehouse was a trial of Hercules, waged somewhere near the North Pole.

To add insult to his tired arms and cold feet, the Ala Company couldn't even pay him half the time. Much of its fleet had been damaged during the War, and owners Bernardino Bausani and Oreste Costanzo were still paying off debt from the repairs. As a result, Ala only paid its employees when it could afford to. That was not often enough for the Procaccinis, who already had too many mouths to feed when one more showed up. Cino in particular couldn't afford not to get paid: he had left all his money in the Santa Marinella post office when he ran away, and had promised his grandparents he would pay his own way. So, being Cino, he figured out a way to pay himself.

It was an easy hustle, really. The fishermen brought their hauls into the warehouse for Cino to pack in ice, then they just left them there for a while. As he packed the fish, he would nick a few for himself, hide them away then sell them directly to the fishmonger at the end of the day. *The bosses must know*, he told himself. *It's not like I'm the first person to do this. It's just part of the job. Probably for the best anyway: Ala's already in enough debt, they don't need to be in debt to me, too*! With Cino, Ala was in good hands: until they could pay him what he earned, he would personally make sure all was square. Still, he always looked over his shoulder as he hurried toward the fish market.

The only good thing about working in the Ala warehouse was that it brought Cino, Trento and Alberto together. They would sit side-by-side on their lunch break, eating whatever Nonna Rosa had prepared for them all, and talk shop. Alberto reveled in his work as an apprentice mechanic, and often the normally taciturn boy would gush as he spoke of the work he and Trento had done.

"You should have seen it, Cino," he said. "This winch came in, totally mangled from that storm a few nights ago. Zio opened it right up and figured out what was wrong, lathed out a new piece, banged the thing back into shape and put it all back together—all this morning!" As he spoke, Alberto's hands moved unconsciously, mimicking his uncle's nimble pulses.

Cino, meanwhile, knew he couldn't last much longer in that warehouse. Cacciucco Day had crystallized in his mind what he already felt in his heart: that he was meant to be out on a peschereccio, hauling in nets with bearded crusaders who spat out ribaldry with their tobacco juice. He was a Chegia, after all, born with saltwater in his veins, and it was time he met his fate out there on the sea.

He told his grandfather so much one day. Alberto straightened up and appraised him with a searching eye.

"You don't want to be a fisherman," he declared.

"Sure I do!" Cino protested.

"No, you don't. Fishermen don't get to go to America. What you want is to get on a merchant vessel."

"Well, someday…"

"Good, good," Alberto said, smiling. "Long time now you've been chasing that dream. Gotta keep working toward it, or you'll end up stuck here for good. But you can't get your libretto di navigazione yet—you know why?"

Cino nodded. "Because I never finished fifth grade."

"Precisely. If you want to get out on the water, you have to prove to them you can do your times tables and conjugate the *passato prossimo*.[64] Knowing how well you paid attention in school, I'd say you had better get studying!"

Two weeks later, Cino sat in the Harbor Office of Castiglione di Pescaia, near Grosseto, staring down at a test cluttered with letters and numbers. He wrote here, circled there, underlined this and that—in minutes, he held a passing grade in his hand. He had studied harder for this equivalency test than he had for anything else in his life, and soon it would all pay off. He handed it to the Harbormaster and waited for the man to present him a libretto di navigazione in exchange.

The Harbormaster stepped out for a moment, then returned.

"Sorry, kid, no luck," he said matter-of-factly.

"What do you mean, no luck?"

"I mean, I can't give you a libretto today. We've already reached our quota."

"But I passed the test! Look at my scores!"

"I see that. But we don't have any left to give this season."

---

[64] Past perfect: the standard past tense in Italian grammar.

"So that's it then?"

"Well, not quite. I can give you this." He pulled a slip of paper out from his desk and slid it to Cino. It was of sturdy stock, and heavy with the ink of the embossed lettering.

"*Foglio di Ricognizione*," Cino read aloud.

"This entitles you to work on local ships, ferries and such. Nothing that goes out on open water. You can't fish, but I bet you'd make a fine deckboy."

Cino nodded and stuck out his hand. Then he ran out the door and around the marina, plotting how to ask Bernardino Bausani to get him on a boat.

They put him on the *Vincere*, a small boat that fished in the waters around Santo Stefano. She was old, patched up, faded down to a dull gray. Torn nets dangled from her deck, and the water's chop revealed a hull studded with barnacles. She was a thing of beauty. He watched from the dock as the men loaded her up—they moved fast, with precision, without speaking. Nothing like the menaita, his uncles cursing as they clumsily stacked boxes in the dark. Cino would have to learn the ropes quickly if he wanted to keep up with these men.

Unfortunately, things didn't get off to the best start. Ever since he moved to Santo Stefano, he had barely stepped foot on a boat—and on his first day, it showed.

"You must be the new *mozzo*," the captain said as they motored out of the harbor. He nodded. "Good. Go make me some coffee."

Cino hurried to the *Vincere*'s small kitchen, eager to make a good impression. He swept the ash from the stove, lit a new stack of coals and set the water on top to boil. As the men packed away the last of the gear and began to haul up anchor for their voyage, he took the pan of ash onto the deck to toss overboard. "But I forgot Rule #1 of life on a boat," he laments, "throw things out *with* the wind, not against it!" The entire pan of ash blew back across the ship's bow, coating everything—and everyone—on deck. The fishermen cursed as they wiped stinging soot from their eyes; the men watching from the dock held their bellies with laughter.

Cino flushed with shame and tried to run back into the kitchen. Before he could get there the captain seized him by the collar, held him against the railing and slapped him hard across the face. Cino never threw anything out against the wind again.

Over the next few months, Cino took dozens of trips on the *Vincere*, hauling up branzini within sight of the shore. As deckboy, his duties were to cook and clean for the men, to swab the deck, to assist the captain, and to be on hand for whatever else was needed. After that first mishap, he worked diligently, and eventually the men took to him. They offered him pointers about fishing and life on the sea: "Pinch the net together like this as you cast it out so it doesn't get tangled." "Don't let your shadow trail over the water, or the fish might see it and get scared." Cino absorbed it all as his brother absorbed the mechanic's trade, filing it away for the day when it became his turn to grip the lines and heave.

After a while, however, life on the *Vincere* became tiresome. The short fishing trips started to feel dull, and it seemed like every time the old boat left port, something else broke down. He yearned for the adventure of the high seas, with nothing and no one to save you but your wits.

To make matters worse, moving from the Ala Company's warehouse to its fleet did nothing to help secure Cino's salary. If anything, it put his pay even more at risk. Ala operated like a partnership: everyone who worked on the boats earned a share of each haul they brought in. Half of all profits went to the owners, with the other half divided among the crew. "Of that money, a part and a half went to the Captain, and part and a half went to the Engineer, and the remaining part was divided evenly among us," Cino says. With five crewmen aboard the *Vincere*, Cino's share worked out to 1/40th of the money the *Vincere* brought in. On good days, that could be enough to pay Cino's way for a week; on bad days, it was barely enough for a bottle of milk. With the Ala Company battling creditors and the *Vincere* in disrepair, there were a lot more bad days than good days.

One day, Cino came home to find his grandfather waiting.

"You still want that libretto?" Alberto asked.

"Of course!"

"Good. Because some just opened up in Castiglione della Pescaia. I pulled a few strings and they agreed to save one of them for you. If we go there tomorrow you can be on a new boat by next week!"

The next day they arrived in Castiglione della Pescaia to find the village sunning itself in the morning light. Bronzed couples lounged on the yellow sand beach while their children flung themselves into the waves, screaming with delight. The town fortress loomed overhead, a living reminder of the days when surprise attacks came from the sea, not from the air. Bypassing the shimmering beachfront, Cino and Alberto made a beeline for the Harbor Office. Cino filled out his application, presented the necessary information, and with a stamp and a cough the thin-lipped woman placed his future right into his hand. Cino stared at the paper. Could it really be that easy? Was such a small, insignificant thing really the key to the life he had dreamed of? How easy it would be for a gust of wind to take it, or a thorn to tear it, or water to soak it through… Cino folded it neatly and placed it in his pocket.

"Come on, let's go celebrate," Nonno Alberto said. "Ever been to a real restaurant?" Cino, fifteen years old, shook his head.

———————

They put him on the *Santo Stefano*, as a deckboy. The fifteen-meter peschereccio was the workhorse of Ala's fleet, and brought in nearly half its revenue. She often went out for a week or more at a time, skipping outside Porto Santo Stefano's waters all the way to Sardinia or the French island of Corsica. Her hold was so big that other Ala ships used it as a waystation, dropping off their hauls before heading out again.

Those first few trips were the most exhilarating of Cino's young life. Far to sea they ranged, whipped by the wind, until home was just a speck in the distance and the only sound was the shriek of birds overhead. After a few hours Sardinia would rear up over the horizon, sprawled out like a fat man face-up in a pool. They would follow the coastline to one fishery or another, eventually dropping anchor and drifting for a while. As they idled, the Captain and the Chief Fisherman would peer and prognosticate, draw circles and nod. Satisfied, the men would roll up their sleeves, drop the net behind them and set the *Santo Stefano* churning through the waves.

When they fished farther offshore, in deeper water, Captain Lofreddo had the men keep the net out for three or four hours at a time. Those days, life was a breeze. The men smoked, laughed, cleaned the fish and played cards, while Cino fixed coffee and sandwiches and practiced tying knots. They swapped bawdy jokes and extolled the virtues of the female form, not minding that their deckboy was the same age as many of their children. Those days, when the sun was high and the men opened their arms to the wind, Cino felt like a prince.

On *scappuzoni* days, however, he felt more like a peasant.

Scapuzzoni is shallow-water fishing, which the crew often did by the town of Alghero, on the south side of Sardinia. The smaller, more tender fish there brought their weight in lira, but they were treacherous to catch. The waters around Alghero were studded with sharp rocks and coral intent on ripping their net, so the crew never kept the net out for more than an hour. That meant that the deck work that usually took three or four hours—sorting and cleaning the fish, packing in ice, swabbing the deck for the next haul—had to happen in about 45 minutes. Those days, the men worked nonstop, barely getting a chance to breathe before the net came up again and another squirming gray mass spilled out onto the deck. Those days there was no laughter, no wheeling and dealing, no freedom. There was only work. "Oh, and did I mention this kind of fishing started at 4 a.m. and didn't end until late in the evening?" Cino adds.

Then there were those days when he felt not so much like a peasant, but like the sickly ass pulling the plow. Out on the open water, with no mountains to break the wind and no shelter from storm, things could get a little rough. The first few times Cino went out, when the rolling got so bad that he could no longer tell whether he or the horizon was spinning, he'd drift over to the railing, struck with the sudden need to get rid of his lunch.

"Man overboard!" the men would shout. "He's chumming the waters!"

"Hey, deckboy: don't get any of that on the boat, or your ass is gonna have to clean it!"

Cino would try his best to smile through the green—he wanted more than anything to buck up, get back to work, earn the respect of his peers. But then the *Santo Stefano* would pitch again, and the world would fold in at the corners. Eventually, though, the young mozzo found his sea legs, and soon enough could serve coffee in a rainstorm without spilling a drop.

And so it went for nearly two years. A week out at sea, back for a day or two to repair and restock, then out again. Alghero, Caloforte, Caprera. Calloused hands and wind-burnt skin, the permanent stench of fish and sweat. Cino's eyes drifting out toward the horizon, following the merchant ships to their unseen destinations across the sea. Someday, he knew he would get there—but for now, the fisherman's life made for plenty of exciting tales.

The Tale of Canapino and the Cow

One tale, for example, began when the *Santo Stefano* set out to do scapuzzoni outside Alghero. To get there, the boat had to go through *Le Bocche di Bonifacio*, a narrow strait separating the northern tip of Sardinia from the southern end of Corsica. The strait ended in a channel they called *I Fornelli*, "the stovepipe"—a strip where the two islands nearly kiss, leaving only three kilometers of water between them. The waves grew choppier there, threatening to crash boats against the tall rocks that jutted out like the teeth of Charybdis. Fishermen never passed through in rough seas, and even whether the weather was calm, they crept through slowly, hugging as tightly as possible to the tiny Sardinian island of Caprera.

Covered in lush grass, Caprera is a popular destination for Sardinian ranchers to bring their cowherds. Every time the *Santo Stefano* brushed past, the men would look out at the gentle giants, who stared back blankly while chewing their cud.

"Red meat!" the men would shout, sometimes leaning out to try to touch them. "I swear, one of these days we should just spear one, carve it up and stick it in the hold. Would bring in a pretty penny at market!" Of course, no one ever did. That is, until someone did.

His name was Canapino. He was a good fisherman, but

pazzo—crazy as the day is long. He used to heft a harpoon as they rounded Caprera and pretend to throw it at the cows. The first time he did it, Cino yelped and rushed to stop him. The tenth time, he figured the man was just full of fluff.

So he didn't think much of it when Canapino called him to the bow one morning, as they passed Caprera about a year into Cino's service.

"I'm gonna get one this time," he shouted into the kitchen. Cino ignored him and went about his business.

Then he heard the grunt, and saw the rope on deck uncoil, and dashed out too late to see the spear flung from Canapino's hand, straight into the haunch of a cow just meters away. The thing bellowed; Canapino squealed. The boat motored on, pulling the helpless creature into the shallows as it scrambled for footing.

"What the hell do you think you're doing?" Cino demanded. "You're going to get us all arrested!"

Canapino grinned savagely. By then, the wounded bleating had drawn the rest of the crew out of the cabin, cursing Canapino for his foolishness. They watched as the force of their motion wrenched the harpoon from the cow's leg, taking a hunk of flesh with it. The poor creature floundered onto shore, its blood streaming into the sea. Three men appeared on the rim of the hill, screaming at the boat as they slid down to tend to their livelihood.

By the time the *Santo Stefano* reached Alghero, the *Guardia di Finanza*[65] was waiting. They had barely dropped anchor when a gleaming steel vessel, its deck studded with machine guns and lined with ominous uniformed men, sidled up next to them.

"Stay where you are," blasted the military ship. "You will be

---

[65] Financial Guard. A cross between Customs and the Coast Guard, the Financial Guard patrols Italy's waters for smugglers and pirates but may also be called in for other maritime disputes, such as a fisherman harpooning a rancher's cow.

boarded and questioned. If you do not comply, we will arrest you."
The *Santo Stefano* complied, and four men wearing we-mean-
business looks stepped aboard. One by one, they interviewed the
crew; one by one, the men denied knowing anything about any
harpooned cow. Even Cino held his tongue—though his insides
churned at the awful thing Canapino had done, the boy was no rat.
The Guardia di Finanza left without arresting anyone, but the
incident left Cino with a bad taste in his mouth. "After that day, I
decided I didn't want to work on fishing boats anymore."

Before Cino could tender his resignation, however, other
adventures remained. The first came in Carloforte, a small island
west of Sardinia. They would fish there when the wind was too
strong in Alghero, and at night go into the little village by the
island's port. The people there were Genovese: they had moved
from the mainland years ago, but still spoke the Genovese dialect,
celebrated their holidays and wore their traditional costumes. To
Cino, who had never before left Tuscany, they might as well have
been from Mars. But they were friendly and hardworking, and they
welcomed the crew whenever they stopped in. The men would
drink coffee and play cards at the *bar*, pause for wine and *frutti di
mare*, then head down the boardwalk on the prowl. The women
batted their eyes at the grizzled outsiders.

One day, one of the men turned to the teenage deckboy. "Hey,
kid, you're coming with me tonight." Cino gulped and didn't ask
many questions. Later, they walked up to a house on the outskirts
of town, surrounded by a tall hedge they couldn't see over. The
windows were covered with heavy drapes, and a dim red light
glowed through their threads. Shoulder to shoulder they stepped
through the door.

Inside, you could hardly see for the smoke. Electric
chandeliers flickered, casting dark, lurid shadows into the corners

of the room. Fat men sat in plush chairs tearing at their seams, while beautiful women with grim faces promenaded past them, swallowing their disgust. Cino and his friend made their way to the bar. He couldn't help smiling as he thought of the women who provided "sensual services" to the soldiers in Porto Ercole. What would they think if they could see him now? Their little errand boy was grown up, and had very different intentions this time around. He gulped down a drink and waved over the barkeep for a refill.

Eventually, a pretty girl sat down next to him. She didn't look too unhappy to see him, and so he let her take his hand and lead him to a room down the hall. "It was my first time with a woman," Cino sighs, "and if I do say so myself, it was a complete disaster."

His next adventure was an even bigger disaster—and not the kind you can laugh at years later with a mixture of embarrassment and pride. It happened off the coast of Corsica, the French island that forms the northern face of the Strait of Bonifacio. The people there are fiercely independent, fiercely French, fiercely protective of their home and their culture. They are lobster fishermen, largely, setting traps called lobster pots in the shallow water surrounding the island. Any fishing vessel that wanted to trawl Corsica's waters had to do so far offshore, where the pots would not be disturbed.

The Tale of the Corsican Lobster Pots

One trip nearly two years in, the sea was too rough to pass through I Fornelli. So the *Santo Stefano* turned north and found a spot off of Corsica.

"I heard the Captain and the Chief Fisherman talking," Cino says. "The Chief Fisherman said we were in a good fishing spot, and asked the Captain if we were outside of France's territorial waters. The Captain said yes, so we began to fish."

Not long after, a loud motor revved nearby and they turned to see another military boat closing fast, calling out to them in urgent and angry Italian. They thought it was the Guardia di Finanza, but they were wrong, and by the time the men with guns stepped aboard they knew they were in serious trouble.

"Do you have a permit to fish here?" one of the officers demanded of the Captain. Unlike the man on the loudspeaker, his Italian ran with a thick undercurrent of French.

"No, I don't," the Captain replied. "I thought we were outside the permit zone."

"Well, you thought wrong," the officer sneered, "and now you're going to pay for it. Pull up your net and follow us to the Port of Ajaccio, or we will seize your ugly little boat."

When the *Santo Stefano* arrived in Ajaccio, the angry eyes of Corsica were upon them. Hundreds of gaunt, unshaven men and squat women in black handkerchiefs stood forbiddingly on the dock, waiting for the peschereccio to arrive. As Cino and his crewmates disembarked from their ship, the crowd began screaming at them in French, hurling insults and death threats at the whole party with astonishing fury. Cino was at a loss for words, completely bewildered by the venomous response. "Many of these people looked like bandits," he remembers. "It was a sight to see, and a sight to strike fear in your heart."

The men followed the officers to a nearby police station, quailed by the jeering horde. Other officers threw them into a large, cold holding room and began firing questions at them. "What were you doing there? Why didn't you have a permit? What are you hiding from us?" The crew just shook their heads, apologizing and casting confused looks at each other. *All this for fishing in the wrong place?*

As the night drew on, the police called each man individually into a private interrogation room. Captain Lofreddo went first, returning hours later with a pale expression and a slight quiver in his gait. "It seemed like they had beaten him," Cino reflects. The Chief Fishermen was next, and as the police took him away the Captain told his anxious crewmen what he knew.

"They think we're after their lobster pots," he said.

"Their what?" asked one of the men.

"Their pots. I think someone's been taking them, and they're on high alert. Besides, they don't want anyone fishing too close or we might break them."

"We were way too deep for lobster pots," Canapino called out angrily. "This is just those damn Corsicans trying to squeeze us for money we don't have. I swear, if I can just get my hands on one of them, I'll—"

"You will do nothing!" Capt. Lofreddo barked. "We're in enough trouble as it is. Let's just ride this out, show them we didn't take any of their lobsters, and get home already." Canapino grumbled but sat back against the cement wall to wait his turn.

They went down through the ranks one by one, each man shuffling nervously into the interrogation room and returning a good deal worse for the wear. Cino, the youngest and lowest on the totem pole, went last. He was in a corner trying to sleep when the police yanked him up by the collar and shoved him into the room.

"This one's just a boy," they said. "No matter, we'll have some fun with him anyway!"

Cino bowed his head to the pain—there was nothing he could say that would stop it from coming, nothing that everyone hadn't already said. The men didn't even ask him questions. As the blows fell, his mind wandered to a land across the sea, where there are no cold stone rooms or men with gaunt faces, and bad things like this don't happen to good people. After an hour, he stumbled out of the room, pitching into the concerned arms of Capt. Lofreddo.

"Are you all right?" he asked. Cino nodded, wiping his eyes.

One of the interrogators addressed the crew with trademark spite. "You vermin are in luck. We found no lobster pots hidden on your ship, and nothing damaged by your illegal fishing. So don't worry, we're not going to lynch you."

The men gasped: since when was that even a possibility? If they had broken a pot or two, what would the police have done? Who *were* these demon people?

The officer cut off their musings and continued. "Instead, we have come up with a fine commensurate to the damage you could have caused, and the disrespect you showed our people. Pay the fine and you're free to go."

"How much?" Canapino called out. The policeman smiled, like he was waiting for someone to ask that exact question.

"More than you can afford, little man," he spat back.

It *was* more than they could afford; much more. Capt. Lofreddo had no choice but to call Ala headquarters and have them wire the money to Corsica. In the meantime, the crew sat sullenly in the lifeless room, stomachs growling and bodies huddled against the cold night fast approaching. "Time seemed to stand still," Cino remembers. "Without sheets to cover us or mattresses to sleep on, we spent a whole freezing night in prison."

The next morning the police arrived again, bringing coffee, milk, and bread "so hard that if you dropped it on your foot your foot would break." They told the crew that the money had come in, and let them go with a final warning: "Come back to Corsica again and we will not be able to hold off the mob."

Cino and his mates did not need to be told that twice, and ran back to their boat as quickly as possible. They set off at full power for Monte Argentario, singing for joy once they crossed back into Italian waters. On their way back, they received another radio message: the Corsicans had intercepted another peschereccio, and this time they were really mad. "Who knows what happened to that crew..." Cino sometimes wonders.

After Corsica, they decided to shut down the *Santo Stefano* for a while. The fine had plunged Ala even deeper in debt, and it was getting harder and harder to keep the whole fleet on the water. Besides, their flagship was in dire need of repair, and a few weeks on dry land would do wonders for the husbands, fathers, brothers, and sons who had shivered on the cold floor of that foreign and forbidding place. They brought the boat into drydock and dug the barnacle scrapers out of storage, readying to return their queen to her former glory.

When Cino found out, he ran shouting to his brother. He had been dreading getting back onboard that rickety thing, turning green the first day out to sea, shrinking in fear from any ship flying a French flag that crossed their path. It was the height of summer of 1951, Cino was 16 going on 17, and he had just been granted his freedom.

"Hey, Albertino!" he called. "I'm staying for the *Palio*!"

The *Palio Marinaio dell'Argentario*,[66] held every year on August 15, is the biggest festival in all of Monte Argentario. Twice the size of the Festival of St. Erasmo, it attracts visitors from across the region and as far as Grosseto. Based on the medieval tradition of horse races and anchery competitions between knights of rival fiefdoms, Italian palios have evolved into grand celebrations of local culture, pitting neighborhoods against each other in a hotly contested battle for bragging rights. The premiere palio is the Palio di Siena, where for two days the city square is converted back to the horse-racing arena it once was, and where

---

[66] Monte Argentario Regatta

the city's best jockeys risk life and limb to urge their steeds across the finish line first. So tight are the turns in the cramped piazza that it is common to see horses finish without their riders.

In Porto Santo Stefano, however, there are no horses. The city's four districts—La Pilarella, La Croce, La Fortezza, and Il Valle—duke it out where they do everything else: on the water. But these are no barrel races or blindfolded regattas: oarsmen train all year for the Palio, bending to their work with the weight of pride on their backs. The winning *rione*[67] will get to hoist the Palio trophy at the end of the day, and see their district flag wave over City Hall until the next Palio arrives.

Despite having lived in Santo Stefano for nearly three years now, Cino had never seen the Palio Marinaio. He had heard stories, but nothing could have prepared him for what he saw that morning: rivers of people streaming toward the harbor, bedecked in wild costumes, tooting horns and beating drums. Banners fluttered from every house and building in the city: red and white for Rione Croce; red, yellow, and green for La Fortezza; pale blue and white for Il Valle; red, white, and blue in Cino's own district, La Pilarella. He wrapped himself in a Pilarella flag and shook Alberto awake.

"Albertino, let's go! We're going to be late for the parade!"

At the parade along the lungomare, candy vendors roamed and children waved ribbons tied to sticks. Good friends who could be found most nights laughing together in the cantina now squared off in feats of strength, gritting their teeth like the most bitter of enemies. The noise, the color, the cacophony filled Cino's every cell with a buzzing lightness, a pride and giddiness he hadn't felt since the Americans marched into Porto Ercole. Gripping his Pilarella flag like a cape, he knifed through the crowds of marching

---

[67] District

santostefanesi, loudly proclaiming the out-of-wedlock births of every resident of their rival district, Il Valle.

Finally, it was time for the race. Cino and Alberto settled in on the grandstands as the teams readied their boats and the Harbormaster raised the starting gun. Nobody remembers who won, and nobody cares. When the contest was over and night fell, they lay down on the piazza to watch the fireworks light up the sky. Townspeople passed wine bottles around and sang drunken songs to the glory of Italy. Their sweat streaked their facepaint, revealing familiar faces beneath.

The next few weeks passed like a lilting lullaby. During the day Cino patched holes and painted the hull of the *Santo Stefano*, and in the evenings he played cards with his grandfather or watched his brother whittle figurines out of driftwood. Soon, it all began to feel like a dream, a long, slow moment of perfect peace, just beginning to toe on monotony. After two years of adventure at sea, he could feel the itch beginning to grow again—the need to be shaken free from the reverie. Then, one day, something woke him right back up.

He could tell the minute he got home from work that something was different. Nobody greeted him at the door; his grandmother and aunt were not in the kitchen cooking. Instead, he found them all in the living room, gathered around a tray of of *antipasti*[68] and bottles of wine. His eyes scanned the room, and then his jaw nearly hit the floor.

"Ah, Cino, there you are!" said Zia Dirce, rising from her seat to usher him in. "You know Angiolino and Clementina Solari, of course. These are their nieces, Giovanna and Lina! You met them a few years ago, I'm not sure if you remember."

---

[68] Appetizers.

Cino remembered—all in a rush, and with a heat that he had never felt before. Angiolino and Clementina, friends of Trento and Dirce, frequent visitors to the Procaccini home…Giovanna and Lina, from Sulmona, in the Abruzzo region far to the east…they had visited before, but it was nothing, nothing like this. Back then, she had just been a little girl—he had just been a boy, too. Now there she sat, Giovanna di Felice, the most radiantly beautiful young woman he had ever seen.

At dinner, he couldn't think of a thing to say—an unusual problem for him, to say the least. The rest of them chitted and chatted, passed trays of food, but he sat and stared, still as a stone. Her hair, chestnut curls that bounced just past her shoulders; her eyes, sparkling as she told of her life nestled in the foothills of the Apennine. Her long legs, which he couldn't see beneath the table but ran up and up in his mind, up and up toward…

"Hey Cino, how's life in the clouds?" Trento burst out. The family roared. Cino turned to him slowly, as if encased in molasses. "I asked if maybe you wanted to take these young ladies for a *passeggiata,*[69] show them around town for a bit."

Cino nodded dumbly, glancing up at the goddess sitting across from him. She looked back at him frankly, her eyes teasing and challenging. The three of them rose and left the house.

Walking down to the harbor, Cino took Giovanna's hand in his. Lina, the elder sister, pestered him with questions about Bernardino Bausani's son, Nando, for whom she had fallen during their last visit. But he still had not retrieved all of his voice, and could only respond with monosyllables—none of which said what he wanted to say, which was *leave me alone and let me gaze on my beloved.* That whole night, no more than a few words passed between him and Giovanna. But still, when he left them back with

---

[69] Walk

their aunt and uncle, he had this feeling that what had begun with a stroll would end with a ring.

For the next few weeks, he and his "Gianna"[70] were inseparable. He reveled in her deft, small movements, she in his broad and masculine smile. They walked for hours every night, retracing their steps until they dug a path into the sidewalk. Along the way, they finally got to talking. She told him that her dream was to live a quiet life in the country; he described to her what he could recall of his mother.

Mostly, though, he talked about America. He talked about traveling so far you feel like you're not moving at all—of coming upon a shining coast marked by a woman with a flame held aloft, beckoning you to safe harbor. He talked of the things he'd see in the order he'd see them: the White House, the Golden Gate Bridge, Mount Rushmore. He could see that she was enchanted by his energy, but when he prattled on too long, her lips pressed into a thin line.

Finally, not long before she was to leave, Gianna took him by the hand. "I think it's time you talked to my uncle," she said.

Angiolino Solari was a garrulous man of average height, with a broad, infectious smile. He was a mariner for the Cosulich Brothers, a Yugoslavian company that staffed international shipping vessels and cruise ships. He had been to America dozens of times, and spent hours regaling Cino with stories of skyscrapers, cornfields, and women in stylish hats. Ever since his young friend got his libretto di navigazione, Angiolino had been keeping his ear to the ground.

"So I hear you want to join a crew?" he said when Cino and Gianna came in.

"More than anything," replied Cino. Gianna squirmed.

---

[70] Short for "Giovanna"

"Good. Because there's a ship coming in next week headed for New York, and they need men. I told them you'd be there."

Cino's face lit up. He threw an incredulous look at Gianna, who avoided his eyes, then rushed to Angiolino and hugged him harder than he'd ever hugged another man in his life.

The next day was a Friday, and the two of them left for company headquarters in Genoa. The hiring manager had to sign off on Cino before he could join the crew, and Angiolino needed to vouch for him. The train ride up took six hours, and Cino spent most of it asking Angiolino every question about seafaring life he could think of. *Do you still get seasick?* Sometimes. *Have you seen anyone go crazy way out at sea?* Not anyone who wasn't crazy on land. *What do you like better: being onboard or at home?* [Pause.]

But once they closed in on Genoa, Cino fell silent. He couldn't believe what he was seeing. The port was enormous— four, five, maybe ten times the size of Porto Santo Stefano. Massive ships jostled for space—workmanlike freighters edging past cruise liners lounging in the sun. People strolled around the docks, looking like ants, taking pictures and tentatively reaching out to touch the marvelous vessels. It was like watching a school of prehistoric fish feeding on a reef, safe in the shelter of a secluded cove. He barely even noticed when the train pulled into the station and Angiolino tugged on his arm.

The man at *Fratelli*[71] Cosulich was burly and kind, and he extended his hand as soon as Cino walked in the room.

"Castelli's the name," he said. "You come highly recommended, young man. You think you have what it takes to make it out there?"

"Sir, yes I do, Signore Castelli, sir. I'm very—I'm ready."

"Well your paperwork seems to be in order, and we had a few

---

[71] Brothers

guys back out on us at the last minute on this one. Can you be back here on Monday? Ship's bound for New York then."

"I, I...yes, I most absolutely can, Sr. Castelli. Thank you, thank you so much! You don't know how much this means to me."

"I think I'm getting the picture."

Cino pumped his hand and pumped Angiolino's hand, and reached across the front desk to where a man was sitting reading a magazine, and pumped his hand too just for good measure. Then he turned to his benefactor and said something he'd only ever said to Gianna and Alberto: "Lunch is on me."

Back home, though, they weren't exactly jumping for joy.

"Cino, where have you been?" his nonna asked. "You didn't show up for work."

"I got the day off from Ala. Nonno, Nonna, Albertino, guess what? I'm going to America!"

"What?"

"America! Finally! Angiolino got me on a boat. I leave on Monday!"

"No, no...tell me you're not serious."

"Of course I'm serious! What's the problem?"

"Our little boy..." Nonna Rosa bent over the sink, sobbing into her hand. Nonno Alberto sat down in his chair with a thud. Even Albertino welled up and grabbed his brother's arm tightly.

"What?" Cino said. "You all knew this was coming."

"Yes, we did," said his grandfather. "We just didn't think it would come so soon. You're only sixteen—it's too fast!"

"Maybe, but what else can I do? I can't be a fisherman the rest of my life."

"Just promise you'll come back," said his brother with a start. "No matter how much you like it. Just come back."

Cino laughed. "Where else would I go?"

Over the weekend, Cino got his things in order and asked to be released from service on the *Santo Stefano*. His last night in town, he stood outside Gianna's door until she came and took his hand. They followed their own footsteps to the gelato stand, and he bought her *straciatella*[72] in a cone. They looked at each other; they knew that by the time he got back, she would be gone. Suddenly, her shoulders heaved and she began to cry.

"Not you, too…" he moaned.

"What if—what if you like it there too much? What if you meet some girl who's prettier than me and wears nice clothes and jewels and—"

"There are no girls prettier than you, Gianna. Not one."

She smiled and sniffed. "It's just that it's all that you talk about. And we've only known each other for a few weeks, and I don't know…"

"Marry me."

"What?"

"Marry me! Not tonight, or even next year…when we're eighteen. Once I'm *imbarcato*[73] for good—when we can start a life together. I'll write to you every day until then."

Her tears stopped; her eyes widened. Laughter sparkled through her.

"Yes! Yes, I will!" she exclaimed. She dropped her gelato on the ground and kissed him, long and slow and sweetly, so he'd have something to write her about.

---

[72] An Italian ice cream flavor like chocolate chip.
[73] "Embarked" – a regular member of a ship's crew.

CHAPTER TWELVE: WHAT A COUNTRY!

"In bocca al lupo"[74]
- Italian saying

September, 1951. Cino races through the moonlit streets of Genoa, looking back over his shoulder to see if the man is still following him. He turns right, left, right, through alleyways he does not recognize, past meowing cats and hungry-eyed dogs. He has no idea where he's going, but he does not care. He just has to keep running, keep going, keep thinking about Gianna—he just has to get out of there and forget that any of this ever happened.

"We've hit a bit of a snag," said Sr. Castelli. "The ship's not here yet. Don't worry, though—we've already worked out your accomodations."

He called to the man behind the desk, who seemed to be

---

[74] "Good luck" (literally, "In the mouth of the wolf")

reading the same magazine as before. "Signore Ricci, take this young man to the Columbus Hotel."

Sr. Ricci nodded, heaved himself out of his chair and motioned for Cino to follow him out. Cino trailed behind him.

"Did he say, 'hotel'?" Cino asked.

He did, and what a hotel it was. Polished wood paneling and curved balustrades; even Cino's shoes, worn as they were, clacked on the marble floor. He gazed around at the fashionable men and women who streamed past, breathing deeply to find out what money smelled like. It smelled like flowers and hair oil. He turned to Sr. Ricci.

"I can't stay here."

"What do you mean? We already got you the room."

"I mean, look at me! Look at these clothes!" He poked his finger through a hole in his shirt. "I've never even been inside a hotel before. They'll toss me out before I get across the lobby!"

Sr. Ricci laughed with surprising softness. "Don't worry, kid. Just follow the bellhop, he'll take care of whatever you need."

Cino made the bellhop take him up and down in the elevator three or four times before stopping at his floor, just to feel it rumble and hear the sharp ding as the gleaming doors opened and closed. He held his breath as they entered the room, then exhaled in a rush.

"Was it ever a marvelous thing," he remembers. "Totally clean, everything smelled fresh, and...I couldn't believe it was only for me!" In all of his sixteen years, he couldn't remember sleeping in his own room for even one night. And the bathroom—well. "Running water and a shower?! I couldn't believe my eyes."

Cino flopped down on the bed, took a nap, took a shower, washed his clothes in the sink, then stood for a while looking out the window, over the marina. Later, the bellhop came back and asked Cino if he wanted to take his dinner in the dining room or his own room. Cino just stared at him with his mouth open.

He decided to eat in the dining room but to do it early, so as to not offend the other guests with his ragged appearance. Afterwards, as the sun was setting, he decided it was high time for a walk. He stepped out onto the Via Balbi and flipped a coin to decide which way to go. It was heads—right. The streets were full of people in suits and ties, coming home from their businesses, coming home to their wives and children in their seaside apartments; eating meat off china dishes served to them by women wearing bandanas and aprons. The late afternoon light cast long shadows of Roman gods and cherubs across the wide, tree-lined boulevard.

A few blocks down there was a park, lined with benches where teenage boys alone in a new city could sit and reflect on their lot. Cino kicked out his heels and, for a while, simply gazed about. "Everything was brand-new to my eyes," he remembers, and he felt astonished by its beauty.

"As I sat there and pondered a man came and sat next to me. He began asking me many questions: where was I from, how old I was, what was I in Genoa for, etc. After not much time, he asked me if I wanted to take a little tour around Genoa with him. I said yes, and we got up and started walking down Via Balbi. He told me we were going to the Piazza Dell'Anunziata...by this time night had fallen, and the streets were rather dark.

"As we walked, strange things started to happen: the man tried to hold my hand, then put his arm around me. After we walked a bit farther, he pushed me into a dark doorway and began to unbutton my pants!" Cino froze, petrified and confused. His hands clenched, his heart pounded, his adrenaline churned furiously. "Then I came back to my senses, shoved him as hard as I could, and ran off like a jackrabbit."

Darting through alleyways, blinded by rage, Cino raced back

to the hotel. Somehow, by grace, he made it there without incident. "I ran straight up to my room and locked the door," he remembers. "A long time passed before I could get to sleep."

The next morning, he could think of nothing else. Why had that man sought *him* out, of all people? Why spread his filth to an innocent boy? Who would commit such an atrocity to begin with? The love of a man for a woman—the love he felt for Gianna—that was holy and pure. But what that Sodomite had in mind was barbarous. He feared to leave his room, and he feared that the memory would never leave him. But then the phone rang, and it all washed away.

It was Sr. Castelli. "Ship's on the dock," he said. "Time to go, kid." Cino grabbed his bag and raced out the door.

Standing next to the ship, it was like being in a dream. Long and enamel-white she stretched out in front of him, so far that he had to turn his head to take her all in. She was a passenger ship, lined with portholes, bustling above and below decks. Sr. Castelli had told him to seek out the ship's purser, who managed hiring and distributed payment to the crew. He took a deep breath and strode confidently up the gangplank.

In the office, the purser looked up from his ledger. "You Cino Chegia? Great. Welcome to the *Atlantic*."

As they walked the halls, the purser explained what was to come. "The ship is bound for New York. Sixteen days there, sixteen days back. We have three, four hundred people onboard— most immigrating, some visiting kin. And around one hundred staff: porters, maids, engineers, the like." He stopped and turned. "You *do not* speak to the passengers. You do not acknowledge the passengers, unless they ask you a direct question. You are to be abovedecks as little as possible. *Ha' capito?*" Cino nodded.

"Good." He stopped next to an open door. "We're here."

Cino looked inside. A long, narrow galley swept out before

him, crowded end-to-end with wooden tables. On the far end was a buffet line, and behind that a full kitchen, already clamorous with the day's activities.

"This will be your home," said the purser with pride. "You will help prepare and serve the crew three meals a day—you will clean up after them, and you will see that their needs are met. You will also do whatever the kitchen staff asks of you: running for supplies, washing dishes, anything. Understand?"

"Like a mozzo in the kitchen!" Cino joked.

The purser looked at him sternly. "Yes, like that," he said after a time. "You can meet the kitchen staff later. For now, let me show you to your bunkroom."

The bunkroom was small and cramped, with just enough room for two beds, two small chests, and a desk stocked with writing equipment. But it had a window that looked out onto the sea, and a little sign on the door with his name on it. Cino thought it was just perfect. His roommate was lying on his bed when they came in, and jumped up to shake Cino's hand. He looked to be only a year or two older than Cino, and spoke with a heavy Genovese accent.

"Paolo's the name," he said. "I'm a server, too. Man, I thought I was the baby of the crew—you just get out of diapers last week or something?"

Cino laughed. "Something like that. Guess we'll have to show these old folks around here how it's done then, eh?"

"You got that right, kid. Think we're gonna get along fine."

Cino didn't have to wait long to prove himself. Within the hour, he was back in the galley, peppering the chef with questions as they walked through the meal routine. An hour later, he was weaving through rows of boisterous men and rosy-cheeked women, dodging gesticulations as he cleared plates and refilled glasses. After the lunch rush, he helped with the dishes and made a list of things to restock in the pantry. The chef nodded as he looked it over, and handed it back to him with a smile.

The next day, Cino woke early to prepare breakfast for the crew, but he found it hard to keep his mind on the task. Soon, they would cast off from shore and turn their nose toward America, far beyond the horizon. He could already hear the hubbub outside as the last passengers boarded and the last arrangements were made. After cleanup, he gave a long look at the chef. Somewhere above their heads, the ship's whistle sounded.

"Go ahead," said the chef.

Cino dashed down the hall and up to the deck. It was a mob scene. All of the passengers and much of the crew lined the railings, waving handkerchiefs and blowing kisses back down to the dock. Cino stood on his tiptoes to see the people below, who wiped away tears as they said goodbye to their loved ones. The whistle blew again, the harbormen cast off the ropes, and with a low groan the *Atlantic* set sail for the New World.

Once they were at sea, the voyage became almost routine. Breakfast service in the morning, lunch at noon and dinner at six; in between, time to learn the ropes, meet the crew, chat with Paolo. "The sailors praised and congratulated me on how hard I worked and how well I got on with other people," he remembers. Of course, "it helped that my job on the ship was a walk in the park when compared to working on the peschereccio!"

Every afternoon, during the lull between meals, Cino would sit by the ship's prow, counting each rise and fall that took him closer to the crystal shores of America. Behind him, mothers nursed their babies and children played hide-and-seek. He envied those kids: they had not had to suffer the obscenity of war. They were on an adventure that would end with a new home in America—and in time they would forget the land of their birth, would learn English, would know what it's like to *be* American. Even as they approached the country he had loved from afar for so long, Cino wondered if he would ever get to know that feeling for himself.

As each day passed, his sleep got more restless. He was plagued with anticipation, excitement and fear built up in equal measure over nearly a decade. What would America be like? Could it possibly live up to his dreams? Would people be nice there or would they scoff at his dirty clothes and rough hands? The *Atlantic*'s helmsman had offered to take all the rookies on a tour of Manhattan, and of course Cino jumped at the chance—but now that the day was nearly upon them, he thought it might be better just to stay aboard and take it all in from a safe distance.

But then, one morning, he awoke to a buzz of commotion. Men ran through the halls, shouting orders; women set trunks and animal cages outside their cabin doors.

"What's going on?" he asked Paolo.

Paolo grinned. "What do you think? Race you to the deck!"

The two friends burst out into the cool air just as the sun rose behind them. For sixteen days its light had stretched over nothing but water, but now there was an end to the sea. Now the horizon was nothing but buildings, dizzyingly tall and majestic—so many buildings, an impossible number of buildings, buildings upon buildings, a forest of buildings on a long, narrow island. And there, in the foreground, an impossibly tall and beautiful woman all in green, draped in pleated cloth, holding aloft a fire of hope and smiling down with the benevolence of the Holy Mother. Tears sprang to Cino's eyes, and he held tight to the railing for fear that his knees might buckle beneath him. It was grander than anything he had ever imagined.

"WHAT A COUNTRY!" he shouted, as the ship inched closer to a world lit aflame by the rising sun.

CHAPTER THIRTEEN: THERE AND BACK AGAIN

"Mi sentivo come vero Americano."[75]
- Cino Chegia

September, 1951. *The noise in Manhattan is crazy, like you wouldn't believe. Even louder than Genoa. Taxis all over, everyone shouting, people on the street selling sausages covered in this strange yellow sauce. At night, all the lights come on in all the buildings and it's so bright, like there's fireworks all around! They call it the city that never sleeps, and I can see why...I don't think I've slept a wink since I've been here!*

Cino sprinkled sand on the paper, stuffed it in the envelope and gave it to the mail carrier. It was last call for mail, time to say a final goodbye to New York City before the *Atlantic* blew its horn again and set off back to Genoa. New passengers had boarded for the return trip, and they looked for the most part forlorn, like the best moment of their lives had just ended. Cino worried that he had

---

[75] "I felt like a true American."

the same look on his face. Three days in Manhattan had given him just a hint of what life in America could be, and he left with a bit of that spirit clutched in his fist. There was a fortune to be made here, and someday he was going to make it.

The whole way home, he dreamed of going back. He wondered if Cosulich would keep him on the *Atlantic*—surely he had proved himself by now. But then, midway through the journey, he woke up to make breakfast and found a shattering note on his door. *Dear staff: We regret to inform you that the* Atlantic *has been sold, and will be dismantled upon your return. Thank you for your service. Sincerely, Signore Castelli*

Cino shook Paolo awake. "Can you believe this?" he asked, shoving the paper in his face.

"Hnnnrkkkh," said Paolo. "What is this?" He read it. "Oh. This happens all the time."

"But I'll have to go back to fishing...those leaky boats, the smell, the long days...I don't think I can do it."

"Take it easy, kid. There are always more ships coming along. They'll get you on to something."

Paolo was right. When they got back to Genoa, Sr. Castelli pulled Cino aside.

"I hear you did a good job, son," he said. "The purser was very impressed."

Cino blushed.

"Would you like to get back on a ship?" Castelli went on.

"Yes sir, as soon as possible, sir."

"Great. Be back here in five days and we'll send you out on the next one. Don't forget your pay on your way out."

Cino was whistling as he stepped on the train to Orbetello, and still whistling when he stepped off the bus in Porto Santo Stefano. He whistled up to his grandparents' front door and matched his pitch to the ding-a-ling doorbell.

Nonna Rosa dropped her spoon when she saw him. "You're alive!" she exclaimed, reaching out to embrace him. Then she smacked him on the head. "And you never wrote, not once."

"What do you mean? I wrote you almost every day. Didn't you get my letters?"

They hadn't; not one. The *Atlantic* had beaten its own letters back—in fact, by the time the mail arrived, Cino would already be gone on his next voyage. His thoughts turned to Gianna. "Uh oh," he said, and took off out the door.

Gianna was staying with her aunt and uncle for the summer, so he didn't have to go far. He found her sitting outside their house, peeling carrots on the porch. Her brow darkened when she saw him, like he was a rival or a doctor bearing news of a loved one. She put the carrot and peeler down slowly, wiped her hands on her apron and stepped haltingly toward him.

"You're not gonna slap me too, are you?" he called from the street. "Apparently my ship was faster than the mail."

Dawn broke on her face. She picked up the hem of her dress and ran down to him, laughing as he spun her around.

"Come, let's walk," she said, and they found their old footprints down to the sea.

Five days later, he was back in Genoa with his battered old suitcase and no idea what awaited him. Sr. Castelli sat him down.

"We're sending you and a few boys up to Ireland," he said. "Oil tanker out of Norway—the *Jenny Naess*—is coming in in a few days. Hauling fuel from the States. You in?"

"Of course, sir—yes, of course."

"Good. Tomorrow you'll all board a train for France, take it up to a ferry to England, then another ferry to Dublin. Then a train to Foynes. You'll be there before you know it."

He stayed in the Columbus Hotel again that night, and in the morning met the rest of the men at the train station. They stamped their feet like restless racehorses. The train came and whisked them northwest, past the jagged ridge of the Alps. Geneva gazed at them placidly, ruddy against the crystalline depths of its lake. The men left fog marks where their noses pressed against the glass.

Eventually, they turned to one another.

"So, uh, anyone know any English?" one asked.

"I do!" said another. *"Uncle Sam want YOU."*

They all applauded wildly, and agreed that he would be their translator when they got to Ireland.

In Paris, the train switched tracks, leaving Cino and his new mates with time to kill. They spilled through the doors in search of bread and wine. The city glowed in the early evening, the cascading sun mingling with the electric haze of the streetlights. The men lit cigarettes and whistled at haughty-looking women with beautiful eyes and soft hair. They found a café that served ham sandwiches smeared with butter, took bets as to who would be the first person to break something on the ship. Off in the distance, a train whistle hooted. They looked at each other, and at their watches. Was it already time?

"Check, please!" they shouted, tossing bills on the table and dashing out the door.

Outside, the night was dark and nothing looked the same. Where was the train station? How had they gotten there? Their laughter died. The whistle sounded again. Blood pumped in their veins. Their feet quickened on the stone streets. This way and that, running now but getting no closer. Finally, an alley opened up onto a large square. The train station. They ran, full-tilt. The third whistle sounded; the locomotive fired. They were too late.

"*Merda!*"[76] said one. "Sr. Castelli is not gonna like this."

"It's not over," said Cino. "Maybe we can still catch it."

There was a policeman nearby, and they swarmed him.

"Speak Italian?"

"A bit."

"That was our train. We're merchant seamen. We need to catch it. Can you help us?"

He pursed his lips. "I'll try...the next station's a few minutes down the road by car. You'll have to hurry." He flagged down a passing taxi and said a few words in French to the cabbie. The men poured in. The cab zipped away.

By the time they arrived at the station, the last passengers were boarding the train. They threw more money at the cabbie, piled out and raced onboard just as the conductor was shouting his last call. Their cabin was still empty, still loaded with all of their possessions. They collapsed into their seats and promised each other that they wouldn't move again for the rest of the trip.

At Le Havre, in the north of France, they transferred to a ferry to Portsmouth. From Portsmouth, it was another ferry to Dublin, then a second train ride to Foynes, in County Limerick. The ship wouldn't arrive for two more days, so Cosulich put them up in a local hotel.

"While we waited for the ship to come, we made our acquaintance with the maids," Cino reports. None of the girls

---

[76] Shit

spoke Italian, and their translator could only recruit American soldiers, "so we did the best we could with hand gestures and body language." That night, the men and the maids went to a local dance, where Italian body language is at its finest. "You can imagine what a sight we were!" Cino recalls. A few of the older men brought their ladies back for a "very nice night," but Cino just sipped his wine and thought of Gianna.

A few days later, the *Jenny Naess* arrived in port. She was long and rugged, workmanlike, with her cabin set far aft and her massive bow studded with cranes and pipes. Her fuel tanks sat underdecks, and when Cino first saw her she was belching oil through accordioned rubber hoses into holding tanks onshore. She didn't sparkle like the *Atlantic*, but she'd do just fine. He glanced up at the flag flying from her prow; he didn't recognize the colors. They had told him the ship was from Norway, but her flag looked like the Stars and Stripes—except that instead of 48 stars for the 48 states, there was only one.

"What the hell's that?" he asked his friend, pointing.

"A flag, son."

Cino gave him a droll look. "From where?"

"Liberia, by the look of it. It's in Africa, on the west coast. Whole country full of freed American slaves. They don't tax overseas trade there, so a lot of merchant ships register there."

Cino let that sink in for a bit. A Norwegian ship staffed by a Yugoslavian company that employs Italians, running oil from the U.S. to the U.K., and flying the flag of an African nation whose ancestors once crossed the Atlantic in the cargo holds of ships much like this. The world was a strange place, that was for sure. But if he'd learned one thing on the high seas, it was that it didn't matter where you were from or what language you spoke, just as long as you got your job done.

The ship departed and Cino, as he always did, got his job done. The *Jenny Naess*'s boatswain assigned him to the same job that he had on the *Atlantic*: cooking meals, cleaning up, breaking up fights in the mess hall. He sprang into it with the vigor and enterprising spirit that had led him his whole life. The men of the *Jenny Naess* quickly took notice, taking their young, garrulous server under their wing. "One of them even wanted me to call him Zio Dario, and would always give trouble to anyone who yelled at me," Cino recalls.

After dinner, the older sailors would gather in the mess hall and deal out five-card draw, three-card lowball, seven-card stud. For the first few days, Cino just watched, soaking in their chatter as they exchanged tricks of the seaman's trade. And looking for tells—always looking for tells, like his father had long ago behind the haystack. Finally, one day Zio Dario invited him into the game.

"This one's called Texas Hold'em," Dario said as he dealt out two cards to each player. Cino just smiled. He was still smiling when he caught on the river and raked in his first pot. The men scratched their heads and glanced at each other.

"I never let on that I learned to play cards at about the same time as I learned to walk," Cino chuckles.

One night, as they sat at cards, Zio Dario taught him a lesson in sailor's economics. "Don't ask for your pay all upfront, or all in lire. Just tell the Second Officer you want $20 U.S. every month, in cash, and have him send the rest back to your grandfather."

"Will that be enough?" Cino asked. After all, they had to buy their own sundries from the ship's commissary, and he wanted to make sure he had enough left over to paint the town red once they got to America.

"Sure! Just do what we do: buy a carton of cigarettes here, then sell them for four, five times as much to the dockworkers on shore. Those guys can't get enough smokes."

Cino wondered again at the strangeness of it all. The War had been over for seven years now and here he was, still selling cigarettes on the black market. *They ought to just make these the official currency of the world*, he thought.

Fifteen days after departure, the *Jenny Naess* neared the American coast. Cino walked the deck with Zio Dario, peering in the distance for first sight of his beloved country. His mind danced with the possibilities: more skyscraping steel marvels like Manhattan? Or maybe green pastures and rolling hills, like he had seen in Ireland. Would it be colorful and cacophonous, or quiet and serene? He realized only then that he had never even asked where they were going.

"So where are we, anyway? New York? Washington? Miami Beach?"

Dario laughed and shook his head. "Son, we're headed to Baton Rouge, Louisiana."

Baton Rouge, Louisiana was not a very nice place in 1951. The *Jenny Naess* drifted a day's ride up the Mississippi River, surrounded by swampland and undistinguished towns. Where was the vibrant city he had seen on his last trip? Where was the land of prosperity, with shiny new cars and kids playing marbles in the street? He had signed up to see the majestic crown jewels of the United States, not its sweaty armpits. *Should have just hopped off when we passed through New Orleans*, he thought.

But still, there was something beautiful about the vastness that stretched out all around them. So much *spazio vitale*; so much possibility in the empty space. This must be what they meant by "the land of opportunity"—this country could still be molded, still be shaped into whatever people wanted it to be. Italy had spent years trying to recapture the glory of Rome, but America's story was still being written.

And it wasn't like there was nothing to do in Baton Rouge. By day, Cino helped restock the kitchen as the *Jenny Naess* filled her belly with crude oil. By night, the men sought out the dark, smoky corners of the city, where Creole jazz slipped through open windows and where a young man didn't have to be 21 if he had a crisp dollar bill to slap down on the bar. "I felt like a true American," Cino says.

They were in Baton Rouge for three days, then turned around again to sail back across the Atlantic to Foynes. As they neared port, the crew started to grow visibly excited, whispering to each other and laughing loudly as they paced the deck.

"What's got you all so riled up?" he asked Zio Dario as they made their approach.

"You'll see, kid," he winked.

That night, Cino saw. After dinner all the men came ashore, and without hesitation made a beeline for the tiny town's only bar. They burst through the door into the warm light of the tavern, and when Cino's eyes adjusted he drew in a sharp breath. Women! Irish lasses everywhere! Blondes, brunettes, and redheads; sitting at the bar, chatting around tables, drinking dark beer with a thick foam head, like the cream at the top of a milk bottle. They all looked up when the crew walked through the door, and they all smiled as one.

"What— What— who are these girls?" Cino asked the ship's steward.

"Nurses, my boy! There's an academy nearby. They all come out here when they know a ship's coming into port. Good luck!" he said, before he was whisked away by a woman with satin curls and a doey look in her eye.

Soon, Cino found himself alone in the corner while grease-stained men gestured wildly to fair-skinned, tittering women. He ordered one of their beers—they called it Guinness—and sipped it as the rumpus unfolded. It tasted like his Nonna's cooking, and it made his head feel all soft and fuzzy. It was the best beer he had ever had.

Eventually, the steward came up for air and found Cino in the crowd. "What in the world are you doing, man? Get in there and meet some lovely ladies!"

"But, Gianna…"

"We all have someone back home, man. They're not here and we're not there. That's life. Listen, my girl has a friend and she wants you to meet her. Yeah?"

Cino nodded and let his friend push him across the room. He drained his beer for courage, wiped the foam from his mouth and looked up—and there she was.

She was quiet, shy; she kept her gaze glued to the floor. Cino's heart melted. He reached out his hand and she took it, looked up at him, her eyes blue-green like the sea. Cino went right to his go-to move.

"Do you want to take a walk with me?" he gestured. She smiled and took his arm.

Outside, the night was warm and the tiny village slept. The young nurse pointed to a tearoom down the street, where waitresses served coffee and cookies. They blew steam over the rims of their chipped porcelain mugs and smiled shyly at each other. Finally, she spoke. Her words were nonsense, but her voice had a pleasant lilt to it. She reminded him of Teresa: kind and bookish, prettier than she knew. They sat there, signing to each other, for over an hour.

On the way back to the ship, Cino felt like he was floating. The beer, the coffee, the smell of her hair—it intoxicated him. As they turned onto a deserted street, he pulled her suddenly toward him and swooped her into a kiss. "She consented," he remembers. "At least, she didn't say anything about it!" She left him at the docks and he told her to meet him there the next night.

The next night, he left the ship and there she was—straw-colored hair swept back into a ponytail, modest dress draped over her slender frame, eyes cast to the ground. Cino had spent the whole day in torment: anxious to see her, then wracked with guilt, then fearful she wouldn't show. He forgot it all when he saw her, and kissed her lightly on the cheek. The men jeered as they scampered toward the tavern, but Cino just laughed and took her by the hand.

On his way home, though, Cino's thoughts turned to Gianna. He thought about what the steward had said—"we're here, they're there"—and about the marriage promise he had made to her. He shook his head in disgust. What would he think if he found out that she had been going on walks with another man, letting a man kiss her and run his hands down her back? He'd knock the guy's teeth out, that's for sure.

"I decided then and there not to see this Irish girl again," he remembers.

The next night, he chose to stay on the ship. "If you see her, tell her I'm sick and can't come out tonight," he told his friends. "Tell her I...tell her I'm sorry."

He watched from his cabin as the men walked down the gangplank; he saw her alone on the dock, searching for him through the crowd. He watched as the steward approached her, put his hand on her shoulder and shook his head. Her face crumpled and lost all expression. She stared down at the ground, then sniffed and nodded without looking up. The men left for the bar and she stood still, hugging herself though the night was warm, before turning back toward the academy. The *Jenny Naess* left the next morning, and Cino never saw her again.

Eighteen months later, Cino stepped off the oil tanker *Jenny Naess* for the last time. He had spent nearly all of his eighteenth year hauling crude oil from the American South to the British Isles. He had cooked thousands of meals, cleaned the cargo tanks dozens of times, played countless hands of poker with the guys. He had seen New Orleans, Houston, and Tallahassee; he had laid waste to pubs in Cardiff and Liverpool. He was starting to wonder if there was anywhere else like New York in the whole world. He had gotten caught in a North Atlantic squall, huddling belowdecks while so many waves crashed overhead that "it seemed like the ship would become a submarine." In late May of 1953, he reached London to find it awash in colors and crests—Queen Elizabeth II was to be crowned in a week.

They were in Baton Rouge when they got the news. The Naess-Melander Company was upgrading its fleet, and had decided to retire its old, weakening tanker. With no ship to sail on, the *Jenny Naess* crew would be sent away too, until Fratelli Cosulich found somewhere else to place them. It was just like the *Atlantic* all over again, except this time it wasn't after his very first voyage…this time it was after he had bled with the men, drunk with the men, stood guard while they snuck women onto the ship. It was his home—they were his brothers—and it was gone, just like that. On the dock in Foynes, he stood quietly with Zio Dario for a moment, then hugged him hard and ran for the train station.

At least there was something worth running toward, some light at the fringe of his sorrow: he was going home. His nonni, his brother, his zii and zie; his cousins, his oldest friends; his father, of course—they all waited for him, even without knowing he was coming. And so did she, somewhere. His soulmate, his goddess, his patient love—she was always waiting. *You won't be waiting long*, he thought, picking up speed.

Back in Genoa, Signore Castelli shook his hand and told him

he had done a fine job. Then he gave him an envelope bulging with bills. Cino counted three hundred thousand lira in there! The image of Gianna slipped from his mind.

"Severance pay," said Castelli.

Cino nodded. "Right. So, uh, when can I get back on?"

"Few weeks, I'd think. Just enough time to see your family, settle your affairs and come back around again."

"I'll be waiting by the phone," Cino said.

At home, Nonno Alberto and Nonna Rosa fell all over themselves to greet him.

"We weren't sure when we'd see you again!" Nonno said. "Every letter you're somewhere else: England, America, England, America. Never Italy—never home! And how thin you've gotten. Rosa, look at this boy. Aren't you a cook?"

"Leave him be, Alberto. But oh, won't your brother be so happy to see you! Alberto, go fetch him."

"Ach," Alberto said. But he went and fetched him.

Minutes later, a tall, lanky boy strode through the door, hair tousled and fingers coated in grease. Cino nearly gasped. It could have been Aldo, striding right out of photos from 1920.

"That you, Albertino?" he said. "What happened to my little brother?"

The mustachioed teen laughed and embraced his brother warmly. "Tell us everything," he said, in a voice that had dropped at least an octave that year.

Cino stayed at home for a few days, then paid a visit to L'Ospizio. Between the *Santo Stefano* and the *Jenny Naess*, he had barely seen his Nonni Chegia in two years. Doretti and Doretta, as it turned out, hadn't changed much. A little grayer, perhaps, with that set, settled look of people in the last stage of their life—but still resolute, hard-working, and satisfied. It struck him for the first time how much they were in Porto Ercole and how much the town was in them: both grew, changed almost imperceptibly, but still stuck fast to their roots. He felt the same way his father must have felt when he came back from the War—like a stranger who knows the city by heart. He was different; they were not. His body had strayed, but part of him remained there; they never moved, but sent their thoughts out to sea. He sat quietly with the people he loved, and remembered the days when the dust of their town caked their palettes.

A few days in, a letter arrived for Cino. It was short, and sweet: *Heard you were back. I'm coming to see you. Forever yours, Gianna.* Cino jumped from his chair, kissed his nonno and nonna and ran for the bus to Santo Stefano.

She was there when he arrived, and more beautiful than ever. He paid her a visit at her aunt and uncle's—Angiolino was imbarcato, but Clementina hovered behind her with a smile that said *I'm so glad you're here, but damned if I'm letting you out of my sight.* They left for a walk, and to be alone.

They caught each other up on their lives, their adventures. They looked at each other, wondering if the other was as real as they seemed. By the waterfront, their conversation turned to marriage.

"It's almost time," she said.

"Almost," said he.

"What are you going to say to my father?"

Cino shrugged.

"I think we should tell the family now," she went on. "The ones that are here. They should know that...that we're serious."

He looked in her eyes. "Would that make you happy?"

She blushed. "Yes. Very."

"Then that's what we'll do," he said.

That night, they gathered the families and made the announcement. Everyone clapped and cheered, though nobody looked surprised. Clementina, the only di Felice in the crowd, wrapped Cino in a hug.

"You will be a great husband," she said. "We will be so happy to have you in the family."

The next day, Cino stood with his betrothed-to-be on the train platform in Orbetello. The whistle blew. They kissed softly, without haste, then she skipped across the platform and swung into an open car. As the doors closed, she leaned back out and waved. Her loose curls caught the morning light. Then the train whistled again, and she was gone.

With Gianna gone, there wasn't anything left to do. Cino had seen everyone he wanted to see. Alberto was fully apprenticed to their uncle by now, and couldn't slip out for joyrides on the Gino Bartali. Cino called Cosulich every day, but still nothing had come up. It was midsummer, 1953, and the heat was beginning to boil his blood like a cauldron.

Finally, he walked down to see Bernardino Bausani. "We've been expecting you," Bernardino said as they shook hands.

"You have?"

"Sure. Your brother told us you were back, and work on a merchant ship can be a long time coming. About half our crew is guys waiting to get back overseas. That's just how it is."

"So...any spots available for a deckboy?"

"Sorry, no. Nothing for a deckboy."

"Oh. Okay, well…"

"How'd you like to be assistant to the ship's engineer instead?"

"I'd—yes! Sure."

"Good. When the ship comes in I'll introduce you to the crew." He winked. "She's got a new paint job, but you'll recognize her."

She had been spiffed up, that's for sure, but her bones were still the same. It was the *Santo Stefano*, back from yet another trip to Sardinia. Cino met the ship's engineer at the dock, explaining that he was to be his new right hand.

The engineer spat gruffly. His face and arms were scarred from too many run-ins with heavy machinery, and his fingers moved expressively as he spoke. Cino wondered how many stories he held in each stitch, each whorl of burnt flesh.

"Ever worked on a ship's guts, kid?" the engineer asked.

"Just a few tweaks to my grandfather's boat, here and there. Lots of engineers in my family, though."

The man nodded, well familiar with the Procaccini men. "All right then. We'll give you a crash course in mechanics tomorrow. For now, I need these." He thrust a supply list into Cino's chest, then strode with purpose toward the cantina. The list unfurled like a scroll, its end nearly touching the ground.

The next day, they walked the ship top and bottom. The engineer pointed out every motorized winch and bilge pump, like he was describing shapes and colors to a toddler. In the engine room, he handed Cino safety glasses and earplugs. "You're gonna need these," he said. Then he flipped a few switches and the beastly contraption spun to life—pistons churning faster and faster

183

in rhythm, gears grinding on their axles. The noise was deafening. Cino jammed the plugs into his ears.

"This is our world," the engineer shouted, grinning maniacally. "Get used to it."

The *Santo Stefano* set out the next day, cradling its new crew member in its belly. From departure to arrival, Cino sat by the engineer's side, handing him tools and checking the pressure gauges regularly. After an hour on open water, the room felt as hot as the fifth circle of Hell. *At least there's no rocking down here*, Cino thought, though it was little consolation at the time.

They stayed out in Alghero for a week or so, fishing scappuzzoni while Cino slaved away in the bowels. After a while he got the hang of the job, and soon found he was even a little bored with the work. Though an engineer's job requires deftness, vigor and skill, being one's assistant requires little more than knowing the difference between a socket wrench and a ball-peen hammer. Every now and again, the engineer would send him up to the deck, to check on things or run replacement parts for broken winches. He stretched those moments out for as long as he could, drinking in the fresh air and cool breeze—though he found that if he stayed out for too long, his eyes would drift toward the horizon, his thoughts to the merchant ships, and his heart would start to sink. In those moments, the cloistered heat of the engine room felt like shelter.

Week after week went by, with no word from Cosulich. Cino was starting to despair, starting to fall back into old rhythms that could engulf a life in their tedium. One morning, he awoke in the shadow of Sardinia to find that he had turned eighteen. The sun shone brightly, though it was October, and the seas were calm. He stood on the aft deck and looked toward the mainland, wondering if Gianna was looking back at him from so far away. Now they could truly begin—now their promises could be kept, now their new lives could take shape. He started composing his letter to her father right then.

Back at home, he sat down and penned his entreaty. *Dear Signore di Felice, I write to you seeking your daughter's hand in marriage.* A week later, there was a letter awaiting his arrival at home. He tore it open while his grandmother stood in the doorway, wringing her hands. A smile broke across his face.

"He gives his blessing!"

So began the engagement of Cino Chegia and Giovanna di Felice. Cino was bound to the ship until the fishing season ended in December, and Gianna couldn't get away from Sulmona, so they planned their union by mail. "We chose Christmas, 1954 as our wedding date, to give us ample time to plan the nuptials," says Cino. "After all, we were in no hurry to marry: I had just barely turned 18!"

When the season ended and they brought the *Santo Stefano* into drydock, Cino asked for a few days off to put a ring on his bride-to-be's finger. He pulled what was left of his Cosulich severance from the Santo Stefano post office, ran to the local jewelry store, and plopped it all down on the counter. The jeweler smiled and reached for the smallest rock in the case.

With his prize in his pocket and his heart on his sleeve, Cino took the train inland to Sulmona. Slowly but surely, the train snaked through the Apennine Mountains and back down again into the Peligna Valley. The Abruzzi region was stunningly rich, but in the winter a heavy fog haloed the hills and the rain fell steadily. Cino gazed out the window in amazement: he had been across the Atlantic dozens of times, but had never been this far east in his own country before!

When the train pulled into Sulmona, he wondered if he would be able to find his beloved. She knew he was coming, of course, but the dusk and the rain made it hard to see. He needn't have worried. The minute he stepped off the train, a cheer went up from a cluster of dark bodies huddled under the awning. As he hurried their way, the crowd opened up to reveal Gianna at its center—surrounded by her father, her mother, her brothers and sisters, her grandparents, her aunts and uncles, her cousins…her entire family awaited him there, beaming and waving like the Prime Minister was coming to pay them a visit.

"What a pleasure to meet you!" they exclaimed through a tangle of limbs and lips. "What a handsome boy. Look at that smile! You're a lucky young lady, Giovanna. What a wedding this will be!"

"Okay, okay, let the boy breathe," said her father, a hefty man with a hefty grin. "Cino, I believe you have something for my daughter."

"I do," he said, digging the ring from his pocket. He took Gianna's hand. Her eyes sparkled. The rain pattered on the awning. "Gianna, I love you. Thank you for choosing me. I can't wait to be your husband." He slipped the ring on her finger and kissed her. It was done.

"Now, we drink!" roared her father. They all walked arm-in-arm through the rain.

At the engagement party, Gianna's father pulled Cino aside. "As you know, I work on the railroad," he said. "It's good work, a man's work, and the pay is steady. Plenty of adventure, too, just like out there on the water! You could work here, live here, have children…just think about it, that's all I ask. Say the word and we'll get you a job." Cino gulped down the rest of his wine.

Two days later, he left again, to tears, kisses, and promises of a speedy reunion. The whole way back, he was awash in emotion: excitement for his life with Gianna, anticipation of the day they would be wed, dread at the thought of months still to come on the *Santo Stefano*. He couldn't leave the boat—who knew when the next summons would come from Cosulich, if ever. But he couldn't stay, either. Something would have to give, but there was no way of knowing what or when. He would just have to be patient.

On April 11, 1954, Cino's patience was rewarded. His life would never be the same.

On April 11, 1954, Cino got home to find his grandmother waiting for him. She held a telegram in her hand, and her face was grim. He snatched it from her.

Come to Genoa immediately, it read. *New assignment begins 13 April.*

"Merda!" he exclaimed. "I need to tell Bernardino."

He spent the next day saying goodbye to friends and family, then caught the night train to Genoa. The car he was in was empty save for one other man, hoisting a suitcase into an overhead bin. Cino had the sneaking suspicion that their trips would end in the same place.

"Headed to Genoa, friend?" he called out.

"Sure am!" came the reply.

Cino left his luggage behind and settled in across from the man. "Let me guess: telegram from Cosulich?"

"How'd you know?"

"Night train to Genoa, right before Easter? Either you're visiting family or leaving them behind, and it doesn't look like you're packed for a weekend trip."

"Sharp eye, kid. Name's Secondo Terramoccia."

"Cino Chegia. Nice to meet you, Secondo." The train sped north through the dark and emerged into a Genoa morning; Cino and Secondo emerged onto Via Balbi as friends.

Signore Castelli met them at Cosulich headquarters. "Have a seat, gentlemen," he said abruptly. "I have a unique assignment for you both. A company we work with has bought a ship in drydock, and they want us to send a crew to fix it up and sail it back here. Here's the catch: the ship is in Alameda, California. In America."

Cino's heart caught in his throat. California, the place where dreams come true! The mariners talked about it all the time, singing songs of its warm sun, sandy beaches, and rolling Tuscan-like hills. There were even Italians there, they said, with little vegetable gardens in their back yards and fresh prosciutto sold in open-air markets. All the way through Houston and Tallahassee, the thought of seeing California someday had buoyed his spirits. Now he would once again get to see the America he'd dreamed about, the one Lady Liberty had promised.

"But California is so far," he said. "How will we get there?"

Castelli slid two slips of paper across the desk. They were printed with a bunch of numbers, departure and arrival times. In the top right corner was a symbol, a gold map of the world with red initials stamped across it: TWA. Cino gasped.

"The rest of the crew arrives on the 15th, on Easter. You will take the train to Milan and fly to San Francisco. A bus will take you to Alameda. The boatswain will assign you jobs when you get there. You'll work on the boat, eat on the boat, sleep on the boat. When she's seaworthy, you'll bring her back here and she'll go into operation. With any luck they'll keep you on as permanent crew. Any questions?"

They shook their heads.

"Good. Let's get you to your hotel."

Cino's head spun. An airplane—a real plane! So many times he had watched them zoom overhead, wondering what it was like on the inside…what it felt like to fly, to cross such incredible distances in no time at all. Now he would feel the power for the first time in his life—not in his hands, sure, but at his back. And when they landed he'd step out into a world he had never laid eyes on before. The possibilities sent shivers from his ears to his toes.

At the same time, there was something eerily familiar about the name "Alameda." He couldn't kick the feeling that he'd heard it before, in conversation somewhere. Suddenly, it clicked. He wrote a letter to his grandfather and stuck it in the evening mail.

A letter came back by return mail. *You are correct, Cino. Signora Perillo's nephew did go to Alameda. He lives in Oakland now, which is right next door. His name is Aurelio—she says that if you have time off the ship, you should look him up. Tell him she sent you. Be safe, grandson. We will pray for you.*

On April 15, 1954—Easter morning—43 men arrived at the Genoa train station. They met up with their two new recruits and set out for the Milan Malpensa Airport. A welcoming committee from Trans World Airlines met them at the gate, ushering them into a private lounge spread with a full Easter repast. The men raised toasts to the Holy Trinity and the Fratelli Cosulich, then tucked in with festive abandon. After an hour or so, they followed the crew to the gate, where a Douglas DC-3 aircraft sat waiting for them to board. Cino trailed his hand along her chassis on his way to the stairs, looking for the bomb bay underneath. The wheels were as big as he was, and the propellors…it hit him just then that they were going to sit inside this machine as it hurtled across the ocean, thousands of meters in the sky. He gulped.

The flight was a blur. Astonishing, exhilarating, terrifying. During takeoff, Cino gripped the armrests so tightly he feared he might rip them right off. On their first landing—in the Azores, to refuel—he and Secondo held hands. In the air, though, it was just like being on a ship, and eventually the men pulled out cigarettes and decks of cards, gossiped and called for wine. Cino felt like he was going to like this crew.

Sixteen hours later, they touched down in San Francisco. Dizzy, delirious, and slightly drunk, they stepped out into the evening light.

"Hey, everyone," one of the men shouted. "I think it's Easter again!"

"Happy Easter!" they cried out, like children. Like people reborn, transcendant, remade. Out here, today, they could be anyone they wanted.

Their bus arrived and they clambered in, weaving through the city and across the Bay Bridge to the Alameda shipyards. The men were glued to the windows, entranced by the beauty they saw around them. Rolling hills, just like they were told. Piers lining both sides of the San Francisco Bay's narrow mouth. A tower shaped like a firehose, and a forbidding building on a lonely island, which folks said was an inescapable prison. In the distance, almost hidden by the rolling fog, the Golden Gate Bridge, shining the color of the Statue of Liberty's flame.

As the sun set over the Cinqueterre-like cliffs of Sausalito, Cino felt that shiver run through his body again. Something was going to happen here, he knew. Something big.

CHAPTER FOURTEEN: FOUR DOLLARS AND A DREAM

"Sempre avanti, senza paura."[77]
- Italian saying

May 5, 1954. 5:30 am. Cino blinks his eyes open and shakes loose stiff limbs. The morning is chilly and gray, like every morning in Alameda has been so far. As if the fog from the Bay slips in through the cracks and envelopes you, even when you're inside. For a moment, he huddles against it, uncertain. Then he's up, and his heart is pounding.

Slowly, silently, he slides out of bed. The Neapolitan snuffles above him but does not wake. Next to his bed are the jeans, the shirt, the socks he will wear. The thin coat he brought with him from home, with more holes in it than he has fingers to put in them. The boots with a bit of one sole dangling off, like a dog's tongue

---

[77] "Ever onward, without fear."

hanging out of its mouth. They are all he will take with him. He puts them on deliberately, reverentially. He ties his bootlace around the sole so it doesn't flap or squeak in the hallway.

Standing, he reaches into his pocket. The soiled greenbacks are where he left them, neatly folded. He thumbs through to make sure all four are there. It's time to go.

Looking back just once, he slips through the door left ajar in preparation. The hallway is deserted. His shoes do not squeak. He runs. Down the hall, up the stairs, through the galley, past the bridge, out the door, onto the deck. Weaving between piles of scrap metal, staying low just in case. Down more stairs to the gangplank, waiting, hardly daring to breath—darting across it when the guard walks away. Then running, just running, to the gate, to the street, to freedom. He drinks the fog and feels strong.

Her name was the *SS Mariposa*. She was 632 feet long, 79 feet wide, and weighed 18,017 tons. She was born in the Fore River Shipyard in Quincy, Massachusetts, and took her maiden voyage on January 16, 1932. Long and sleek, she was a luxury liner first: for ten years, she ported the rich from California to Hawaii, Fiji, and New Zealand. Then the Japanese divebombed Pearl Harbor, and her number came up in the draft. She ran her first naval mission on December 26, 1941, carrying survivors from Hawaii to Melbourne. She didn't stop running until Fat Man fell and the War was over.

Like the soldiers she hauled, the *Mariposa* came home from war scarred and almost unrecognizable—no longer fit for the life she once led. The Matson Company, her owners, had no use for her anymore, so they mothballed her. She sat in drydock at the Bethlehem-Alameda Shipyard for seven years. But then a Greek man named Eugen Eugenides founded a shipping company called Home Lines, and with help from his investors at Fratelli Cosulich bought several former liners from around the world. One of those ships was the *Atlantic*, which took Cino on his first adventure. Another was the *Mariposa*.

By the time Cino and the crew arrived in Alameda, the drydock workers had already overhauled her engines, and were nearly done extending her hull by nine feet. When they were done, she would be a whole new vessel—the *SS Homeric*, a mass transport ship, soon to be a staple of Home Lines' Caribbean fleet. The crew would have their work cut out for them, that was clear: in twenty days she would be greeting the water again, and when that happened she had to be ready. It was a challenge they all relished, and they raced aboard to get briefed and get going.

The First Officer put Cino on kitchen duty, which suited him just fine. Kitchen duty meant free evenings, meant people to meet, meant trips into town for ingredients. His mind raced imagining what might be out there, what the sniffs of garlic and snatches of Italian that he caught through the bus window might mean. He could barely contain himself—there was so much exploring to do.

His bunkmate was from Naples, and not much older than Cino himself. "We used to throw rocks at your kind growing up," said Cino as he settled back on his bed.

The Neapolitan chuckled. "You and everyone else...how do you think we became such good sculptors? Take those rocks, carve 'em up, sell 'em back to you for a hundred times more. Shake your hand and tell you to shove it up your ass as you walk away."

Cino paused. "I think we're going to be good friends," he said.

At breakfast the next morning, the men were already buzzing about the neighborhood.

"*Tutti Italiani,*"[78] they said. "Everywhere you look."

"I got a cousin lives just down the road from here. Says he's gonna come by with *cannoli* first chance he gets."

Cino snooped. "Where does he live? Where do they all live?"

"Brod Wai," they said. "You have to go to Brod Wai."

After lunch, when the men were gone and the galley bleached clean, Cino cast the Neapolitan a look.

"Brod Wai?" he asked.

"Brod Wai," his friend nodded.

They caught a ride from the Navy men at the base next door. Cino asked each of them if they ever served in Porto Ercole; they hadn't. He asked them if they had met Joe DiMaggio or his new wife, Marilyn; they hadn't. But he only had to ask once about Brod Wai to get the answer he wanted.

"We're going there now!" one said. "And it's pronounced 'Broadway.' Broadway Avenue, in Oakland"

Brod Wai a Venu was a staggering place. Twice, maybe three times the size of any street in Porto Ercole, it thrummed with the sounds of produce hawkers and passing cars. Every store they passed had an Italian name: A.G. Ferrari, G.B. Ratto, Genova Delicatessen. Long shanks of pork hung from windowsills, next to salame logs split down the middle to show their marbled insides. Old men sat on stoops, smoking and playing cards. And outside—on the sidewalks, in the cars, everywhere—there was only Italian. Genovese, Piemontese, Toscano—even Napoletano, to his roommate's delight. Dismounting from the Jeep, they stood still and gawked like small children. If they hadn't flown halfway across the world to get here, they could have mistaken it for home.

---

[78] All Italians

Suddenly, a voice cut through the wonder. "Corriere della Sera! La Repubblica, *da solo due giorni fa!*"[79]

Cino turned to the man, who stood by a newsstand behind them. "You have *La Repubblica* from two days ago? Let me see."

The man handed him the paper. Cino scanned it, checking first to see where Juventus stood in the Serie A table, then glancing through the headlines and obituaries. He held it up to the light, like a *carabiniero*[80] examining money that might be counterfeit.

"Where did you get this?"

"I have an arrangement with the newspapers. They print out a few copies nearby, and I sell them," the man said. His Italian was crisp, polished, suspiciously lacking in dialect. He extended his hand. "Leonardo Marabella,"

"Cino Chegia. May I ask, Signore Marabella, where are you from?"

Leonardo—Leonard—blushed like he'd been caught. "Good ear, kid. I was born and raised on these streets. Parents came over from the motherland long ago. Can you believe it—I've never even been to Italy!"

Cino lit up. "So you can tell me things about America? Please, Sr. Marabella, tell me—I want to know everything. I'll tell you whatever you want about Italy in return!"

Leonard laughed. "I think that can be arranged, son."

Just then, the Neapolitan checked his watch and tapped Cino on the shoulder.

"Right," Cino said. "Sr. Marabella, it was a pleasure to meet you. I'll come back and find you soon."

---

[79] "*Evening Courier! The Republic*, from only two days ago!" [*Evening Courier* and *The Republic* are two of Italy's most popular newspapers.]
[80] Member of the Italian special police force, the *carabinieri*

"I look forward to it, my boy," said the older man with a smile. But Cino and the Neapolitan were already across the street, tracking down adventure before they had to trek back to the ship for the dinner rush.

From then on, every day went about the same way. The Tuscan and the Neapolitan served breakfast and lunch, went out, came back to for dinner, and left again. They visited Jack London Square, Lake Merritt, Oakland Chinatown; they gambled with the enlisted men at the naval base. They even popped across the Bay to North Beach, the Italian neighborhood in San Francisco, once or twice. But, mostly, Cino sat with Leonard Marabella on Broadway Avenue, swapping tales. Cino told Leonard about the bombings, and the time he saved that drowning boy; in exchange, Leonard told him how the neighborhood grew up.

"They call this place Temescal, because of the little creek that runs through it. *Temescalli*—that's what the Indians called it. Runs up to a lake not far from here. Nice place to take a pretty girl to," he said with a wink. "Used to be the estate of this rich Spaniard named Vicente Peralta, then Oakland swallowed it up."

"When did the Italians get here?" Cino asked.

"Early in the century, oughts and teens...my parents came before the Great War, because my mother didn't want my father to fight. Folks settled in North Beach first but in 1906 there was a huge earthquake, and the whole city burned down. People came here to start over."

"Funny, I met so many Italian-Americans during the War, but they were all from New York or New Jersey," said Cino.

"Lotta Italians over there, yep. Southerners, mostly, like your friend. Warmer summers out there, so it seems to suit them. But here? Feels just like home, no?"

Cino had to admit that it did. The green hills, the cool nights, the lapping waters—nowhere he had been in America reminded him more of the Tyrrhenian coast. That palpable, portentous feeling settled over him again.

Back on the *Mariposa*, Cino wrote rapturous letters to his family and fiancée. He was enamored and enlivened by what he saw: the tender community of home, dropped into a land of adventure and possibility. Given *spazio vitale* and a chance to forge a life not already defined by history. "My thoughts lie with you all, of course," he wrote, "but I know that someday I'll be back here." Then he dashed out to catch the bus across the Bay before the sun set too low.

Imagine the chagrin, then—the utter, contorting agony Cino must have felt—when one day, after dinner, the galley refused to clear. The meal was long over: pots drying, tables scrubbed to a shine, all the men gone for the night. All except two, who sat at a table and laughed uproariously while passing a bottle of wine between them. Those two, and Cino, who had to wait for them to go before he could close up the room. He glared at them as they tipped their glasses. One, Gino Appennini, he knew from the boat—a seasoned crewman and someone he considered a friend. The other was a visitor, an outsider, and therefore completely at fault. Whoever he was, he had just made a new enemy.

The bottle ran dry, and the visitor gestured Cino over. "More wine," he demanded, in guttural Genovese.

"We're out."

"Ha! You're full of it. More wine, boy."

"I'm not your boy. Get out before I call the night watchman."

"Actually, I was thinking I might just stay here for the night." The man yawned and stretched out on the bench. "Be a good boy and bring me a blanket, will ya? Then you can sing me to sleep."

Cino glowered but bit his tongue, and swiped the empty bottle from the table.

"Come on, let's go," said Gino Appennini from behind him, grunting as he helped the other man up. They tottered out the door.

"My brother-in-law, you know?" Gino remarked, by way of explanation. "Hasn't seen his family back home in ten years. Didn't think he'd stay so long or drink so much, but that's Tony Vignale for you!"

"He's an ass," Cino said, then he closed the door and locked it behind him.

By then it was too late to go out, so Cino crawled into bed. He lay awake playing through the scene like a record on repeat: the red-faced man; his broad, drunken smile; that look, like nothing could please him more than making sure Cino had no fun at all that night. There was something gleeful in it, and that troubled him. But what troubled him more was that he missed one of the last nights out on the town before they had to go back—and then it troubled him that it troubled him, because after all it was just one night, and if his real life awaited him in Italy, then what did one night out in America really matter? And so he was troubled, and awake, when the Neapolitan barged through the door in the wee hours, drunk and troubled.

"What's wrong with you?" Cino asked.

"Nuthin, s'nuthin, snuthin. Iss just—well shit, then, what was it all for?"

"What are you talking about?"

"They're gonna dump us. When we get back home. We come all the way out here, fix her up, n' bring her all the way back, n' they're gonna dump us. Got a whole new crew ready."

"WHAT?" Cino sat up.

"First Mate told me. Don't think he meant to, but what does he care, right? We're all back t'twistin' in the wind."

"Screw that," said Cino. "You know how long it was between my last run and this one? No way I'm going back to peschereccio work. No way I'm going back there just to be cut loose again."

"Whaddya mean? What choice've you got?"

Cino thought for a moment—about America, about home, about what he wanted to look back on when he was an old man. Maybe it was his anger, or the tang of the harbor that had followed the Neapolitan into the room, but suddenly his mind drew sharp.

"Only one, I guess," he said.

Two days later, the plan was set. Leonard Marabella would pick Cino up at the newsstand and take him to meet a woman he knew, who ran a hotel and would rent him a room in exchange for some help around the grounds. That way, he could get on his feet and earn a few dollars while he planned his next move. After that, it was anyone's guess.

Cino told his roommate his plan. "Come with me," he said.

The Neapolitan shook his head. "No way, man. It's a bad plan. How you gonna make a living? What you gonna do when Immigration comes around? You got no money, no papers. You don't even speak English. How you think you gonna make it here?"

Cino shrugged. He pulled four soiled dollar bills out of his pocket—all the money he had left from his cigarette sales. He was saving it for one more cheeseburger and beer before he left. "We could pool our money," he suggested.

"Sorry, kid. I got people back home. Can't just leave 'em. And you—what about your girl? Your nonni? Your brother?"

"I don't know," said Cino. "All I know is this is where I was meant to be."

The Neapolitan stuck out his hand. "Then good luck to you, my friend. If you want to write any last letters, leave them on my desk and I'll see that they get there."

They shook hands, then the Neapolitan climbed into bed. Cino dipped his pen into ink, thinking of the nibs and Teresa and Porto Ercole, and Gianna and Alberto and the future. His hand shook as he touched pen to page.

Dear Gianna, I'm sorry, he wrote. That was as far as he got.

A few hours later, Cino slid out of bed and into a stained T-shirt, ripped jeans, and worn shoes with floppy soles. He pulled the four crumpled dollars from his pocket, looking George Washington in the eye for assurance that things would work out. The old man gave him no sign.

Stepping onto the dock, in the gray kiss of morning, Cino felt something fly from his chest and hover overhead. It was the dream he had followed since the death of his mother, since the bombs blew his world apart and let in the light from the far reaches of the Earth. Cino followed it, eyes up, imbued by a hopeful spirit that he knew well, though he could never capture its shape. *Sempre avanti, senza paura*, he thought, as he strode confidently into the fog.

Porto Ercole and Porto Santo Stefano

Old Porto Ercole and Le Grotte (view toward La Rocca)

Le Grotte and Forte Filippo

Fishing boats in Old Porto Ercole

Porto Santo Stefano, date unknown

The Chegia and Procaccini Families

Annunziata (Doretta) Chegia

Sebastiano (Doretti) Chegia

Rossirosa Procaccini

Pietro Chegia

Alcide Chegia

Piero (Vittorio)
Chegia

Dirce & Trento
Procaccini

Aldo Chegia

Laura Procaccini Chegia

Cino, Alberto, and Aldo Through the Years

Cino in 3rd Grade, 1946. 3rd row, 7 from L. (Sig.na Carbone in middle, Teresa on her right)

Cino photo for Foglio di Ricognizione, 1951

Wedding photos (from L):
Franco & Madeline, Cino & Josephine

Aldo in Navy, 1934-35

Alberto in Navy, 1960s

Cino Chegia and Family, 1960s - Today

Cino, Jo, and sons, 1970s

Cino, Jo, and sons, 1980s

Cino and Jo on train, 2004

Cino, Alberto, and Cory, Porto Ercole, 2010s

Cino and
Alberto,
2000s

Chegia Clan at Cory's wedding, 2014

Cino, John, Cory, and Eugenia Chegia, 2014

CHAPTER FIFTEEN: ONE MAN'S TRASH

"Hotcakes and eggs."
- Cino Chegia

May 20, 1954. Gianna di Felice sits at her parents' home in Sulmona, sipping a steaming hot espresso. She stares at the envelope, hastily addressed in his chicken-scratch scrawl. He never quite got the hang of handwriting; or grammar; or school. Her letters to him are always in perfect cursive, strung straight across the page like she held a ruler under her pen.

She doesn't want to open it. She already knows what's inside, just from the heft in her hand. His other letters are heavy with radiance, page after page soaked in light. This one weighs next to nothing, like a raincloud. She opens it.

"I knew it," she says to an empty room.

Leonard picked Cino up where they arranged, and drove him right to the woman's hotel. By 7 a.m. he was standing in front of her desk, thrusting his chin out and shoulders back like they taught him in Figlio della Lupa camp. Next to him, Leonard spoke English to the woman, who had kind but shrewd eyes and a tight, gray bun. She looked at Cino and half-nodded, half-shrugged. His mouth went bone dry.

"How are you at washing windows?" Leonard asked.

"Good! Yeah, good. I don't know. We didn't have many windows growing up."

"No problem, son. You'll get the hang of it. I gotta go pick up the papers, but I'll be back at noon and we'll have some lunch."

With that, he was gone. In his place was the old lady with the tight bun, holding a sponge and a bucket. She didn't speak Italian, but gestured for him to follow her. She led him to a small room complete with a bed, a nightstand, a lamp and a wash basin. She swept her arm across it and handed him the key. Cino pumped her hand vigorously. Then she thrust the bucket and sponge into his arms and pointed to the bay windows at the end of the hall.

Sponging and soaping, washing and drying, Cino couldn't believe his good fortune. The spring sun smiled at his reflection, and the smell of May flowers wafted past him on the breeze. He wondered what the men on the ship were doing. By now they would have realized he was gone. Were they looking for him? Did anyone care? Were they upset, or secretly cheering him on? If only they could see him now—just a few hours into his new life in Oakland, and already he had a job and a place to live. It felt like a dream, and if it was, so be it—he would stay asleep for as long as he could. But time stretched on and he didn't wake up, and at noon Leonard came back to take him to lunch, so eventually Cino accepted that this was all really happening. That made everything so much more meaningful, and so much scarier.

The two men—mentor and pupil, leader and led—walked a few blocks down to a diner, where Charlton Heston, Audrey Hepburn, and Frank Sinatra posed on the window. Inside, teenagers sipped malts and dropped pennies into a jukebox blaring Chubby Checker.

"What is this place?" Cino asked, as they slid into a Formica booth.

"It's a diner," Leonard said. "Like an American *bar*."

"Huh." Cino looked at the menu, which was emblazoned with American flags, Uncle Sam, images of soldiers and exploding fireworks. "I didn't know they had propaganda like this here!"

Leonard chuckled. "So, what'll it be?"

Cino scanned his menu. It looked something like this:

Atbbwefn Ijebnapdsk...................$2.00

Nawgpoijqgnojkoawef.................$3.50

Qwe uoh Mw3rjn9......................$1.25

"Uhh..." he said.

"Right, sorry."

The waitress arrived, and Leonard addressed her in English. "*I'll have a cheeseburger and fries, and some hotcakes and eggs for the kid,*" he said.

"What was that?" Cino asked. "What did you order?"

Leonard pointed to the top item on the menu. "*Hot-cakes and eggs,*" he said slowly. "Say it with me: *hot-cakes and eggs*. Good. You'll like it."

Their food came, piping hot. Cino stared at it, unsure of what to do with this stack of flat, floppy pizza crusts. Leonard laughed and showed him how to smear the hotcakes with butter, drizzle maple syrup on top, pierce the eggs so the yolk ran down like lava. Cino dove into his plate and didn't emerge until it was clean.

"That was the first time I ever ate hotcakes and eggs," he remembers, "but it would not be the last!"

When the meal was over, Leonard called for the check. Cino pulled out the four Washingtons in his pocket, but his friend waved him off and, instead, put one ten-dollar bill on the table and another in Cino's hand.

"We take care of each other in this neighborhood," he said. "Don't forget that."

Before they left, Cino looked one more time at the laminated menu with its garish Americana. It now read like this:

Hotcakes and Eggs.....................$2.00

Nawgpoijqgnojkoawef................$3.50

Qwe uoh Mw3rjn9.....................$1.25

"What a country!" he said, kissing Uncle Sam on the lips.

Back at the hotel, Cino moved inside to clean the walls and floors. Working his way through the lobby, he overheard two men speaking flawless Italian.

"*Paesani!*"[81] he called out. The men hollered back and they struck up a conversation.

"We're just in town for a visit," they said, "but our family lives here. You know, they said they were looking for help in their garden. Think you can come by tomorrow? They'll pay!"

"Then I'll be there!" Cino chirped.

---

[81] "Countrymen!"

The next day, he cleaned the family's garden and mowed their lawn. "When I was done," he remembers, "they paid me a full 15 dollars! I felt like a real man that day, and went to the same restaurant to buy my own plate of hotcakes and eggs."

Little by little and piece by piece, Cino assimilated himself into American life. Leonard took him to buy new clothes, then doubled his culinary options at the diner by teaching him the words *"hamburger steak."* A few days later, they registered Cino for Social Security so that he could get a real job. "I returned to the hotel happy and feeling like a true American!" he says.

With a Social Security card in his hand and a growing nest egg under his bed, Cino decided it was time to settle in. But there was only so much he could ask of Leonard Marabella. Though the man's generosity seemed unbounded, Cino's dignity would not allow him to keep coming back for handouts. He needed to find another connection, one who could link him to Oakland's Italian-American network. It was then that he remembered the note his grandfather had sent him, the name that had been crouching in the back of his mind: *Aurelio Perillo.* He flipped through the hotel's phone book, found the entry for **Perillo, A** and dialed the number.

"Pronto!"[82] came a voice on the other end of the line. Cino figured he had the right Perillo.

Two hours later, Cino sat at the Perillos' dining room table with Aurelio, his wife Colamba, and their children Rita and Joe.

"I haven't been back to Santo Stefano since 1940," Aurelio explained. "Can't go back, really. If INS finds out I'm here, they'll arrest me. Or worse—they'll deport me and never let me back."

"But why?" asked Cino.

"Let me tell you."

---

[82] "Hello?" [Italian way of answering the phone…literally means, "I'm ready!"]

The Tale of Aurelio Perillo

"It was 1940. I was a merchant seaman, just like you. Working on a tanker going back and forth to the States. Stopped in New York City around June of that year—you remember what happened in June, I figure?"

Cino remembered all right. The blackshirted paraders; the rallying cries. *Il Duce* in his epaulettes, pontificating from the balcony. Doretta cursing by the wireless.

"When Mussolini declared war, suddenly we were the enemy. America wasn't in the fight yet, but they sure weren't out of it, either, and that fuel we were carrying could be going into tanks or trucks fighting the Brits. We men, too. If we go home, they're giving us guns the next day. So they closed up the ports, wouldn't let us leave.

"We sat there for months, going nuts. Nothing to do but wait. Finally, word got around that FDR—he was President back then—had signed this thing called Lend-Lease with Churchill. The U.S. was gonna send food, oil, guns, what have you to England, in exchange for space on their military bases if America ever got in the War. So now they're looking around for ships to carry all the stuff and they say, 'Hey! Got a bunch of Italian ships right here!' They start getting ready to seize the boat and send all us crewman off God knows where.

"Meanwhile, the Italian Navy finds out all this is going on and sends out a secret signal to all the captains: 'Scuttle the ships.' Toss whatever odds and ends we got into the engines and blow 'em out so the Yanks can't use 'em. So, we do! *Credere, Obeddire, Combattere*, you know? Besides, we're none too happy with America for keeping us around for almost a year.

"Here's where things go wrong, though. We knock out the engines, U.S. Coast Guard comes storming in, arrests everyone, asks who the ringleaders are…most captains, all the good captains, say, 'It was me. My men had nothing to do with it.' But not my captain, no! Damn coward says, 'Don't look here, my men made me do it!' Now we're all on some list, enemy combatants or something, and INS wants nothing better than to get us off their shores."

"So why are you still here? Why didn't you go home?"

Aurelio shrugged. "By the time the war was over, things had changed. I came out here, started a whole new life. Met me a beautiful American gal, had a couple great kids, figured I'm here to stay. But still, I'm hanging by a thread; I have to drive to San Leandro just to mail letters to my family, so the INS can't trace them back to me. So should you, for that matter—if you want to contact your people, give me your letters and I'll mail them with mine. You're an illegal now; these are the kinds of things you gotta do. Fortunately, I know a place where they don't much care if you're legal or not. I'll take you there tomorrow."

The following morning, Cino stood outside the hotel as a heavy sedan with bucket seats and chrome wheels swung around front. Aurelio beckoned him in and they set off through the winding streets of his new home. As they drove, Aurelio pointed out landmarks that Cino would come to know well: the Tower Theater on 51st and Telegraph; the Colombo Club; the Bilger rock quarry; Buon Gusto Bakery.

"All Italians around here," he explained. "Mostly Genovese, some Toscane, like us. The Siciliani and Calabrese, they work in the quarry and dance at the Colombo Club on weekends. We Northerners, we go to the Ligure Club. And we all work right…here."

Aurelio turned onto Peralta Street and pointed to a two-story building that dominated the block. It looked like an oversized garage with offices on top, and at 7 a.m. it was already buzzing with activity. Huge, belching trucks rolled in and out, their aft ends wide open like hungry mouths. Above them, men with wild mustaches leaned out of the office windows to shout instructions down to the street. Here, there, everywhere, the patter of Genovese and other Italian dialects. It reminded him of his days with the Ala Company: semi-organized chaos, always threatening to fall apart but somehow holding itself together. It was a dazzling, awe-inspiring sight.

"Welcome to the Oakland Scavenger Company," Aurelio said with a certain pomp.

He led Cino through the oil-slicked garage and up the stairs to the offices, greeting everyone they passed. They walked into an open room with a window overlooking the street.

"Cino Chegia, meet Joseph Biasotti," Aurelio said. "Joe here is the Hiring Manager of Oakland Scavenger. Joe, Cino's santostefanesi like me, and he's looking for a place to work. Think we can get him on a truck?"

Joe Biasotti looked Cino up and down. "He's just a kid," he said. "Looks like he can barely haul his own balls around, much less walk a beat."

"I've been working since I was nine," Cino interjected. "I've been a deckboy, a cook, a ditch-digger for the troops. I've hauled coal and washed fish guts out of crates in the freezing water. I can handle—whatever this is."

Joe smiled. "All right then, you've got the job. Gino, was it?"

Cino nodded—it wasn't the first time someone had gotten his name wrong. Besides, they could call him whatever they wanted, as long as they paid him.

"Great. You start tomorrow. Come by at 5 a.m. and I'll give you the rundown."

Cino shook Joe's hand and walked out as light as a feather. He couldn't believe it—a real job! No more washing windows! He beamed at the roughshod men in the garage, who shot him a *just you wait* look in return.

"I've got another surprise for you," Aurelio said once they got back on the road.

"What is it?"

"You'll see," said Aurelio mysteriously.

They drove east out of Temescal, past a large, curved lake dotted with small islands. Nearby, a small amusement park was just rousing itself, shaking off the morning dew. "Lake Merritt," Aurelio said. "That there is Children's Fairyland. Rita and Joe love it there."

Deeper into Oakland they went, until the sounds of Italian streets were far behind. Here, the faces were darker and the eyes seemed wary. Aurelio smiled reassuringly.

"We're here," he announced, pulling up to a small house on 38th Avenue. An old Italian woman came out to meet them, looking for all the world like Nonna Rosa Procaccini.

"Cino, this is Maria Sinibaldi. Maria, this is the young man I was telling you about."

"*Piacere*,"[83] said Cino politely.

Mrs. Sinibaldi looked at him but spoke to Aurelio. "He got a job?"

"With Oakland Scavenger," said Aurelio.

"Great." She led them inside the house and down a flight of stairs, flicking a light on at the bottom. A room sprang into focus— a whole apartment, really, empty and waiting.

---

[83] Pleased to meet you.

"Bedroom's in here, kitchen through there, bathroom just down the hall. Keep your showers under ten minutes or the hot water runs low. I'll take first month's rent after you get your first paycheck, give you some time to get on your feet." She looked at Cino expectantly. "So, you want it or what?"

Cino blinked. "Sorry, what?"

"She's asking you if you want to rent the apartment," Aurelio prodded.

"The whole thing? Just—just for me?"

Mrs. Sinibaldi tapped her foot impatiently.

"Yes, of course! I'll take it!" Cino finally blurted out.

Aurelio smiled. "Let's go get your stuff, then."

Lying awake that night, Cino stared at the ceiling in his very own bedroom, in his own apartment, in a brand-new city, in America. Soon, he would be joining a team of men who worked on dry land, who spoke (some) English, who had houses and families and driver's licenses and didn't have to sneak onto trains. What a world he had stepped into—what generosity they'd shown him! The young gambler couldn't believe his luck.

At the same time, there was a sadness. A hotel room was one thing; an apartment was another. And though the letters had been sent and the job had been taken and the *Homeric* had long since left the dock, in a way none of it had felt permanent until now. Like he could just turn to Leonard and say, "I want to go home," and be back at Nonno and Nonna's in no time.

Cino awoke with a start. Where was he? What time was it? And what was that pounding on the door?

"Let's go, kid!" Mrs. Sinibaldi shouted. "There's a man outside waiting for you."

In a heartbeat, it all rushed back: new life, new job, first day, running late. He dashed out of bed and up the stairs, to where Aurelio's friend Gino Cerruti shivered in the pre-dawn fog.

"I'm sorry," Cino said, by way of introduction. "It won't happen again."

"That's right, it won't," said Cerruti, and he drove off.

At 5 a.m. sharp, Joe Biasotti ushered Cino into his office.

"So, what has Aurelio told you about the Oakland Scavenger Company?" he asked.

"Well, nothing," said Cino.

"Good. Then I'll start from the beginning."

The Tale of Oakland Scavenger Company

"Right now, as we speak, Oakland Scavenger Company is the biggest garbage collection agency in the East Bay Area. We have about 500 employees running dozens of trucks across Oakland, Alameda, San Leandro, Berkeley, you name it. About 100 of them are partners, who own equal shares of the company. Our territory covers over 750 square miles—that's like 2,000 square kilometers. We even bought our own private dump over in San Leandro not long ago. If you're talking about waste disposal in the East Bay, kid, you're talking about Oakland Scavenger.

"But it wasn't always like this. Back at the turn of the century, when people were just starting to settle here, a few teams of Ligurians started up their own routes. Groups of brothers and friends, each with their own horse and buggy, making their own deals with people and businesses to pick up their trash. My father, Giuseppe, was one of them. He and his partner would go around piling garbage up on these burlap sacks, then toss it in the cart and take it out to the dump. For a while there weren't too many people around here, so these little two-man jobs didn't really bump into each other. But after the earthquake in 1906, when the City burned, people started moving out here in droves. Suddenly these little family businesses are getting way more work than they can handle, and stepping on each others' toes trying to take more turf.

"So they merged up. Formed a collective called the Oakland City Garbage Company. Equal shares for everybody—all Ligurians, too. Speaking Genovese, like you hear now. They bought this place in 1916, changed the name to Oakland Scavenger Company, and the rest is history."

"But how did it—you—we get to be so big?" Cino asked.

"Great question. A few ways. One, we got some good contracts early on. Working with big manufacturers and city governments just as the area was building up. Two, right place, right time. World War II kicked things to a whole 'nother level around here, what with the Naval shipyard and the Port of Oakland bringing in loads of cargo. Lots of waste coming out of those places. Three, the partnership thing: guys like you can buy a share of the company after a while and become owners with the rest of us. That gives people incentive, you know? And pride.

"Four—and I think this is most important—we've been *smart* about it. Men like my father knew that trash wasn't just trash; like it wasn't all created equal, you could say. Some of it could be turned back into money. Food waste, for example. We've got this hog farm out in Byron, and when we collect food scraps from restaurants we bring it out there to feed the pigs. Then, we sell the pigs off for slaughter! Bottles and rags, too, we can wash and re-sell. We make a huge profit, save room in the landfill, then can turn around and use that money to win more contracts. Took us right to the top! There's some real smart cookies here, Gino—you remember that. And not a high school diploma between 'em."

"So everyone here is Italian?" Cino asked.

"Not everyone. During the War, lots of our boys went off to fight. We were growing then, too, so we needed more men on the trucks. Eventually, there just weren't enough Italians around anymore. So we started hiring blacks, Mexicans, you name it. They've done good for us, helped us grow. But they can't be partners. That's just for us, you know? *Cosa nostra.*" [84]

"Any more questions?" Joe asked. Cino shook his head. "Good. Let's get you out on a truck."

Thirty minutes later, Cino clung to a pole on the back of a truck that wound through the Oakland hills, billowing smoke and grinding gears. The hills were steep, steeper than the ones back home, and the houses were tall and broad-shouldered. Across from him, his trainer, Lou Alberti, dangled out into the street and waved to the driver.

"Hold up!" he shouted. He turned to Cino as the truck slowed to a halt. "Grab the can—we're walking from here."

Cino drew a heavy metal can from the mouth of the truck and slung it over his shoulder like Lou had taught him. The steel handle dug into his shoulder blade; he bent down like an old man trying to find a comfortable position.

Lou laughed. "You ain't seen nothing yet, son—there isn't even any trash in there yet!"

As they walked, Lou explained the garbageman's trade to Cino. "On trash days, you see, people leave their bags out on their stoop. You go in, throw the bags in the can, take the can to the truck, up the steps and into the back. Lather, rinse, repeat. Got it?"

"Sure, yeah," said Cino. The sun had broken through the fog, and beads of sweat had started to dance on his forehead.

"Now, some of these house aren't customers, you see," Lou

---

[84] "Our thing"—the name the Italian-American mafia gave itself.

continued, breathing normally. "So you gotta learn the map—they'll give you a map. You stick around long enough and become partner, you get your own route, you gotta come and collect from these people before *conti*[85] day every few months. That can be a real pain in the ass, trust me. People give you the runaround, they don't come to the door, they sic their dogs on you...and if you show up short to conti, it's on you. Listen: these folks think they own you 'cause you pick up their trash. Put you own them, remember that. Don't take nothin' from 'em but their money."

They went on that way for several blocks, Lou pointing out where the longest driveways were and what houses gave good tips at Christmastime. Eventually, as the sun moved past its apex, they hopped back on the truck and rolled down to headquarters.

"That's really all you need to know, kid," Lou said when they got back. "The key is you just gotta get out there every day and do it. You may find out that's easier said than done."

It didn't take long to find that out. Every morning from then on, Cino got up at 4:15, hopped into Gino Cerruti's car, pounded a cup or two of espresso at the truck barn and headed for the hills. Like all the newest guys, he got the toughest routes—and from morning dew to high noon, it was him and his footsteps, and the can on his back. A can that got a lot heavier, he learned, once it actually had trash in it.

Not that he ever regretted it, though. The job was steady, the pay was good, and the Scavengers embraced him like a member of their family. Work ended by 1 or 2 p.m., so nearly every day Cino and the other newcomers—guys like Leandro Giacomelli, Tony Bavoso, and Giuliano Fontana—could spend their afternoons exploring the city. They took the ferry to San Francisco, went to the pictures in Berkeley, found bars that served 18 year-olds. They

[85] Accounts/accounting

taught each other new English words, whistled at ladies in skirts on the street, then rode the bus home since none of them could afford a car.

"We all became fast friends," Cino recalls fondly. "They were some of my closest compatriots at the Oakland Scavenger Company." But as close as they were, they weren't his real family. They weren't his cousins or his brother. And every day since jumping ship, Cino wondered what had happened to his family since they found out he wasn't coming back.

"I knew it!" Nonno Alberto exclaimed, looking at the hastily written letter in Cino's chicken scratch. "Didn't I tell you, Rosa. Good boy." Rosa shrugged.

Albertino, peach fuzz on his cheeks, squinted impassively. It was official. His big brother was gone, and he may never come back. Alberto wasn't sure if it hurt or not. Sure, he would miss him, but Cino was a man now. They were both men. And he had been waiting for this moment his whole life. So, in a way, had Alberto. They all knew it was coming. So it wasn't a hurt, so much. Just a hole.

"Excuse me," he said. He walked to his room and pulled out a large map of the world's shipping lanes. Diligently, he traced all the ones that went from Europe to the Port of Oakland.

Word of Cino's abandon-ship spread swiftly through Monte Argentario. In L'Ospizio, Doretti and Doretta consoled each other quietly, knowing they may have seen the last of their beloved grandson. Cino's friends toasted his fortune and imagined what world he must be seeing. On the *Santo Stefano,* they shrugged their shoulders and settled bets.

On the mainland in Santa Marinella, Aldo sat at the dinner table with his family.

"I heard something today," he told Anna.

"What?"

"Cino jumped ship in California. He's not coming back."

She reached for his hand. "Oh, Aldo. I'm so sorry."

"It was bound to happen. I just wish I had had the chance to say goodbye."

"Who's Cino?" piped Pino, sitting next to his father.

"Cino is your brother. You remember him, don't you?" Aldo said. "Perhaps not. You were just a little boy when he left."

Pino looked at his mother, confused.

"He's your half-brother," she explained. "From your father's first marriage. Like Mario, but on your dad's side."

"Oh," said Pino. "Okay!"

"I'm going to Santo Stefano tomorrow," Aldo announced. "I'm going to see Alberto."

Anna squeezed his hand. In her lap, baby Mara cooed happily.

The next day, Aldo took the train to the promontory, hat in hand. He knew that Alberto was apprenticed to Trento, so he wouldn't be hard to find. Once the sun dipped behind the hill, he went to Ala headquarters and stood out front, reading a newspaper. He wondered if he would even recognize his son; it had been so many years. He wondered if Alberto would recognize him, or would look at him like a stranger.

Finally, the doors swung open. A tall, lean boy stepped out, squinting as his eyes adjusted to the light. He started walking home, wiping his hands on a greasy rag then stuffed it in his pocket. Aldo's heart skipped like a flat rock across the water; it was him, no doubt about it. His father's long, aquiline face; his mother's soft brow. Aldo breathed in tremblingly, then put on the broad Chegia smile and strode forward.

"Hey kid," he said, matching Alberto stride for stride. "Who's your daddy?"

The young man glanced at him once then kept walking, looking straight ahead. They never saw each other again.

CHAPTER SIXTEEN: THE PLUNGE, PART II

"Sex, please!"
- Cino Chegia

Summer, 1954. Cino Chegia stands outside Maria Sinibaldi's house, fidgeting nervously in a white shirt with a starched collar. He clutches the small bouquet uncomfortably tight, worried that it may slip through his damp palms and scatter on the ground. He checks his watch: they're five minutes late.

Just then, a large sedan pulls up in front of him. The driver's side window rolls down, unleashing the sounds of "Rock Around the Clock" from the car radio. A young woman in large black sunglasses, scarf thrown gaily around her neck, turns to him.

"Giuseppina?" he asks.

The woman laughs and jerks her thumb behind her. Cino peers in through the open window. The car is full of young ladies, tittering and whispering to each other. In the backseat, scrunched up against the passenger-side door, one of them waves at him.

Cino draws in a sharp breath. Aurelio had said she was beautiful, but nothing like this. Ringlets of blond hair frame her soft cheekbones; her wide, affable brow slopes down to a button nose. Her doe eyes hint at a teasing defiance, that beckons and then evades. For a moment, Cino loses himself in them.

"Hello," she says, in flawless Italian. "I'm Josephine. This is Joanne, Beverly, Angela, and Angela. It's...nice to meet you." Cino blushes.

"Now what are you waiting for?" demands Joanne, the driver. "Get in—we're going to be late to the movie!"

Cino opens the back door and crams himself in next to Angela and Angela. He thrusts the bouquet into Josephine's hands, daffodil petals falling across the other girls' laps. She nods politely then looks out her window.

"Here we go!" shouts Joanne, and they zoom off, tires squealing.

Earlier that day, Cino sat around a Saturday lunch spread with Aurelio Perillo and family.

"So, Cino," Aurelio said. "'Bout time we get you a girlfriend, don't you think?"

"Huh?" Cino looked up from his prosciutto and melon.

"A girlfriend. You know, one of those pretty little numbers with nice hair and big...smiles and all that. Time you met a nice Italian girl."

"I've met some nice Italian girls."

It was true, he had. Nearly every weekend since he arrived, Cino had visited the Italian clubs, dancing and drinking and chatting up girls. The Ligure Club played the old accordion tunes his uncles used to play, but the Colombo Club had those dark-eyed Southern girls, and the *Fratellanza*[86] Club—well, let's just say it lived up to its name. Cino had met many lovely women at these dances, and had even taken a few out on dates, but none had been able to shake Gianna from his mind. He hadn't heard a word from her since he jumped ship.

"I'll bet you have," Aurelio continued. "But I have a special one in mind for you. She's sweet and beautiful, and sharp as a tack. Quiet when you first meet her, but once you get to know her well, sharp as a tack."

"Okay, sure. I'm in. It's just…"

"I know, you had a gal back home. But you're here now—you made that choice. And you have to marry, Cino. That's the only way you can ever build a real life here. Without an American wife, you'll just be running in circles until they catch you."

"You're right—thank you, Aurelio. I'd love to meet her."

"Great. I'll call her father now!"

Before Cino could protest, Aurelio picked up the phone and spun the rotary.

"Yeah, Baci," he said. "Got a boy here who wants to take out your Josephine. Yeah, tonight. No, he won't get any funny ideas. Yeah, he's a good kid. A Scavenger, one of the new helpers. Italian boy, yeah. Doesn't speak a lick of English."

He fell silent for a moment, listening and nodding. "Sure, sure, I'll tell him," he said finally. "Okay. My love to Maria. Ciao."

He hung up and turned to Cino. "She's going to the movies with her friends tonight…so I guess you're going to have to pay for all five of them!"

---

[86] Brotherhood; camaraderie.

Cino clapped his hands and smiled. "Better go check my couch cushions then!"

Six hours later, Cino stood in front of Mrs. Sinibaldi's house, waiting for the girls to pick him up. He thought about how he'd tell Alberto the story in his next letter: *Just got back from a date with five women—can you believe it? America: what a country!*

In the car, Cino leaned across both Angelas to talk to Josephine.

"So, were you born here?"

Josephine nodded. "My parents came here from Liguria in 1931. My sister Madeline and I were both born here. You're from Porto Santo Stefano, like Aurelio, right?"

"Yes. Well, Porto Ercole, but I lived in Santo Stefano before coming here. They're all basically the same, anyway. Just little fishing towns, until the War at least."

"I hear they were..." Josephine trailed off. The car fell silent for a moment. "How did you end up here?"

"Was a merchant marine, flew here on Easter, jumped ship on May 5! What do they call it, Cinco de Mayo? *Ole!*"

All the girls laughed. Cino smiled broadly.

"We're here!" said Joanne.

They were seeing *Three Coins in the Fountain*—a film, ironically enough, about American women looking for love in Italy. When they pulled up, Cino dashed out of the car to open the door for Josephine, but by the time he got there she was already standing on the curb.

"What are you doing?" she laughed. "I can open my own door, you know."

"Oh, okay, sorry. Uh, stay here—I'll go buy the tickets."

"Stop! You can't do that. They don't speak Italian here."

"I know! My English is pretty good, actually. Not as good as your Italian, but I've been practicing a lot. *May I please hamburger steak?* See?"

Josephine smirked. "Maybe I'll go with you, just in case."

In line, Cino felt a thrill run down his neck. Here he was, standing next to the prettiest girl he had met since Gianna, and now he had a chance to show her how American he could be! Pulling a clump of bills from his pocket, he strutted to the box office window like Baby Ruth at the baseball plate. He knew exactly what to say; had counted the number over and over again in his mind. He stuck out his chin, looked the ticket vendor straight in the eye, and said, in his loudest voice and best American accent:

"Sex, please!"

The ticket vendor goggled at him, shocked through her spectacles. Josephine turned white as a sheet. Joanne, Beverly and the Angelas doubled over with laughter.

Josephine darted past him to the window. "He means 'six'!" she exclaimed. "Six tickets to *Three Coins in the Fountain*, please." She glared at Cino, who blushed brilliantly, though he didn't quite understand the difference between what he had said and what she had said.

"In the almost 60 years of marriage that followed that night," Cino says, "my wife Josephine never let me live that down."

After the movie, the girls dropped Cino back at Mrs. Sinibaldi's house, and he stood outside of the car with Josephine for a moment.

"I'm sorry about…whatever happened back there, but I still had a nice time with you," he said. "Can I see you again?"

"Probably, if you try hard enough," she smiled.

"Where do you work?"

"At the bank during the day, and Buon Gusto Bakery at night. You know where that is?"

"Yeah! I pass it all the time. I love stopping in to look at all the beautiful cakes I can't afford."

"Well, maybe some time you'll stop in and I'll be there. No guarantees, though."

With that, she ducked back into the idling car and was gone. Cino watched the car until it drove out of sight.

A few weeks later, he worked up the courage to "casually" stop by Buon Gusto one evening after work. When he walked in, Josephine was piping a cake.

"Ah, it's you," she said, not looking up. "I was wondering when I'd see you here."

"Hello," he replied eloquently.

She wiped her hands on her apron. "So, do you want anything?"

"Um, yes."

"Okay, what?"

"Another date?"

A wisp of a smile blew across her face. "How about an éclair?" she asked. "Cup of coffee? Cream puff? Cookie?"

"How about I just call you sometime?"

"Ooh, you have to try these brownies! Double-fudge walnut."

"Okay, okay, I get the picture. And yeah, give me one of those double-fudge walnut brownies."

Walking home alone, Cino's only consolation—aside from the decadent brownie—was the thought that, perhaps, Josephine was softening. Perhaps, with persistence, he could get her to see that he was more than a poor garbageman who couldn't speak English; he was witty and charming, and a hard worker. So he went back, and back, and back again. He bought cannoli for Mrs. Sinibaldi, cupcakes for Aurelio's kids, a little something for the guys on the truck. Each time he went, he asked her out in a different way; each time, she gave him a different excuse.

"It's my cousin's birthday," she would say; or, "I have to cover a shift at the bank."

Once, he ran into her at the Ligure Club, and spun her around the dance floor to some of the old Genovese folksongs. As they danced, he asked her out again.

"Listen, Cino," she replied. "You seem nice and all. All the ladies in the bakery like you. But, well—you're just not really the kind of guy a girl would want to go steady with right now. Heck, you don't even have a car! Sorry, but it's just not going to work."

The next day, Cino set out to buy a car. His first stop was the DMV, where with his Social Security number he was able to apply for a driver's license. The test was all in English, but he had been practicing, and, "Much to my surprise, I passed!" Two days after that, Cino and his neighbor Jim Perata went to see Jim's friend, who was selling his 1949 Ford for $175. Cino emptied his savings and bought the car right then and there, keeping just enough money for two tickets to the Ice Follies in San Francisco.

In November, 1954—not long after his 19th birthday, and not long before he was supposed to have married Gianna—Cino pulled up in front of Buon Gusto Bakery in his new car. Wordlessly, he walked in, leaned across the counter, and handed Josephine the tickets. She looked at them, glanced behind him at the parked car, and nodded.

"Pick me up on Saturday at 6," she said. "Don't be late."

Cino walked back onto the sidewalk, made sure no one was looking, and clicked his heels in delight.

That Saturday, Cino washed and waxed his car until he could see his own reflection in it. He washed himself, put his white shirt with the starched collar back on, picked up more flowers and drove to Josephine's house. He had to walk up the steps three times before he got the courage to knock on her door.

Her mother, Maria, answered. *"Sex, please!"* she exclaimed. A burst of laughter came from the room behind her. Cino turned red to his ears.

"I'm sorry, son, I had to do it. Come in, come in, please. Josephine's almost ready."

Cino followed the friendly, square-shouldered woman inside. "Baci! Come meet the boy!" she called out. "He brought us more flowers!"

They turned through a doorway into the living room, and came upon two men playing cards. The one facing them looked up, his merry eyes framed by oversized ears.

"Welcome, kid. Gino, is it?" Cino opened his mouth but said nothing. "Come here, have a seat. This is my friend, Tony."

The other man swiveled around to face Cino. Cino froze in his tracks. It was *him*! The man from the ship, who kept him in the kitchen for hours while gabbed with his friend!

"Hey, I know you!" the jerk said. "Weren't you on the *Mariposa* with Gino Appennini? You gave me dirty looks that whole night! Hey, Baci, this kid gave me dirty looks. You can't let him take Jo out! He's a no-good dirty-look-giver!"

Baci eyed Cino accusingly. "Is this true, son? Did you give my friend Tony dirty looks?"

Cino gulped. The bouquet felt limp in his hand. This was not exactly the impression he had hoped to make.

"Well, did you?" Baci demanded again. "I tell you, Tony, the kids these days. When I came here in '21, young men showed respect to their elders. Those boys out in Iowa, why they said 'sir' to you even if you were a lowly farmer like me. Nowadays, young guy meets a man he can learn a thing or two about life from, and he just gives him the stink eye."

"I—I'm sorry." Cino finally gasped. "I didn't—I didn't mean any offense. I just wanted to go out that night, and I couldn't until he left. You know? I didn't mean anything by it."

The room fell silent, heavy. Cino wished he could dissolve into a puddle and sink through the floorboards.

Finally, Tony cracked. "Ha ha ha! We're just pulling your leg, boy. You did give me dirty looks, but I deserved it! And I've seen you since then, too. You're a Scavenger now, aren't you?"

"Y—Yes," said Cino, as he remembered how to breathe.

"Ah, one of us!" chimed Baci, throwing a friendly arm around Cino's shoulders. "Tony and I have been Scavengers since the War. It's good work—men's work. Now go, have a good time with Josephine. Josephine, let's go! Your boyfriend's waiting!"

"I'm coming, Papa," she said, as she appeared in the doorway. "And he's not my boyfriend." She was radiant in a simple blue dress. Cino forgot how to breathe again.

On the drive over, Cino and Jo chatted about their families and friends, about life in Italian Oakland. At dinner, they glanced shyly into each other's eyes, then looked away, then looked back again. Cino could feel himself falling deeper and deeper under her spell. At the Ice Follies, some people skated around in sparkly costumes, but Cino mostly noticed how Josephine's faced shone in the warm glow of the spotlights.

After the show, the fun really began. She took his arm as they walked across the parking lot, buzzing with excitement at the spectacle. He was buzzing, too, but not about the Follies. He turned his collar up against the cold night air, and to hide the smile spreading across his face.

At the car, she allowed him to open her door for her and help her in. "Let 's get you back home before your father changes his mind about me," he said.

He slid behind the wheel, threw her a smile, and turned the key in the ignition. *Bub-bub-bub-bub-bub*, said the car. He coughed, smiled again, and turned the key again. *Bub-bub-bub-bub-bub*, it said again.

"Everything all right?" she asked.

"Sure, sure, it's fine. Sometimes she has a little trouble getting started. We…we may have to push."

"Say again?"

Bub-bub-bub-bub-bub.

"Yeah, we definitely have to push."

Josephine sighed, and her face twisted into this wry, exasperated expression—"a look I would come to know very well," Cino remembers. She kicked off her heels, got out of the car, and stood by the passenger door.

Cino released the brake and put it in neutral. "On three, ready—one, two, THREE!"

They strained their backs against the doorjambs, pushing with all their might. The car rolled ever so slowly forward. As it picked up speed, Cino hopped in, turned the key and the engine revved to life.

"Bravo!" they shouted into the night air. Jo flung her arms up like a victorious boxer, then climbed in, face flushed with exertion.

"What a country," he beamed, as he shifted into gear.

Back at her house, they sat in silence for a moment. The only sound was the idling of the engine, which Cino was afraid to turn off lest it not turn back on again.

"So, would you like to—" he began.

"Yes," she said, without hesitation. She darted in and kissed him on the cheek, then hopped out of the car and up the stairs.

After that, it was him and her. Gino and Jo. He took her dinner, to the dances, stopped by the bakery almost daily. She brought him lunch and helped him with his English, darned his shirts when they got ripped. He grew close with Baci, pampered Maria, and eventually met the rest of her family: her older sister Madeline, Madeline's husband Franco, and their two young daughters, Vickie and Valerie. He even made friends with Tony Vignale—a friendship that would later springboard Cino to the forefront of Temescal's Italian community.

When next Cino looked up, he was crossing the threshold of his first year in America. He couldn't believe it had gone by so fast; he couldn't believe all he had been able to pack into a year. New place, new job, new friends, new woman, new life. He had been safe, so far. Protected. But every day was still a risk, and every shadow held the prospect of capture and deportation. It was time to make things official, make this new place his true home. There was nowhere in the world he would rather be, he was sure of that. And no one he would rather be with than his beloved Jo. So, as the winter of 1955 crept into spring, Cino turned to her one night at a party.

"Josephine," he said, in his serious voice. "I—I love you, you know. Very much. And I have something I've been meaning to ask you. Will you—um, you know. Will you—?"

"Yes," she said. Her smile bloomed like a daisy.

"You have to let me finish the question."

"Fine, go ahead."

"Will you—?"

"Yes!" She laughed loudly. People nearby turned to look.

"Stop! Give me a second. Will you marry me?"

"Yes, yes, yes!"

He swept her into his arms, lips pressed tightly against hers. The party erupted into applause.

The next day, Cino and Lou Alberti drove to San Francisco to buy the ring.

"What are you, 19?" asked Lou.

"Yep."

"And this is the second engagement ring you've bought."

"You got it."

"Better be right about this girl, kid. You're gonna go broke trying to get married."

Cino smiled. "I'm right about this one," he said.

Cino Alberto Chegia and Josephine Maddalena Accinelli were married on April 15, 1956, at St. Augustine's Church—two years to the day after Cino's plane landed in San Francisco, and five years to the day after Franco and Madeline (Accinelli) Petri were married. The ceremony was simple, but the church was packed to the rafters. The whole Oakland Scavenger gang was there, and about everyone who lived within a five-block radius of Baci and Maria. Spring flowers burst from white plaster sconces, and the rough-hewn *romentai*[87] fiddled with their ties. Joanne, Beverly, Angela, and Angela were among the bridesmaids, and smiled at the groom they now called their friend.

The organ blared the first strains of "Here Comes the Bride," and all rose to see Josephine process toward her future. She hung on her father's arm, radiant in a cotton and lace dress with a long train. To Cino's eyes, she seemed to float down the aisle on angel's wings.

For a moment, he couldn't help but feel a slight sadness: here he was about to embark on a new adventure with this magnificent woman, and he didn't have a single family member there with him. How he wished to see Doretta sitting in the front row, dabbing secretively at her eyes. How he yearned to have Alberto by his side, ramrod-straight. He sent them all his love, and then Jo was in front of him, and nothing else in the world mattered. The priest gave the blessing, the man kissed his wife, and the wild party began.

The wedding reception tore up the Ligure Club. Tony Vignale, who, when he wasn't a garbageman, was Italian Oakland's favorite "Singing Chef," catered the event, and unveiled the wedding cake while singing "That's Amore" in his boisterous baritone. The sound of dancing feet echoed through Temescal all night.

Before the bride and groom left for the evening, Baci pulled them aside and pressed a key into Cino's hand.

"For you," he said.

"What is it?" asked Cino.

---

[87] Garbagemen [Genovese dialect]

"Your wedding gift. You know that empty apartment in my building on Claremont? It's yours—all bought and paid for. You go enjoy your night, and when you get back tomorrow, it will be ready for you."

Cino could hardly speak. Josephine's eyes filled with tears.

"Thank you, Papa," she whispered, and wrapped her arms tightly around him.

"Thank you, Papa," Cino said, kissing his cheeks.

Later that night, in a motel bed in lovely Hayward, California, Cino lay awake as Jo slept softly on his chest. Once again, he held up the pieces of his life. A key, a ring, a hand to hold; a home, a bed, a life to share; a job, a future. A marriage certificate, stamped with the Great Seal of California, that stated before God and the United States Government that he belonged in this place. He felt like a new man, reborn in the light of the American Dream. Whatever happened next, nothing was ever going to be the same. His eyes drifted shut, and the first chords of "Here Comes the Bride" carried him off to sleep.

CHAPTER SEVENTEEN: GINO CHEGIA

"Whozzat guy?"

- Cino Chegia

April 16, 1956. Cino and Josephine Chegia stand on the stoop of their new apartment, peering inside. With one hand, he idly strokes the nape of her neck. The key his father-in-law gave him dangles from the doorknob.

"You ready?" he asks.

"Yes!"

"Here we go!" In one swift motion, he sweeps her off her feet and carries her across the threshold.

"Honey, we're home!" he calls out.

She smacks him lightly on the chest. "You know there's no one here."

"Sure about that? Your father could have changed his mind."

He puts her down and they survey the living room. It's empty, save for a few boxes in the corner, but spotless. Maria and Iole (Franco's mother) have been here, scrubbing and mopping so that the entire place gleams.

Jo hugs him close. "It's perfect. Let's go see the kitchen."

"Oh no you don't," he says, grabbing her arm. "I have another room in mind."

She giggles and coos as they make their way to the bedroom, stepping gingerly in the darkness. He flings the door open, draws her toward him, and they fall together onto the bed.

"HEY! What's the big idea?" the bed calls out, grumpily.

Josephine screams. Cino stands up in shock.

"Who's there?" he yells, groping for the light switch. "You've got three seconds to tell me what's going on. One, two—TONY!"

Cino finds the switch and floods the room with light. Two lumps wriggle on the bed, one peeking out just enough to reveal his face: Tony Vignale.

"It's just us," Tony mumbles, wiping the sleep from his eyes. "Me and"—he glances under the covers—"Melvin Piombo."

"What the hell are you doing here?" Cino demands.

"Honestly, I'm not sure. Must have been Baci's idea. See, after you two left last night, we kept the party going: me and Melvin, your father, Franco, Lum, all the guys. No work today, so why stop drinking? After a while we couldn't see straight, so I guess Baci took us here to hide us from the wives."

Suddenly, Tony's face turns green-gray. He holds a finger to his lips, then his eyes go wide and he dashes off into the master bathroom, slamming the door behind him. Laughter bursts from Josephine's throat and she buries her face in Cino's shoulder, but that does nothing to drown out the sound.

On their way out, Tony pulls Cino aside. "Sorry about all this, kid. I'll make it up to you, I promise. You're family now, you know? Family looks out for each other. So if you need anything from me, just name it."

Cino nods. "Actually, I do have something in mind…"

With the wedding over, Cino and Jo were free to start building their future. Couches and chairs were the first thing, and between their wedding gifts and the money they had saved up, they filled their small apartment in a week. Kids were another thing, but they would come later. What remained was perhaps the most important step left, for both of them: making sure that Cino became a legal resident of the United States of America. Without that, none of the other pieces could fall into place.

During their engagement, Cino had started taking trips to the International Institute in San Francisco, to gather the proper paperwork for his marriage certificate and green card. Jo worked days, so her sister Madeline would often go with him, explaining the finer points of American bureaucracy and translating words like "triplicate" and "authorized signature" into Italian.

When they got to the birth certificate, however, things got a little tricky. In order to be listed as an official resident alien, Cino had to provide proof of live birth in his country of origin—his original, authentic birth certificate.

No sweat, he thought. *It must be in comune records. I'll just write to them and have them send it to me.* He mentioned this in a letter to his grandfather, then got back to work and promptly forgot about it.

It's a good thing he did, too. Days later a letter from Nonno Alberto arrived, blaring like an air-raid siren.

STOP! Don't contact the comune, if you haven't already. There's something I haven't told you: the military has been looking for you. Your mandatory service was supposed to start two months ago, and when you didn't show up to boot camp they came to our door. We said we don't know where you are, of course, but they keep coming back. If you write to the comune, they'll find out where you are and deport you back here right away. Leave it to me. I'll get your certificate and mail it straight to the Institute.

Your grandmother and brother send their love. I pray that you haven't mailed that letter yet—if you have, I'm afraid we'll be seeing you soon.

Love,

Nonno

Cino breathed a sigh of relief. In all the rush of his new life in America, he had completely forgotten that, back in Italy, he owed his country two years of service in the Navy. Cino's plan before he jumped ship had been to marry Gianna, settle in for a few months, and then set sail for wherever they sent him. He grimaced at the irony of his forgetting—his own name, of course, only came to be because his father was in the service when Cino was born.

Suddenly, he was struck with a panicked realization: Alberto would be 18 in just over a year. When the Navy got tired of looking for Cino, they would surely just take him instead.

I'll make it up to you, brother, Cino thought, though he wasn't yet sure how.

Eventually, Nonno Alberto managed to smuggle out his birth certificate, and Cino's road to citizenship was paved. By the time he and his new wife stood on their doorstep, only one hurdle remained between Cino and a green card: he needed to cross the border legally.

"They gave us two choices of where we could go, Canada and Mexico," he remembers. "We had heard stories of people who went to Mexico for three days but then weren't allowed to leave for six months, so we decided Canada would be safer!"

A few weeks after their wedding, Cino and Jo packed up his 1949 Ford and drove nearly 1,000 miles to Vancouver, British Columbia. Snow-capped mountains loomed on the horizon, criss-crossed with rivers of runoff. The small, pristine city hugged tight to the water's edge, as inviting and warm as its people. The newlyweds spent a few days seeing the sights, then visited the United States Consulate.

"I wish to immigrate to America," said Cino.

"And I wish to sponsor him," said his wife.

The consul looked over his paperwork, asked them a few standard questions, and stamped him through to the border. "Good luck," he said as they shook goodbye.

At the border, the immigration agent looked up at Cino, then down at the paper, then up again, then down.

"You're Gino Chegia?" he asked, in English.

"Yes. I am Gino," Cino replied haltingly. His papers clearly said "Cino," but he had given up on trying to correct people long ago—they just seemed more comfortable saying "Gino." Besides, the American border was no place for pedantry.

The man flipped through his paperwork, checking boxes and scribbling numbers. Satisfied, he reached into a drawer and pulled out a small green card. He took Cino's picture, wrote down his information, and slammed a red rubber stamp down on the back of the card. When he peeled it off, Cino could see a word taking shape. *A-P-P-R...APPROVED!*

"Congratulations, young man," the agent said, handing him the card. "Welcome to the United States of America."

"Thank you, sir—thank you, thank you. This a dream come true." Cino's eyes filled with tears, and he hugged his wife tightly to him. Then they ran to their car, drove across the border, and began the long journey back home.

They came for Albertino in 1958. Same bemedalled epaulettes, same mirrored sunglasses, same crisp uniforms that had been showing up at Alberto and Rosa's door for four years.

"Like I told you before, Cino's not here," Alberto said.

"We know," they said. "His papers came through from America months ago. Your other grandson, however—he is nearly 20, is he not?"

"Yes, he is. But he's not here either."

In fact, he wasn't. By 1958, Alberto the Younger was imbarcato on a ship of his own, running freight up and down the west coast of Europe. The engine room was his home, his studio; the steaming pipes played like music in his ears, each strand carrying a different meaning. He tuned them until they hummed in harmony. The churning pistons kept a steady rhythm by which he counted the days. As Assistant Ship's Engineer of the freighter *Enrico Insom*, Alberto was finally doing the work he had studied for years—and he found that its movements were already in his fingers.

As he learned her inner workings, Alberto learned, too, the life of the *Enrico Insom*. She was born to fuel the war machine: built in America under the name *Forbes Road*, she brought much-needed gasoline to Allied forces in Europe. Back then, not much was expected of her—they hoped she would make it across the Atlantic and deliver her payload, and that was about it.

"They built these ships for one day," Alberto says. "Fifty to one hundred ships in a convoy. Of one hundred ships, only fifty would make it." The rest would be lost to bad weather, bad machinery, and U-Boats in the North Atlantic. Of those that made it across, very few ever saw the sea again—except as scrap metal built into other ships. But *Forbes Road* endured, and after making multiple runs during the War, she was purchased by the Cleveland Petroleum Company and then by Rinaldi Transport, which renamed her *Enrico Insom*. Four years later, Rinaldi placed its new employee, Alberto Chegia, in her heart.

Alberto spent eleven months on the *Enrico Insom*, shipping goods all over the Mediterranean and Western Europe. He came to love her, for her foibles as well as for her resilience. But the nineteen-year-old was not satisfied. Like his brother, Alberto wanted desperately to see the whole world, not just the little part he called home. On those dull days riding the same seas he always had, Alberto read Cino's letters and thought of the places he'd seen: New York City, New Orleans, San Francisco. In between trips, Alberto reached out to Fratelli Cosulich and all the intercontinental shipping lines, offering his services as a long-haul engineer. Then, one day, he came home and found out that he was joining the Navy.

"Nothing to be done about it, I'm afraid," said Nonno Alberto over dinner.

"Nothing needs to be done," Albertino said. "I'll serve for my brother."

In fact, he was excited about the prospect: a few months on land, followed by a year or more at sea. Who knows where they would go! He prayed that they would send him somewhere exotic, like Brazil or Indonesia. A few days later, he reported to the local Navy base and they shipped him off to boot camp.

A few months, as it turned out, was more like a year: eleven months of early wakeup calls, rifle training, and hospital corners.

Alberto didn't see the point—he was an engineer, not a soldier—but they asked it of him, so he did it dutifully.

The day bootcamp ended, Alberto's superior officer introduced his cadet class to their new home.

"I'd like you to meet the *Sterope*," he said. "She's the newest member of our fleet. She may not look like much, but she's been at it for 15 years now. So be nice to her!"

Alberto squinted up at the massive freighter. His jaw dropped. It couldn't be. It had to be. He leaned forward for a better look. It was the *Enrico Insom*! She had a new paint job and official *Regia Marina*[88] lettering, but it was definitely her. His keen eye picked out weld marks in the hull, where he and the crew had replaced a few panels; in the whirring of the motor, he heard the telltale sound of a replacement part he had lathed out, that never fit quite perfectly into place. He grinned at the old girl and ran up the gangplank, straight to the engine room.

Fifteen months later, Alberto stepped off the only ship he had ever truly known, and sent a letter to his brother in California. *Your military service is complete*, he wrote, with only a hint of bitterness. *You're welcome.*

Back in Temescal, back in 1956, Cino and his new green card made the rounds of the neighborhood. Leonard Marabella clapped him on the back when he saw it, shouting from his streetcorner that the boy who jumped ship had finally made good. Leandro and the other new Scavengers held it gingerly, like it was the Hope Diamond. Aurelio brought his kids in to say congratulations—they looked at Cino shyly, as if he were a new person.

In truth, he felt like a new person. The man in the card was

---

[88] Royal Navy

more than a poor fisherman from Porto Ercole: he was a husband and a Scavenger, an Oakland man. He was not just the boy who had seen bombs fall on his town, who had watched his mother's body lowered into the earth. He was not just the butt of an inside joke, someone who lived in memory and across the sea. He was something more, something bigger—he had become the person who had lain dormant inside of himself for years. From that day forward, he was *Gino Chegia, American.* With his new life laminated in plastic, Cino began doing all the things he couldn't do as an illegal alien. He opened up a savings account; he sent his family letters from his own address. He started speaking English as much as he could, defaulting to it even on the truck and in the Italian clubs. And he laid the groundwork for the next two steps of his ascent to manhood—steps that his in-laws and friends never failed to harp on.

"So, when's the baby coming?" they would ask him.

, "So, when are you going to buy a share in Oakland Scavenger?" they would ask next.

Cino would shrug and turn the conversation, but later that night he would lie awake and wonder the same thing.

They got their first answer late in 1956, with the holidays on the horizon. One day, Cino came home to find sitting on the couch, fiddling with her hands.

"What are you doing here?" he asked. "Aren't you supposed to be at the bank?"

She looked up at him, eyes gleaming. "I'm late!" she announced.

"No you're not, you're early! Four hours at least."

"No, you fool...I'm *late.*" She rose from the couch, walked slowly toward him, grabbed his hand. "Late, late." She put his hand on her belly.

"Oh! Late, late! As in, late late? As in…"

"Yes! I'm pregnant!" A vast smile burst from her lips.

"You're pregnant?"

"I'm pregnant!"

"She's pregnant!" Cino howled like La Lupa, tackled his bride to the cushions, and smothered her with laughter and kisses.

While new life grew inside of Jo's small frame, Cino set about answering the second question, too. A family needed stability, a future they could rely upon. A man needed something that he could call his own, that he could point to on his deathbed and say, "I did this." For Italians working with the Oakland Scavenger Company, that meant buying a share of the business—an ownership stake in a company that had been growing since before Cino was born.

When Oakland Scavenger was founded, there were only a handful of partners. Now, there were over 100—so many that the company had stopped issuing new shares for people, and now required that helpers who wanted to become partners buy their shares from retiring partners. The waiting list was long and the price was steep, but Cino knew it was worth it. With so many shares of equal value, he could only hope for a small slice of the pie—but the bigger the pie got, the bigger each slice grew. Cino was determined to help make that pie as big as it could be, and to make sure that when it was ready to be eaten, he had a slice with his name on it.

Early in 1957, at the ripe old age of 21, Cino got his chance. One morning, OSC Vice President Dewey Vittori tracked him down by the espresso machine.

"You've been here, what, three years now?" Dewey asked.

"Almost," Cino said.

"You've done good work for us. You're part of the family now. And you're planning to be with us for a while yet."

It wasn't a question, Cino noticed. He nodded.

"You're on the top of the list for a share, did you know that? I didn't think so. Well, you are. And one's come up: Carlino Alberti, Lou's uncle. He's ready to retire, and his son doesn't want his share. It's yours if you want it."

"Of course I want it! This is all I've wanted since I joined OSC."

"Great. Then it's settled. You can start paying Carlino for your share next month."

"Right, that. Can I ask: how much does it cost, exactly?"

"Seventeen thousand, five hundred dollars."

A bit of espresso dribbled down Cino's chin. "I'm sorry, did you say, 'Seventeen thousand, five hundred dollars?'"

"I did, yes."

"Sure! No problem. I got that right here in my pocket!"

Dewey laughed. "You don't have to pay it all now. All you do is sign a few forms, and we'll start taking money out of your paycheck every month. After a few years, you'll pay off your debt to Carlino and be a full partner in Oakland Scavenger! It'll be hard for a little while, but trust me, it's worth it. If all these lazy bums around here can do it, I know you can, too."

Cino closed his eyes. In his mind, he saw that little sliver of pie growing and growing, until it could feed an entire family. He saw himself, his wife, their child—their children—all enjoying their share.

"Okay," he said. "Let's do it."

John Albert Chegia was born on August 23, 1957—a healthy baby boy with a healthy mop of blond hair. His whole family gathered around him, like Cino's had 22 years before: Baci and Maria; Franco and Madeline; Vickie and Valerie standing on tiptoe to peer over the edge of the hospital bed. In the middle of it all, Jo smiled serenely, spent but elated, while her son slept in her arms. Cino, meanwhile, paced back and forth, unsure of what to do with his hands.

"Okay, so, now what?" he said to no one in particular.

Baci looked up at him slowly. "Now you get to work, son."

And so he did. With Jo on maternity leave, a new mouth to feed and his paycheck slashed suddenly almost in half, Cino had to pick up every extra job he could. He started working as a night janitor, subcontracting with a company that cleaned office buildings in Emeryville and Oakland. He learned to sleep only between the hours of 2 and 5 (a.m. and p.m.). Every spare moment he had, he spent with his son, playing with blocks and swooping him around like an airplane. But he simply did not have many spare moments. Things were hard just like Dewey had said, and the wellspring of energy Cino once thought inexhaustible seemed to run drier every day. But still, he worked.

Two years later, another boy: Joseph. Dark-haired and dark-eyed, smart and savvy. Cino would bounce him on his knee while pulling crushed crayon out of Johnny's hair, as Jo ladled risotto on everyone's plates. They would eat, he would kiss them all, and he would leave again—back to work, back to the sting of the trash can or the slosh of the mop. Some days, he would curse himself for ever fleeing the *Homeric*; other days, he would wonder how on Earth he had gotten so lucky.

As the months went on, Cino and Jo found it harder and harder to make ends meet. She had given up her jobs to take care of the boys, and even working 12-hour days, Cino's paychecks weren't enough. So, he called in a favor he'd been saving for a rainy day: a favor from Tony Vignale, the Singing Chef.

"Listen, Tony. Remember how you crashed in my bed the night of my wedding? I'm still getting your drool out of my pillow, you know. On your way out, you said that if I ever needed anything, I should call you. Well, I need something."

"Shoot."

"You know that ICF[89] thing next week at the Ligure Club?"

"Sure, yeah. I'm catering it."

"I know. I want you to hire me as your assistant."

"Why should I? How do I even know you got chops? You were just a server boy on the ships."

"Ask my wife, old man! I make a mean *cacciatore*, *cioppino*…anything you need. I'm your guy. Can't sing a lick, but I'll cook you up a storm."

"Okay, kid, you got a deal. But if I hear any boo birds come out next week, I'm kicking your right out on your backside."

The night of the event, Cino and Tony swept through the Frat kitchen like two ballerinas in tandem. They were a natural pairing: Cino had never been a cook, but he'd watched them for years, and he knew just where to be to make Tony's life easier. Cino prepped, Tony cooked; Cino chopped, Tony sauced.

While they worked, they swapped tales of their lives back in Italy.

"You know, I got a brother out there still, too," Tony said.

---

[89] Italian Catholic Federation

"In Portofino?"

"Yeah. His name's Giulietto. He's a master shipbuilder."

"That so?"

"It is. A real engineer type, like your brother. When the Nazis took over, they made him build a pulley system to send artillery shells up to the guns on the cliff. When the thing broke, they thought he sabotaged them. He had to run away to the partisans to escape them."

"My father fought with the partisans, too."

Tony nodded and salted.

"You know, you never told me how you ended up here," Cino said. "You come over after the War?"

Tony grunted. "That's a long story. Put those loaves in the oven and I'll tell you."

The Tale of Tony Vignale

"Before the War started, I was a merchant seaman just like you. Young kid who just wanted to see the world, working as a *mozzo* on a freighter. It was either that or be a *gotze*[90] fisherman, you know?

"Anyway, I'm out on this ship called the *Santa Rosa*, back and forth from the States to home, and one run we wind up in Camden, New Jersey. You ever been to Camden? Don't bother. Once was enough for me. But we get there, and it's…June. Yeah, June. June, 1940."

Cino looked up from his loaves.

"One day, we wake up and find out Italy declared war on the

---

[90] A Genoan night-fishing boat, pointed at both the bow and stern.

Allies. All of a sudden, we're surrounded by Coast Guard ships, guns on 'em and everything. And they're saying, 'By order of the President you are to remain in American waters. Prepare to be boarded and searched.'"

Cino interjected. "Aurelio told me about this. Said the captains all scuttled the ships."

"That's right. Orders from on high, and all that."

"Did you help out?"

"Ha! I didn't even know it was happening. One minute I'm out drinking with a friend in Camden, next minute we hear these boom, boom, boom, booms, and everyone's running around like the War's on or something. Nobody knew what it was, but I turned to my friend and said, 'Let's go. Something's not right here—something smells funny. Let's get out of here.'

"He said, 'Yeah, okay, I got a cousin up in NYC, let's go there.' So we *run*. Seriously. Run. Out of the bar, trying to catch a boat or a train to New York, just trying not to get seen. But by then, the place is swarming with cops and Coast Guard, you name it, and they round us up with the rest of them. Send us over to—what's it called, that little island where they do the immigration."

"Ellis Island?"

"Yeah, yeah. We're out there for a month, maybe more—thousands of us, by my count. Aurelio, too, and a few other guys from Scavenger. They're using the whole place as a jail until they can figure out what to do next.

"Finally, one day they gather everyone together and say, 'Okay, listen up. We're sending you out to this camp in Missoula. Gonna put you boys to work.' Us guys got all scared, like it was one of Hitler's camps."

"Missoula? Where in the world is that?"

"Montana."

"Montana? Where in the world is that?"

Tony ignored him and went on. "They crammed us onto a train, hundreds of guys in these wooden cattle cars. No seats, not enough food, nothing to do. A lot of cards, a lot of arguing, you know. Guys with guns watching over us all the time. We were on there for three, four days I think. Rough days, I can tell you.

"But then, just when we think we're gonna die on this train, it stops! Guards say, 'Okay, we're here, get out.' Everyone tenses up; this is it, you know? No one knows what it will be like.

"Then the first guy steps out, and we all hear him shout, '*Ai! Che bella vista!*'[91] And boy, was he right. High up in the mountains, deep valley right there in front of us, farmland and green hills, river running right through it all…it looked like we'd died and gone to Heaven. So that's what we called it from then on: Camp Bella Vista.

"They led us down to this old Army base, right there in the woods: big concrete barracks, parade grounds, old cannons, everything. They called it Fort Missoula. Built it during the Indian Wars in the late 19th century, when all these settlers were moving out here and had to be protected from war parties. We walked all over, just stretching out, breathing the fresh air—don't get me wrong, we were prisoners, but it didn't feel like it. The camp didn't even have a wall! Just a fence and some barbed wire. It was kinda like Alcatraz, you could say: you could escape if you really wanted to, but then where would you go? Some guys broke out once, but they got lost in the woods and just turned around and came back.

"So, anyway—check the beans, will ya?—they get us in this camp, and right away they start putting us to work. They'd take teams out into the sugar beet fields nearby, or out on the railroad

---

[91] "Ah! What a beautiful view!"

tracks clearing brush and the like. Me, I got put in the kitchen mostly—I was only 21 then, and the older guys got first pick of the jobs. They wanted to be out in the sun. Worked okay for me, too: how do you think I became the Singing Chef? By the time it hit midsummer and was hot as the devil, they all wanted to switch with me, but I wasn't going nowhere.

"After a few weeks of working every day, they rounded us up and said, 'Okay, come collect your pay.' 'Pay?' we said. 'We're getting paid? We thought we were prisoners!' Turns out we were 'alien detainees.' Not enemy combatants or suspected spies, just citizens of enemy countries. So the Geneva Convention said we had to be 'compensated for services.' It wasn't much, but we got to send most of it home—not much to buy in the camp, you know? That was nice, because without me to make money, my family was really suffering. Papa was long dead, and Giulietto was just a kid.

"Those first few months, things were great. Autumn rolled around and all the leaves changed color, and it felt like we were inside God's painting. Colors like you've never seen, colors like we don't get around here. But then winter came, and suddenly we started thinking maybe it wasn't God with the paintbrush after all. Cold like you wouldn't believe: snow and ice whipping around, temperatures twenty below zero, everything dead, everything covered in white. Our coats were too thin, the boots all had holes in them—it was miserable. Thank God I had figured out how to make toilet hooch out of raisins and berries by then. That was about the only thing got us through those days.

"By 1942, it was pretty clear we weren't going anywhere. Italy was up to its neck in it by then, the Japs bombed Pearl Harbor so Uncle Sam finally got involved, and we all figured we might as well just settle down and wait. Some of the guys started meeting local American girls, started taking them out, started talking about sticking around even after the war...you want spazio vitale? Go to

Montana! Wide open spaces, enough to build a whole new life from scratch. But I was done with that place: tired of being cooped up, cooking potatoes all day—those guys eat so many potatoes, you wouldn't even believe. I still wanted to see the world, you know?"

Cino, listening intently, held up a *tortellino* for Tony to taste. He slurped it down, chewed thoughtfully, and patted his protégé on the cheek.

"Almost done. Anyway, early '42 we started getting these visitors: guys from companies all over the U.S., looking for cheap labor. See, America had called up the draft, so now all the young men were shipping off to war and there was no one left on the home front. No one except these dumb Italians and Germans with nowhere else to go, who you can pay cents on the dollar to do your dirty work. Not a bad deal, eh? Everyone who wanted to would put their name in to be selected for these jobs, and they'd pull as many names as they needed and that was that. I put my name in for just about every job I could, but it never got called.

"Then, one day, a bunch of Italian guys in suits show up. They start right in talking Genovese to guys in the camp, and my ears perk up. *Who are these guys, and how can I get in with them?*, I'm wondering. So I go up and say, 'Hey, who are you?'

"They say, 'We're from Oakland Scavenger Company, out near San Francisco. We haul waste, and we do it real good. We're looking for 37 guys to replace good men of ours who went off to fight. We're Italian owned and operated, we offer competitive pay and we'll help you get back home after this ugliness is over. You want in, line up over there to drop your name in.' No joke, I'm fighting people off with my spoon to get to the head of that line. When they called my name, I ran around cheering like I'd just won the World Cup or something."

Cino and Tony went through thir final pre-meal check.

Outside, the rumble of voices was growing, awaiting them, summoning their bounty.

"We took the train here in '42, and they put us up in headquarters. You know the conference room above the garage? I slept there for almost two years. My first day on the job was shit: it was raining, they had me up in the hills with those heavy cans…all I wanted that day was to go back to Missoula. But the next day was better, and so was the day after that. This place started to draw me in, just like it did for you—Italians everywhere, making something of themselves, helping each other and treating everyone with respect, no matter if they were a newcomer or an illegal or whatever. We didn't have guards on us, so after a while we started to go out to the clubs, go to dinner, take day trips to the City. As long as we were here every week for our check-in with the INS guys, they basically left us alone.

"Couple years go by, and we're starting to look at the end of the war. Italy had surrendered, Hitler was falling back, and the American boys were starting to come home. Suddenly I realize: I don't want to go back. There was nothing for me at home. Portofino was in ruins, my brother was on the run, and I could do more good sending money from here than going there. Plus, I just didn't feel like I belonged there anymore. My life was here. I started talking to some of the guys about buying their shares, and Giulio Biggi said he would sell me his if I could figure out how to stay. Gave me the same advice Aurelio gave you: 'Find a nice American girl and marry her, quick.'

"So, I started going out. Hard. I chatted up every girl I could, spending my tiny savings on taking them out on the town, but nothing clicked. Then, one night, I came to this very club for a dance, and there she was. Dina. So beautiful, so kind. It took me all night to ask her to dance, but I did it. And she said yes! I don't think she's ever stopped regretting it.

"On the day they released us, I wrote to my family in Portofino. Said, 'I love you all, but I'm not coming back.' Then I marched over to Dina's place, pulled her into the living room and got down on one knee. We got married a couple days later, I bought Biggi's share and that was that. Been thirteen years, and I love that lady more every day."

"Wow," Cino said. "Hell of a story. Is that the end?"

"I'm still alive, ain't I? Doesn't feel like the end to me. But it's enough for tonight, that's for sure. Now let's go—we've got some mouths to feed."

With that, Tony hefted the giant pot of minestrone, belted out the first few bars of *Funiculì, Funiculà*, and backed through the swinging double doors into the crowded dining room, with Cino right on his heels.

By the mid-1960s, life was taking shape for Cino. He had his own route with the Scavengers, his own truck, his own crew. He paid off his debt to Carlino Alberti, quit his job as a janitor and became a full-fledged partner, at age 24. On the weekends, he would arm himself with a wad of cash, a handful of new jokes and a keen eye for a winning bet, and arrive at the racetrack or card club to a flurry of welcoming "Gino!"s. He wouldn't leave again until his cup runneth over or the well ran dry. In 1960, he humbly accepted Tony Vignale's chef's hat and took up the mantle of the new club cook. To everyone's relief, he did not attempt to sing.

The boys just kept coming, too: Jay in 1963, followed by the fourth and final, Jimi, in 1964. At nights, seven-year-old John would chase Joe through the house with bugs or baseball bats—Joe would use Jay as a human shield—Jay would squirm out of his grasp and hide underneath Jimi's crib. Sometimes, when Cino came home from work, he would find Jo sprawled out on the couch, while the kids orbited her like little Sputniks. On Sundays, when the family gathered with Baci and Maria and Franco and Madeline and their five kids, and Franco's parents Iole and Vittorio, and his little sister Sandra, it felt just like Cino was back in L'Ospizio. Sometimes, he imagined he was Ward Cleaver, and his sons said, "Yes, Father," and helped the neighbors paint their white picket fences. But he didn't really think he would like that, in the end.

By 1963, there was only one thing left to do. Everything in Cino's life looked American: the car, the clothes, the job, the salary. Everything except the green slip of paper in his wallet, that still read "Resident Alien." He had been in the country for almost a decade, and it was time to make things official.

At the International Institute, they told him that he would need to pass a test to earn his citizenship.

"There are night classes you can take in American Government," they said. "You'll need to know about the Constitution, the electoral college, that sort of thing."

"Sure, sure," Cino said, never having heard the words "electoral college" before.

"And it might not hurt for you to brush up on your English a bit," they hinted.

"Sure, sure," he said.

The next day, he enrolled in night courses at Oakland Technical High School. Set in the heart of Temescal, the school fed into Oakland Scavenger—many of its graduating seniors announced, "I'll be attending OSC in the fall"—and many of its night classes were taught in Italian. Cino settled in among familiar faces and worked through six months of schooling with an intellectual enthusiasm he had only shown once before: studying for his libretto di navigazione exam. "By the time I was done with my classes, I knew more about America than most Americans did!" he proclaims.

In early 1964, Cino sat for the test that would decide how American he could be. A few weeks later, an envelope came from the United States Immigration and Naturalization Service. He eyed it suspiciously, sure it would contain word that he had done so badly they were sending him back to Italy. He tried to gauge by its weight whether it contained good news or bad. Finally, Josephine—Jay on her hip, Jimi in her belly—couldn't stand it any more.

"Just open the damn thing!" she exclaimed.

He did, and scanned its contents. He sighed. She stared. He read it again. She tried to grab it, but he yanked the paper away.

"Well?" she demanded.

He read it slowly, in English. "Dear Sir, Your application for citizenship into the United States of America has been…accepted!" He threw his hands in the air, danced his wife around the kitchen, kissed his sons as they ran in to embrace their father.

On February 11, 1964, Cino stood with his family at the citizenship ceremony and recited the Pledge of Allegiance with gusto—in comprehensible, if thickly accented, English. Then they sat, and he waited for his name to be called.

"Gino Chegia?" said the man at the podium.

Cino stood. "That's me," he said with pride.

On the way home, he took his family to Fenton's Creamery for ice cream, and as the boys scarfed down their sundaes, he tousled their hair like Ward Cleaver did on TV.

Chapter Eighteen: Homeward Bound

"One hand washes the other; both hands wash the face."
- Cino Chegia

Summer, 1965. Cino paces outside the Chevron oil refinery in Richmond, checking his watch every thirty seconds or so. One cigarette after another powers through his lungs, billowing forth like the smokestacks behind him in miniature. He scans the horizon for approaching ships.

Finally, it arrives. A tanker, as unassuming as it is massive, led in by a tugboat straining against its cables. It looks just like the *Jenny Naess*, except for the Chevron symbol stenciled on its side. He positions himself so he can be seen and fiddles with his dress shirt, chiding himself again for having put it on in the first place. The gangplank lowers—he throws his shoulders back into a position he imagines looks distinguished.

It doesn't take long for a tall, lean man to emerge from the ship, carrying a duffel bag and wiping grease from his hands. He glances around with a keen eye, taking everything in all at once. Cino's heart swells like a balloon.

"Hey, Procaccini Alberto!" he calls out.

Then he's running, full-speed, leaving his distinguished pose in the dust…running like they used to run through the cappanne. Alberto spreads his arms wide and braces for impact. Even so, his big brother nearly tackles him to the ground.

For a while, they say nothing—they merely kiss cheeks and stare, drinking in over a decade of separation. The babyish features that Alberto once had have been drawn tighter by time, scored through with adulthood: furrowed brows and sleepless nights, hard work and heat and sweat. Cino wonders what changes Albertino sees in him.

Alberto answers his question. "You're getting fat," he says flatly.

Cino laughs heartily and hugs his brother tight. "Come with me and I'll show you why."

At home, the boys line up next to Josephine, scrubbed to a polish.

"Boys, this is your Zio Alberto," Cino says.

"*Piacere nostro,*"[92] they say, as their mom had instructed them.

Jo kisses Alberto's cheeks and takes his bag to the living room, where she has lain sheets on the couch. Alberto simply smiles at everything and everyone.

At dinner, Alberto pulls out pictures of his wife, Piera, and their toddling son, Lauro, named after his grandmother.

"He's big now, like Jay here. Getting harder to keep up with

---

[92] "Our pleasure to meet you."

him. You're lucky, you know, to stay here with them. Hurts more and more getting back on that ship."

"At least it gets you away from your wife!" Cino laughs.

Alberto casts him a rueful look and spears an anchovy. "She's pregnant again...I'm already keeping my distance. She's desperate to meet you, though. We really missed you at the wedding."

"Me too, me too. Wish I could have been there."

"Told Doretta and Nonna Rosa I was coming to see you, they wanted to stow away on the boat. Said if I couldn't convince you to come visit them, I might as well stay here, too!"

"Josephine, make up the couch—I guess we're going to have a guest for a few years! You know I want to come home, Alberto. Nothing I'd rather do. But I just can't right now. Someday, you know? Once these guys don't need me to wipe their butts anymore."

"Don't know how much longer they'll last, Cino. Don't wait too long, or there won't be anyone left to see."

"Boys, clear your plates," Josephine says. "Let's give your father and uncle some alone time."

In the living room, she brings them brandy and cookies. The lights are dim and the room soft with secrets.

Cino hesitates, then asks. "How was the funeral?"

Alberto swirls the amber in his glass. "You know. It was what it was. Everyone came, people said nice things about him, that was that. No tears, no hugs. Everyone just went home."

"And now?"

"You know the situation. Anna's mother, Ernesta, keeps demanding we give her our share, but we got a kid to feed now too, you know? Piera won't let her have it. It's gotten a bit ugly...I don't know if we'll be seeing them again. But that money is ours, Cino. After all these years, it's the least he owes me."

Cino sighs. "We'd better get some sleep, brother. Early morning tomorrow."

At 4 a.m., the Chegia brothers rise and drive through the darkness back to Richmond, so they can both be at work by dawn.

In the 1960s, as Cino and Jo were building new lives for themselves, things were changing fast across the sea, too. In 1962, Alberto married Piera Schiano, the daughter of a Monte Argentario miner. They had their first of three children in 1963: Lauro would be followed by Laura in 1965, and Luca in 1968. Alberto started working for Chevron, traveling all over the world as a ship's engineer. Doretti and Alberto Procaccini retired, and whiled away their final days in much-deserved peace. Monte Argentario grew and grew, wealthy vacationers filling the ports until they had to build a new one in Cala Galera just for their yachts.

For the most part, word from home was cheerful: babies born and jobs taken, weddings attended and marriages plotted. But, as the years drew on, the news got worse and worse.

From Doretta: *We lost Doretti last night. He went in his sleep with his family around him, just how he wanted it. Wish you could have been here to say goodbye.*

From Nonna Rosa: *Strange to be writing you a letter on behalf of your Nonno Alberto, like he did for so many for so long...He wanted me to tell you that he won't see you again before he goes, but he'll always be watching over you.*

From his father: *Cino, Anna is dead. Cancer or something. Came out of nowhere, just like with your mother. I can't get off the boat right now, so your nonna and a few zias are moving out here to take care of the kids. Honestly not sure what I'm going to do. I miss you, son.*

Each time, Cino hung his head and said a quiet prayer for those he loved back home. If only he could be there with them, he could at least lend a hand...but he couldn't, he knew, not yet. All he could do was hope that that was the end of the bad news.

It wasn't. In 1964, with baby Jimi just around the corner, Cino opened a letter from Doretta and his whole world suddenly stopped spinning.

Dear Cino,

How terrible it is to have to write to you with this news. What malaccio *lies over your father, I will never know. I prayed for him every day, like I pray for you, but it seems the Holy Mother never answered.*

Cino, your father is dead. He was riding his Vespa, and just fell over, just like that. The doctors say something in his brain popped, so he lost control...they don't know if it was the pop or the crash that killed him, but they don't think he felt any pain. Thank God for that, I guess.

The young ones are all alone now, just like you and your brother were. We don't know where they will go: everyone already has enough mouths to feed. Ernesta says she wants to take them, but I'm afraid her body is not as strong as her spirit these days...

Your father left some money behind, too: a pension at the capitaneria.[93] *He wanted it split between all four children. It's not much, but it's something. You all can do what you want with it. If you and your brother don't need your shares, maybe you think about making a* procura[94] *to Ernesta? You decide.*

---

[93] Harbor office
[94] A financial gift – in essence, relinquishing his share of the money.

I am tired now, from the writing. Soon I'll be sleeping. I love you, son of my son, and will see you someday in the Kingdom.

Love,
Nonna Doretta

Cino twisted the letter and brought it to his lips, like a thirsty man wringing water from a damp cloth. In his mind's eye, he saw his father standing at the tiller of the menaita—racing down from the haystack to the water's edge—upending a sack of dog tags in front of the American troops. He said a prayer for the man he loved first.

Josephine appeared behind him, her warm hand on his shoulder. She always knew when something was wrong.

"My father's dead," he said. Her grip tightened. "He left a small pension for us, but I'm going to give Ernesta my share to help with the others. The weird thing is, my grandmother said, 'all four children,' like it's more than just me, Pino and Alberto...guess her mind must be going. Either way, we don't need that money. I'll try to convince Alberto to give his up, too."

Jo didn't say anything: she just wrapped her arms around him and nestled her face into his neck, listening to his silent sobs.

"Are you out of your mind?" said Alberto over the phone. "I'm not giving them a damn lira. You and I are his real sons, remember? I don't see why they should get anything."

Cino shook his head. He was paying an arm and a leg for this call, and he didn't have time to butt heads with his brother. He had figured Alberto would be a *testa dura*[95] about it—he still had never even met Pino, after 16 years—but something else was going on

---

[95] Stubborn, hard-headed person

here. And he knew where it came from, too: Piera. She was by all accounts a pugnacious woman, clashing with the rest of the family over everything from child-rearing to who would host Christmas dinner. Alberto was imbarcato when Aldo died, and while he was away Piera wrote Ernesta a scathing letter, attacking her for taking money that belonged to her husband and barring Anna's family from coming to Santo Stefano. By the time Alberto returned, his father was dead and the family was at each others' throats.

So when Cino found his brother siding with his wife, he gritted his teeth.

"Come on, Alberto, you're not using it."

"That's not the point. The point is, what have they done to deserve this money? You—you were his son. You defended him to Nonno, you tried to make things work in Santa Marinella. I lived for years not knowing who my father was, and pretending not to care. What have they ever done?"

"Okay, hold on: what do you mean, 'they'? Nonna keeps saying it, too. Who are 'they'?"

"They! They! You, know, Pino and—" The line went dead; their time had run out.

That night, Cino sat down to write Ernesta a letter, and an official notice of *procura*. Alberto's money stayed where it was.

Seven years later, in 1971, Cino stepped onto the streets of Porto Santo Stefano for the first time in seventeen years. He couldn't believe what he was seeing: apartment buildings and luxury hotels stretching high into the hillside; the marina grown to double its original size; ferries bobbing at anchor and a cruise ship on the horizon. He was home, at last—back in a motherland he barely recognized. Seventeen years since he took his last, long look at its green hills and sparkling water, from the window of an airplane leaving Milan. Nearly half his life on American streets, learning the American tongue, raising American kids. John was going to high school in the fall, for Pete's sake. Here in Santo Stefano, a whole new generation of Chegia and Procaccini ran the streets. Aside from stories and the occasional photo, Cino had never met any of them.

He was here, he would tell people, for his Nonna Rosa. She was the only one left—Doretta had passed a few years before—and her time was running out. Cino was finally in a place where he could take some time off to come home, and he vowed to see his last remaining grandparent one more time while she lived. When he called her to tell her he was coming, she simply muttered, "Thank you, God," again and again, as her voice filled up with tears.

The other reason he was there was to settle the feud once and for all. In the seven years since Aldo's death, tension had simmered between Piera and Ernesta—the two sides barely even exchanged words. Alberto still had not met Pino, though they lived less than an hour apart by train. With the older generation dying, somebody had to step in and nudge the family in a new direction. Perhaps the prodigal son could do the job.

Nonna Rosa opened the door before he could even knock, squealing with delight and cupping his face in her hands.

"My baby, my baby," she said. Cino noticed that the apartment was cluttered with Catholic icons, which seemed to have multiplied since her husband, the great atheist professor, died. She kissed her statuette of St. Christopher and made the sign of the cross over Cino as he walked in the door.

"I never thought I'd see you again," she said.

"I know. Neither did I, Nonna. But I wanted to every day."

"Nonno Alberto, Doretti, Anna, your father, Doretta...you

have a lot of cemetery visits to make this trip. You can come back again in a year or so to see me there."

"I'm seeing you here now," Cino smiled. She gripped one of his hands tightly in both of hers.

The next day, Cino laid flowers on the graves of his father, his grandparents, and the other family members who had died while he was gone. Then he walked all around Monte Argentario and Orbetello, trying to map the boutiques and restaurants onto the fish stalls, net repair shops and dingy bars he had once known. Hiking up to Forte Filippo, which had housed Fascists and Nazis and where his cousin once nearly blew himself up with a flare, Cino couldn't believe his eyes. They had turned it into luxury apartments!

That night, he went to Alberto's house. Alberto was once again imbarcato, but Piera had insisted that he come over for dinner and meet his nipoti. *No matter what happens,* he reminded himself, *you're not here to argue. You're just here to listen.* When she flung the door open, however, he flinched instinctively, like a boxer steadying himself to take a punch.

The punch never came. "At last!" she exclaimed, kissing Cino on both cheeks. "Kids, come meet your Zio Cino. Oh, I can't believe it's you!"

From behind her came a pattering of feet, then a trio of heads peeked out: first Lauro, the man of the house, who shook Cino's hand and held out a drink; next Laura, who curtsied and blushed; last Lucca, who at three years old was more interested in his shoes than his uncle. Cino marveled at how beautiful, how magnificent they were. His own flesh and blood, an ocean away. Is this how Alberto felt when he first met Cino's kids? He could only hope so.

That whole night, Piera and the kids were delightful. Lauro regaled him with tall tales from the fourth grade, and Laura performed a dance she had learned at school. Piera, too, was accommodating and friendly. Cino wondered if this was really the same woman who wrote such terrible things to Ernesta and her family. *Maybe things have changed,* he thought. *Maybe this won't be as hard as I thought. Could it be that they're all ready to reconcile, just looking for someone to break the silence?*

Ernesta didn't think so. "I'm surprised you survived that witch," she said, when Cino called to tell her he was coming. "She's a devil woman. And I'm sorry, but that brother of yours is no better. I have nothing to say to either of them, and I doubt that you coming will do anything to change that."

Cino feared that she was right: the feisty woman who once took on Mussolini's wife in court (and won) would not likely be swayed. But he wasn't out to change her mind—she was an old woman, and had no Chegia blood in her. It was Pino he had to convince; not just for himself, but for the whole family. Come hell or high water, Cino would make things right.

He drove out to Santa Marinella with a friend who said he knew where to find Anna's people. The whole ride, his friend stole strange, sidelong glances at him, as if he wanted to reveal something to Cino but knew that he shouldn't.

They pulled up in front of a seaside *bar* with tables and chairs on an open-air patio. "Here we are, Bar Gabbiano," said his friend.

The memories flooded back to Cino: stopping by here for a cool drink after a long day of biking coal; meeting up with his friends and whistling at the teenage girls walking by. Anna's sisters, Lorenza and Mirella, owned Bar Gabbiano, and it seemed like you could always find one of them there.

Cino's friend left him there and set off to run an errand. As soon as he sat down, a young waitress came up and asked him if he wanted a drink.

"Campari soda," he said, as it was only 11 in the morning. She left and came back shortly with his drink, a bowl of green olives and a bowl of pretzels. She had brown curly hair and smiled shyly at the unfamiliar man sweeping his gaze across the dining room.

"Need anything else?" she asked politely.

"Actually, yes," Cino said. "Do Lorenza and Mirella still run this place?"

"They sure do."

"Are they here?"

"I'm afraid not, they're off until the end of the week. Is there something I can help you with?"

"I'm not sure…I'm looking for their nipote, Pino Chegia. I'm his half-brother, Cino. From America."

The girl took a step back, and the empty tray crashed to the ground. "Cino?" she cried. "Is that really you? It's me, Mara! Mara Chegia!"

"Mara Chegia? Are you his wife or something? You seem a little young to be married…"

"What? No! I'm his sister, Cino—your half-sister, Mara Chegia!"

This time, it was Cino's turn to drop something. "A half-sister? But I didn't even know I had one!"

"Well, you do—surprise! Here I am!"

Cino rose to his feet, hesitant at first to even touch this strange apparition. Then he threw his arms around his half-sister, embracing her as if he had come all this way just to see her.

"You must tell me everything," he said.

She sat down across from him. "I was born in 1951. You had

been gone a few years already, out on the ships—you must just have never gotten the news. You know how Babbo was: forgetful, always on to the next thing. Besides, those were different times!"

Cino laughed. "You have no idea."

"Anyway, I grew up here with Mama, Babbo, and Pino for a few years. Went to school, spent time here, the usual. Everything was fine until Mama died. I was nine, then. Just a little girl. Nonna Ernesta moved in to help take care of us. Then Babbo went four years later, and ever since then I've been pretty much on my own."

"I'm so sorry, Mara. If I had only known…"

"Forget about it! It wasn't your fault. Nothing you could have done, anyway! Now let's go see my brother."

Minutes later, Mara knocked on the door to Pino's apartment. She glanced back at Cino, excitement dancing in her eyes. He swallowed his anxiety and smiled broadly.

The door swung open, revealing a tan, muscular man in his early twenties. His hands were caked in concrete dust.

"Mara! Didn't know you were coming over. You want some dinner? I'm just making dinner. Who's your friend? I—" He looked at Cino and froze, his face a flickering mask of emotion. Disbelief mingled with nostalgia; hope and hurt elbowed for room. He opened and closed his mouth.

"Little brother!" Cino exclaimed. Without thinking, he wrapped his arms around Pino's shoulders. Pino stiffened, then relaxed—in an instant, the years melted away, and a new kinship began to form.

"What took you so long?" Pino demanded, laughing and embracing his brother.

Over dinner, Cino sat and listened as Pino and Mara said everything they needed to say, to empty out their sadness and begin to forgive. He could not believe how far things had gone, how completely the bridges between their families had been burnt. So many battles, so many grievances...he vowed again to break the curse his father had brought down on them.

"I will talk to Alberto for as long as it takes," he said. "Until then, don't go to Santo Stefano unless you have to. Alberto is a stubborn man; it may take me a while to convince him. But I'll wear him down...I'm his big brother, he has to listen to me!"

The next morning, he took his leave of his half-siblings with kisses and promises, assuring them that he would be back in just a couple years. Back in Santo Stefano, he said goodbye to Nonna Rosa, sitting with her in quiet contemplation until his taxi pulled up outside. He had no way to tell her all the things he felt, no way to wish her well in the world beyond. Next time he came back, she would be lying in a grave of her own—next to the one that her husband shared with their beloved daughter, Laura, taken so long before her time.

Finally, she spoke, as if reading his mind. "Don't worry about us. We're so proud of what you have become over there, and what you're trying to do here. Just remember: it's not about your father. It's not about Alberto. It's not even about you. It's about Lauro, Laura, Lucca; John, Joseph, Jay, Jimi. Bring this family back together for them, so that they can know what family is."

The taxi honked its horn. Nonna Rosa clutched her rosary, kissed her grandson for the very last time, and sent him back to the life he built from nothing.

CHAPTER NINETEEN: CHANGING TIDES

"We Shall Overcome"
- American Civil Rights anthem

March 25, 1987. Cino Chegia sits at his dining room table, *drinkino*[96] in hand. His eyes skim the first few lines of the article, narrowing quickly into a grimace.

"The founders of the Oakland Scavenger Company, once themselves 'social outcasts,' have become the oppressors of their black and Hispanic employees, a lawyer charged in federal court yesterday,"[97] the article reads.

Cino flings the paper across the room and downs his drink in a swallow.

———————————

[96] "Little drink": in Cino's case, a brandy Manhattan
[97] Ayres, Gene. "Race-bias lawsuit goes to judge". *Oakland Tribune*, B-5. March 25, 1987.

In the 1960s and 70s, the life that Cino and Josephine built grew taller and sturdier, like a mountain rising from a small slice of earth. His sons grew bigger and stronger, faster and smarter; his wife grew keener in her role as head of the Chegia Family Fraternity. As a partner in Oakland Scavenger, Cino ran his own truck, which picked up industrial-sized dumpsters from local businesses. He was also on the OSC design team, and helped engineer innovations like wing-tipped loader forks and a dumpster "turntable" to easily replace damaged bins. All around him, his community grew and excelled: in 1971, Vickie Petri—Madeline's daughter, who was flower girl at his wedding—became the first person in her family to leave home for college.

Outside of the comforts of home, however, the winds of change blew fiercely. The self-satisfied American Dream of the 1950s gave way to the turbulent 60s, when the Vietnam War awoke young peaceniks to the reality of atrocity, and the Civil Rights movement reminded the world that freedom in America was only granted to those whose skin was a certain shade. As the Bay Area transformed into a hub of hippiedom and a battleground for social justice, the Temescal community turned further inward to protect its values and heritage. It wouldn't be long, however, until the Italians of the Oakland Scavenger Company would be forced to reckon with race in a way that few had imagined.

It started in 1964. The fight for civil rights had been raging for nine years, and the tide was finally turning in favor of the proud black men and women who stood in solidarity against bigoted mobs, riot police, fire hoses, and the forces of institutional racism. In 1963, Reverend Martin Luther King, Jr. stood on the steps of the Lincoln Memorial and declared before all his dream of a free people and a united nation. His words, carried by microphones and TV cameras and whispers, drifted across the National Mall to Lyndon B. Johnson in the White House.

One year later, Johnson proved that he had heard Dr. King. On July 2, 1964, he signed into law the Civil Rights Act of 1964, which banned any and all entities—public or private, company or individual—from discriminating against another based on race, gender, or religious creed. The Civil Rights Act eliminated discriminatory voting requirements, segregation of public and private spaces, and, in its crucial Title VII, "discriminat[ion] against any individual with respect to his compensation, terms, conditions, or privileges of employment because of such individual's race, color, religion, sex, or national origin." With the passage of the Civil Rights Act, all American citizens—black, white, or other—were granted equal protection under the law and equal opportunity in the workplace.

Across the country, people rejoiced. The visionaries of the Southern Christian Leadership Conference, the Student Nonviolent Coordinating Committee, and the NAACP toasted their success, as the burgeoning anti-war movement in the San Francisco Bay Area applauded its allies in the South. But inside Oakland Scavenger headquarters, panic set in.

"What are we going to do?" the partners wondered, at an emergency meeting a few days after the Act passed. "They're going to take this whole thing away from us."

"Maybe it won't be so bad," said others. "Maybe they'll understand our situation. We've had this partnership for years: it's a way for us Italians to support each other, create opportunities, you know? Besides, we treat our helpers well, everyone gets along…maybe they won't say anything."

"We have to be ready if they do, though. We have to have a plan."

So, they set out to make a plan. For days and weeks, all 122 partners debated and argued, plotting every contingency. It was sad, somber work: the business they and their fathers had built from the ground up, with their own sweat and muscle and savvy, could be rent apart at any minute. And it was all due to the one thing that made the Oakland Scavenger Company special.

The key to OSC, of course, was its partnership structure. Men like Cino, fresh off the boat with four dollars, a fifth grade education and not enough English to order breakfast, could work their way up and buy into something that was real—something that grounded them, gave them purpose and community. They could learn valuable skills, make lifelong friends, earn wages they never would have been able to make back home. But only if they were Italian.

For 44 years, that structure had held true. Under Italian leadership, the company grew to become one of the largest privately-owned garbage companies in the United States. They expanded and innovated, competed and won. They integrated early, and by the 1960s over half of Oakland Scavenger's 500 employees were people of color. "It was definitely an integrated company," recalls Bob Biasotti, grandson of founder Giuseppe Biasotti and de facto OSC historian. "A lot of camaraderie…just having beers after work. It was wonderful." But no one who was not of Italian descent—Asian, black, Latino or white—could ever become a partner. With one stroke of a pen, the Civil Rights Act rendered that structure illegal.

In the meetings, the partners looked around at each other. All across the room, they saw faces they knew: weatherbeaten, scarred, red-nosed and square-jawed. Faces of men they had grown up with, had bled with, had stood next to at the wedding altar. Brothers, fathers, cousins, neighbors. Paesani who always had each other's backs. All committed to doing what was best for the Oakland Scavenger Company, for the legacy they had built. And all undeniably white.

In the end, they chose a wait-and-see approach. The Civil

Rights Act was brand-new, and no one knew quite how it would play out. Until the federal government came knocking, there was no reason to do anything rash. So they got back to business, and waited to see what would come next.

As it turned out, they had a long time to wait. After a historic signing and tumultuous response, the Civil Rights Act came into effect in 1965 with more of a whimper than a roar. Thrown together hastily to calm a nation that was threatening to unravel, the Act contained very few actionable steps to combat discrimination in the workplace or in public life. What it did instead was create the Equal Employment Opportunity Commission (EEOC), a government body whose mandate was to "receive, investigate, and conciliate complaints where it found reasonable cause to believe that discrimination had occurred." Notably missing from the EEOC's original charter was the word "enforce"—in a major compromise to get the Act passed, its authors stripped the EEOC of its power to litigate against, or in any way punish, those employers it found to be discriminating against their employees. The EEOC could dig into discrimination claims, try to resolve them through settlement or out-of-court negotiations, and could refer lawsuit-worthy claims to the Department of Justice, but otherwise its hands were tied. In other words, when it came to workplace discrimination, the Equal Employment Opportunity Commission was a "toothless tiger."[98]

It was also a very busy tiger, gumming on far more cases than it had expected. Estimated to receive about 2,000 charges of workplace discrimination in its first year, the EEOC received 8,854. The following year, that number was nearly 13,000; by 1970, the Commission was receiving over 20,000 discrimination claims per year. With a Thermopylaen backlog of cases and little

---

[98] "Milestones in the History of the U.S. Equal Employment Opportunity Commission." EEOC Website: http://www.eeoc.gov/eeoc/history. Accessed 12/02/2015.

ability to do much about any of them, the EEOC shifted its focus to gathering data on the worst employment offenders. Its findings were staggering: in the Carolinas, 99% of African-American textile workers were in the lowest-paid job categories. Of the 4,000+ New York City corporations with 100 employees or more, 1,827 did not have a single black person working behind a desk. In the aerospace, utility and pharmaceutical industries, race and gender discrimination ran rampant.

Finally, in 1972, Congress gave the tiger some teeth: the Equal Employment Opportunity Act granted the EEOC the authority to file lawsuits against companies, employee unions, and even the government itself. With that power, the EEOC immediately began bringing charges against its most systemic offenders: General Electric, United Airlines, and more. This top-down approach put millions of dollars in the hands of underpaid, deserving employees, and sent a message to companies across the U.S.: once we're done with the big guys, we're coming for you.

Meanwhile, the partners at Oakland Scavenger had made a few concessions of their own to fairness and workers' rights. In 1967, they joined the Teamsters Union, ceding employee benefits and hiring practices to them. But the company was not yet willing to part with its management structure, and for years cast about for a way to keep control in the hands of the people whose people had founded the business.

In 1971, OSC's long-term attorney, Ed Moore, made a simple suggestion. "Why don't we just stop selling shares?"

"What do you mean?" they said. "We stopped issuing new shares years ago."

"Not issuing new shares: I mean selling off the shares you already have. Rather than finding some guy to buy them off you when you retire, just pass them down to your sons. That way, we can say they're being inherited, just like any other property."

The partners began to stir and nod. Property was protected under the Constitution; maybe if they kept it in the family, they could squeak by the law. Could the solution really be so simple?

"What about daughters?" one called out. "I don't have any sons."

"No way!" said another. "This here is man's work. Not gonna sell shares in trash to no secretaries."

"Don't let my wife hear you say that," said the first.

Cino listened to the debate with interest, but not anxiety. Many of his fellow partners were victims of their own success. As Oakland Scavenger grew and the partners made more money, their sons had opportunities they never had—and they tended to choose those opportunities instead of spending their lives hauling trash. But Cino was only 36, he owned his share outright, and he had four sons. Surely one would want his piece when he retired. Tony Vignale, sitting to his left, was not so lucky: his only son, Leon, had just bought a share, and no partner could own more than one. Cino patted his back, reassuring him that they would figure something out when the time came.

Ultimately, like they did for every important decision, the partners took a vote. The vote was close, but the resolution passed: partnership shares would only be passed down from father to son. A son could split the share with his sisters and mother, but no woman could ever own a share outright. The shareholding son did not have to work for the Oakland Scavenger Company, but it was easier if he did—that way, he could have his wages garnished like the rest of them did, rather than having to pay his way in cash. Those partners who did not have sons, or whose sons didn't want to buy their share, could sell their holding back to the company for its full value.

In an instant, a new era dawned. Never again would the

Oakland Scavenger Company seek out Italians to join upper management; never again would a share be created for a *cugino*[99] with enough money to make a down payment. The company that welcomed Cino into its arms was gone. In its place was a network of 122 men who wanted to hold on to what they had built, just as they had built it—and who knew that doing so would probably sink their own ship within a generation or two. Their hope was merely to stay afloat for long enough for the fog to clear, or until they could find another solution. Instead, that vote would bring about the death of the Oakland Scavenger Company less than fifteen years later.

Things began to unravel in 1975. While Oakland Scavenger was paving the way for its own expansion—buying a landfill in the Altamont Pass, moving its headquarters from Peralta Street to a full-service transfer station in San Leandro—five of its minority employees sued for racial discrimination. The company settled with them quickly out of court, but by then word had already gotten around. In 1978, sixteen more black and Latino employees intervened in the case, suing the Scavengers for upward of one million dollars.

As the case of *Bonilla v. Oakland Scavenger Company* picked up steam, Ed Moore realized he needed some help. For that, he hired Stephen McKae, a young attorney fresh out of San Francisco's Hastings College of the Law. While McKae handled the Scavengers' commercial affairs—including pursuing contracts in an emerging South Bay region known as Silicon Valley—Moore focused his attention on the discrimination cases. "I really knew nothing about [those lawsuits] early on," Mr. McKae recounts years later. "That was Ed's thing."

---

[99] Cousin

Soon, however, it would become Steve's thing. After a lifetime of service to the law, and to the Oakland Scavenger Company that loved him like one of their own, Ed Moore passed away peacefully in 1980. Suddenly, Steve McKae—five years out of law school, and better suited to negotiating labor contracts than arguing civil rights cases—became lead attorney in the *Bonilla* case. McKae briefed himself on Moore's defense, and in 1982 the case went to the District Court of Northern California.

McKae's strategy was simple: get the judge to throw the case out on the grounds that, because Oakland Scavenger stock only went from father to son, the company was technically a family business and therefore not subject to Title VII of the Civil Rights Act. "There was no statutory reason for the suit," he continues, "no law against keeping stock ownership in your family." District Court Judge William Ingram agreed with him, and summarily dismissed the case.

Attorneys for the plaintiffs immediately appealed the decision, and found that the Ninth Circuit Court of Appeals did not see the case the same way as Judge Ingram did. "Since the [Oakland Scavenger] Company ties preferential wages, hours, and job assignments to ownership of its stock, the shareholder preference plan constitutes a condition of employment subject to the mandate of Title VII," reads the judgment of the Honorable Shiro Kashira. "Title VII case law has from the beginning made clear that nepotistic concerns cannot supersede the nation's paramount goal of equal economic opportunity for all."[100] With that, the Appellate Court reversed the District Court's decision, and remanded the case back to where it began.

That is when things started to get a bit odd. When the Court of

---

[100] Kashida, Shiro in Shanoff, Barry S. "Discrimination or nepotism?" *The management of WORLD WASTES* Mar. 1990: 48+. *General OneFile*. Web. 29 Aug. 2012.

Appeals sent the case back to trial, the plaintiffs' lawyers had to file another complaint in District Court. In doing so, however, the secretary for one of the lawyers accidentally omitted one of the plaintiffs—a helper named Juan Torres—from the paperwork. Once Torres realized the error, he filed his own lawsuit to try to get his name back in the plaintiff group. But the case had already been filed, and United States law was clear that, once filed, it could not be amended. So Torres took his lawsuit to a higher court, then a higher one, until it finally reached the Supreme Court of the United States of America.

"I actually argued this thing in front of the Supreme Court!" Steve McKae laughs. "I couldn't believe they actually took the case; it seemed so procedural." But the Supreme Court saw it as a substantive challenge to the letter of the law: should a man be denied his right to proper restitution just because a secretary forgot to type in his name? In an overwhelming 8-1 decision, the Court decided that yes, he should. "We recognize that [the decision is]...a harsh result in this case," Justice Thurgood Marshall said. "But we are convinced that the harshness...is imposed [by law] and not by the judicial process."[101]

With the Juan Torres question settled, Steve McKae, OSC President Peter Borghero, and the rest of the team turned their attention back to the discrimination suit itself. A lot had happened since the suit was dismissed and then re-opened in 1983, and the lawsuit now demanded the company's undivided attention.

"They were able to certify a class [for a class action lawsuit]," McKae recalls. As a result, the number of plaintiffs ballooned from 15 to 280—all the black and Latino employees of the Oakland Scavenger Company, except for Juan Torres. Though many of Oakland Scavenger's 800 employees were white, non-Italian men

---

[101] Marshall, Thurgood in Yoshikawa-Cogley, Linda. "Clerical error wipes worker from race bias lawsuit". *Oakland Tribune*. 1987.

who also never had a chance to become partners, they were not included in the class. Undoubtedly, plaintiffs' attorney B.V. Yturbide thought that including white employees would dilute the charge of racial discrimination; Oakland Scavenger, for its part, did not argue the point. Much better to settle with 280 people than with 500 or more.

After the Juan Torres case, *Bonilla v. Oakland Scavenger Company* began attracting local and even national attention. One of the heads that turned toward the case at this time belonged to Marshall Krause, former Chief Attorney of the American Civil Liberties Union. Arrested in 1964 for protesting the House Unamerican Activities Commission, Krause had grown over the years to become one of Northern California's most prominent civil rights activists. And though he never argued the *Bonilla* case in court, he made it his duty to sway the court of public opinion. In a series of interviews with Gene Ayres of the *Oakland Tribune*, Krause lambasted the Scavengers for operating in what he called "apartheid-like conditions." He demanded that Oakland Scavenger pay out $35 million in lost income and damages; Yturbide took up the call as well, claiming that the company was in "dogged defiance of the law."[102]

Under mounting pressure in the courtroom and the newspapers—and, in truth, knowing that they were on the wrong side of history—Oakland Scavenger began to look for a way out. Simply put, they had no defense: once the Court of Appeals overturned the partners' right to reserve the best jobs and pay for their shareholding sons, they had no ground left to stand on. For a while, they pursued alternative structures like an Employee Stock Ownership Program, in which every full-time employee owns an equal share of the company. But with 800 employees stretched across a half-dozen counties, most of them with no management

---

[102] Yturbide, B.V. in Ayres, Gene. "Race-bias lawsuit goes to judge". *Oakland Tribune*. 25 Mar 1987: B-5.

experience or education, the venture would have been far to unwieldy to succeed. So, the partners did the next best thing: they started looking for buyers.

Fortunately for Oakland Scavenger, despite its courtroom drama, the company continued to grow by leaps and bounds. Purchasing the Altamont Pass landfill turned out to be a master stroke: in the 1980s, a number of other local dump sites shut down, and suddenly companies and city governments were lining up to dump their trash in the Scavengers' landfill. While the civil rights case was still gearing up for the final showdown, the company inked a lucrative deal with the City of San Francisco, to dump *all* of the city's trash in the Altamont Pass. With Oakland Scavenger's stock still on the rise, Pete Borghero and Vice President Lou Alberti—Cino's former supervisor—called another meeting of the partners.

"Fellows," they said, "now is our chance. The helpers have their hands in our pockets, and one way or another they're gonna get what they're owed. But we can get out of this right now if we want to, once and for all."

A murmur swept through the crowd. "What do you mean?" one partner asked.

"Waste Management has made an offer," said Borghero. "They want everything: the transfer station, the landfill, the trucks, everything. Our employees, too. Whoever wants to stay, helper or partner."

"How much?" asked another.

"Eighty-five million dollars, give or take. They'll pay us out in Waste Management stock, so we'll have to wait a few years to claim the money—all in all, though, it'll work out to about seven hundred-fifty thousand for each of us. We'll have to pay about 10% off to the class, but still, that's a nice chunk of change."

There was a long, still pause. Then all 122 partners began talking at once, animated and optimistic and guarded.

"Seven hundred and fifty grand? Can you imagine?"

"I could pay off my mortgage with that."

"I could send my kids to private school!"

"But what about our ancestors?" a few said. "What about *our thing*?"

"It's not our thing anymore," the rest reminded them.

In the flurry, Cino thought about that boy who had jumped ship over thirty years earlier. That boy had nothing: four crumpled bills, a t-shirt and a pair of jeans. Now, the man he had become had the chance to make, with the stroke of a pen, more money than he had ever dreamed possible. What Doretta would say if she could see him now!

Three weeks later, the partners convened again, this time in the company of corn-fed Texan executives with WM pins in their ties. They voted one by one, in secret, then clustered together to share and tally their votes. It was a landslide: a no-question-about-it, no-going-back kind of vote. In October, 1986—right around Cino's 51st birthday—the co-owners of the Oakland Scavenger Company sold the business their grandfathers had built to the largest waste collection corporation in America, and collected their handsome reward.

Selling the company made the trial a breeze. The case resumed in early 1987, and settled by the end of March. Marshall Krause and the defense still wanted $35 million, but the law only required that Oakland Scavenger pay out the money that minority employees could have gotten if the company had opened shares up to them in 1972. Given that only a few shares would likely have come available in that time, the final sum was closer to $8 million—around $28,000 for each member of the class. For the legal team, that number was a disappointment, but to the 280 black and Latino helpers of the Oakland Scavenger Company, it represented a sort of vindication—a recognition of their value as workers, and as people.

Not long after, nearly all 800 employees of the Oakland Scavenger Company—partners and helpers alike—went back to work, now as members of Waste Management. Their famous "blue wagons" now gleamed green and yellow, just like thousands more across the country. Their unofficial uniform of overalls and floppy hats—the same outfits they'd wear in their gardens or at the flea market—were replaced with official uniforms and neon green vests. After sixty years, Oakland Scavenger was no more. But in its place was a new opportunity for all: the opportunity to put their heads down and do good, honest work, together.

Cino stayed at Waste Management until 1993, then retired to enjoy the fruits of his labors with his beloved wife, his four sons and his grandchildren. With the settlement money, he followed his father-in-law's example and bought apartment buildings around the East Bay. Josephine didn't want him to, but in the end, the income from those properties helped keep them secure. He still owns and operates each of them, at age 80. After 47 years of working on fishing boats, oil tankers, bicycles and garbage trucks, Cino settled back to focus on the three things he loved most: his family, a good hand of poker, and the Rockridge Soccer Club.

CHAPTER TWENTY: AN ORANGE TREE IN A BANANA GROVE

"You gotta live your own life; everyone has their own style."
- Cino Chegia

Spring, 1972. Cino Chegia sits in the office of Dr. Hank Klopping, Superintendent of the California School for the Deaf.

"You see, Mr. Crappy," he says, oblivious to how the man flinches. "This—this is for my sons. They've never been back in Italy, and who knows if they ever will. Lots of kids around here the same way. This is my chance to bring a little bit of it here—and to teach them, you know? Competition, sportsmanship, discipline. All we need is someone to say yes. Will you say yes, Mr. Crappy?"

Doctor Klopping sighs and scratches his chin. He searches Cino's eyes for falsehood or greed, and sees nothing but love, passion, and commitment. How on Earth could he refuse?

"I must say, Mr. Chegia, you're very enthusiastic. I'd be remiss if I didn't support your boys. You may use our field. Good luck with your little soccer thing."

"Thank you, Mr. Crappy, thank you! You won't regret this. We'll get it going real soon." Cino pumps Dr. Klopping's hand, then dashes out the door to tell Jo and the boys.

Dr. Klopping shrugs, far less sure than Cino seems to be.

In 1970, with the boys in school and the Scavengers still in a legal gray area, something began to gnaw at Cino. It felt like a part of his was drifting away, rudderless, like a broken-down boat…For a long time, he couldn't put his finger on it.

Then, one day, his sons helped him figure it out.

"Dad," they said, shoulder-to-shoulder like a Roman phalanx. "We want to change our name."

"What you mean, change? You are John, you are Joe, you are Jay, you are Jimi. Why you want to change that?"

"Not those names, Dad. Our last name. Nobody knows how to pronounce it: they say, 'Che-ja,' or 'Che-gee-a,' or they just look at it and don't even try. Why can't we change it to Smith or Martin, something American?"

Before he could stop himself, Cino let out a laugh. When he was their age, he was dodging bombs. Their biggest worry was people pronouncing "Ke-ja" wrong. And did they really think that they were going to convince their father, Chinaman Chegia, that their name was too embarrassing to keep?

But, in the next moment, it hit him. Here were his children, as Italian as he could make them: going to school with their cousins; eating *focaccia* and *fiori fritti* at their nonni's house; beating the neighbors' kids at cards; serving *cioppino*[103] at the Ligure Club. But still, they were as American as the land of their birth. Their

---

[103] Fried dough; fried zucchini flowers; seafood stew

English was flawless but their Italian poor; they pushed away "yet another plate of pasta" and clamored for burgers and fries. All around them, Oakland was changing: new languages cluttered the Genovese streets, and new faces, markets, and churches popped up on every corner. Now his sons wanted to scrub away the most Italian part of themselves, the one that faces outward and declares, "This is who I am." They wanted to be like everyone else—just the way he had hoped they never would be.

"Listen, boys," he finally said. "You know what happens when you plant an orange tree in a banana grove?" They shook their heads. "You get oranges. See, a tree can only ever be what it is, even if it's surrounded by all different types. You can be surrounded by Smiths and Martins your whole lives, but you'll always be Chegias."

Most of the boys shrugged and walked off. But Joe, sharp and pensive, lingered for a moment. He looked like he wanted to say something—something that he could only say now, when the time was ripe for saying things. But then he set his jaw and left to do his homework.

Years later, Cino would think about this moment, when Joe, then in his thirties, sat his parents down in the den.

"Mom, Pop, there's something I need to tell you," he said. "I've wanted to for a long time, but I haven't found the words to say it. It's been...hard...to accept, I guess—to say it out loud, at least. Mom, Pop, I'm gay."

There was long silence. Finally, Josephine spoke up. "It doesn't matter. You will always be the same son to us."

Cino sat, too stunned for words. Joe had always been different, but this? This he didn't know what to do with. Didn't the gays all live in San Francisco, and dance around on floats wearing feather boas and leather pants? That didn't seem like the son he knew. The one who started his own T-shirt company and could beat anyone (except him and Franco) in five-card draw. It wasn't right; it had to be a mistake.

"Gino, say something," said Jo. "Did you hear what he said?"

"Sure, sure, yeah. It's, uh, it's okay, son. You're okay. You're just confused."

"I'm not confused, Pop. I was confused for a long time, but not anymore."

Cino breathed deeply, a tear welling in his eye. "Okay then. It's fine with me. But…" he grasped for words. "You're not…sick, are you?"

"No, Pop," Joe replied. "I'm not. And you shouldn't worry about that. Just get used to the fact that I'm different in this one way."

They talked later, and again after that, and over time things became more comfortable. Joe was gay. He loved a man like Cino loved Jo. And, somehow, his father and mother—who were traditional is so many ways—would have to accept that.

Eventually, Cino embraced his son, and when the time came, he embraced his son's partner, Christoph. Nowadays, when he talks about Joe, tears sparkle in his eyes—just like he was thinking back to that day long ago, when Joe gave him the first sign that he, too, was an orange tree in a banana grove, and that he would never grow anything but oranges.

———————————

Not long after the incident with the name and the orange trees and all that, Cino hatched a plan. If he couldn't bring his sons to Italy—and, in those days, he certainly couldn't—he'd have to bring a piece of Italy to them. But not another dish or another song: something they really wanted. Something they would work for, would invest themselves in, that would tie them to the motherland and their homeland at once. Cino and his sons would start a soccer club.

Since the boys were born, they had been playing soccer. As soon as they could toddle, Cino showed them how to kick a ball, how to dribble, how to read the field. They kicked the ball around in the backyard, in the park, on the streets of Oakland. Whenever *Il Corriere dello Sport*[104] showed a Juventus win, he'd pick them up and carry them around the living room like a trophy. Jay and Jimi had even joined a league recently—but, in the Bay Area in the 1970s, the youth soccer pickings were slim.

"At that time, there were only three clubs [in Oakland]— Montclair, Oakland Soccer Club, and a Mexican team," Cino recounts. The two boys were playing for Montclair and already showed promise, but they were outsiders on a team full of kids they didn't know, with little room to progress their game. *What these kids need is a team of their own*, Cino thought that night— and he knew just the man to make it happen.

His first thought was to go through the CYO, the Catholic Youth Organization. An arm of the Oakland Diocese, the CYO organized sports leagues for local Catholic programs and schools, as "a vital instrument for the moral and spiritual elevation of the human person."[105] Its basketball team dated back to 1912, and it even offered girls' sports long before Title IX passed, but it had no soccer program to speak of. In 1970, with all four boys enrolled at St. Augustine's School, Cino approached the school's principal.

"Catholics around the world play soccer," he said. "Don't you want the kids in your diocese to do the same?"

---

[104] A popular Italian sports newspaper.
[105] "CYO Philosophy." Diocese of Oakland Catholic Youth Organization. http://www.oakdiocese.org/CYO-and-scouts/cyo/cyo-philosophy (accessed 12/3/15)

The principal shrugged. "If you can get it off the ground, be my guest. You'll need to get support from the other schools, though—the kids will need someone to play against, after all."

So Cino took his show on the road, cajoling and sweet-talking and arguing with the administrators of St. Teresa's, Corpus Christi, and St. Columba's to try to convince them to form a team. They each had a different excuse—they didn't have the money for a coach or uniforms; there was nowhere to play; the insurance premiums would be too high—but the same answer. Thanks, but no thanks. Behind their words, Cino heard a similar theme: *You're not in Italy anymore. This is America, and no one here wants to play soccer.*

Meanwhile, though, the boys had spread the word, and soon dozens of their friends were clamoring for a team. Italian, Latino, Irish, and black, they all yearned for the same thing: a chance to run, to play, to learn together. A chance to be part of something bigger than themselves. They were enthusiastic and spirited, ready to dive into the sport—they were everything that a coach, and a father, could ever hope for. There was no way that Cino was going to let them down.

Not long after giving up on the CYO, he sat down with the boys. "We're going to get this soccer league going," he promised, "but we may have to do it on our own."

And so they did. By 1971, the Chegias had rallied enough support and raised enough money to fund one team, which they entered into the Alameda-Contra Costa Soccer League. That same year, the family moved from Baci's apartment to their own home on Chabot Road, in the Rockridge district of Oakland. Now in a new neighborhood, Cino could easily form a new team without stepping on anybody's toes. Furthermore, their new house was just a few blocks from Chabot Elementary School, which had its own baseball field with plenty of green space in the outfield for a soccer match or two. The school agreed to let them practice on it, and soon young people from all over Rockridge swarmed Chabot in soccer cleats and shinguards.

Despite its early success, the Rockridge Soccer Club did not have many of the things that real teams had: trained coaches, regulation balls, and most importantly, uniforms. Cino called every sporting goods store in the East Bay looking for a bulk deal, but walked away empty-handed. Unbeknownst to him, as he led the kids through drills on the Chabot field, the answer to those concerns was watching from across the street.

"Rockridge Realty was nearby, and one day, the owner's wife walked over and offered to sponsor the team," Cino says. He agreed right then, and the next day ordered the first run of jerseys for the new Rockridge Cougars: green and white, reversible, with the Rockridge Realty logo printed on the front.

That first year, they only fielded one team: Under-14, with John Chegia and friends leading the way. Cino was the team's coach, general manager, equipment manager, match secretary, field coordinator and referee. With no game field of their own, the Cougars traveled as far as Walnut Creek and Concord to play against teams that were far more experienced, better prepared and better equipped than they were. "They demolished us," Cino chuckles.

Despite the grass stains and hung heads, demand continued to grow, and by the 1972 season the Rockridge Soccer Club fielded a team at every age level within the ACCSL. But they still had no home turf, and Cino's many meetings with the Oakland Department of Parks and Recreation went nowhere. "[They] would say, 'Oh, you can't play, you're messing up the fields,'"[106] he reported years later to Pete Elman, who wrote an article about him

[106] Elman, Pete. "Italian immigrant finds dream on soccer pitch". *Alameda Journal*. 17 Nov, 2006: C-2.

JEFF GILLILAND AND CINO CHEGIA

in the *Alameda Journal*. Facing yet one more roadblock, he turned—as he often did—to his friends and relatives. As they often did, one came through.

Evelyn Vega, Madeline and Franco's neighbor, was a secretary at the California School for the Deaf. The school had been built over 100 years ago on a large plot of land in Berkeley, with a sizable field that would be perfect for Saturday games. So Cino paid Mr. Crappy, or whatever his name was, a visit, and worked out a deal.

Forty-three years later, what was once the Rockridge Soccer Club is now East Bay United: at 2,500 participants, one of the largest youth soccer clubs in Northern California. Under Cino's guidance, the club established a Board of Directors, worked with the City of Oakland to build fields for its kids, and started a spin-off franchise called Bay Oaks—a traveling team for talented youth who wanted to take their game to the next level. From the kernel of Cino Chegia's love for his sport, fed by the heat of his love for his sons, popped a revolution in Bay Area soccer that has helped usher in a new era of fandom in America.

Cino retired from Rockridge in 2000, but not before coaching his sons and grandchildren to dozens of championships. He helped guide East Bay United into a partnership with the Jack London Youth Soccer Sports League, a regional league boasting over 7,000 players. Soon after that, the soccer club that Cino gave so much of himself to gave something back to him: the chance to see his family united, for the first time in nearly fifty years. It just didn't happen *exactly* the way he imagined it.

Chapter Twenty-One: Full Circle

Sempre Famiglia[107]
- Italian saying

July, 2004. Cino Chegia writhes in a hospital bed in Orbetello. The pain stretches and grinds, threatening to tear through his skin. He clenches his toes, his fingers, his eyes, trying to bottle it up and pack it away. His breath comes short and ragged; a hot, sharp something lances through him, and he reaches for a hand to hold.

A hand reaches back and clutches his. Gnarled from years in the engine room, less and less able to carve the wooden owls its owner loves—but still able to clutch, and clutching hard. Another clasps his shoulder, firmly and tenderly. Yet a third hand pats his leg. A woman's voice sings and soothes.

"Open your eyes, Cino," the voice says. "Look who's here to see you."

---

[107] Family Forever

Cino pries open his eyes and looks around. The room is crammed with people—half of Monte Argentario, it seems, has come to see him. To his left, Alberto channels strength through his hand, his children and grandchildren gathered behind him. In one corner, Zio Trento's sons, Alberto and Roberto Proccacini, laugh heartily with Beppino Bertocchini. In another, Zia Faustina Chegia, 85 years old and still feisty, whispers to Cino's niece, Anna Tosi. Perched on the bed, singing and soothing: Vanna, Alberto's *acompagnata*, whom he met a few years after Piera's sudden death in 1996.

Cino smiles as he sweeps his gaze to the right, then stops short. Could it be? Was that really them? Pino, hand on his shoulder, with Mara by his side!

"But—" Cino starts, but Mara shushes him.

"It's okay, Cino. We're here for you—*all* of us. As a family."

Tears flood Cino's eyes. He embraces his brother, his cousins, his nieces and nephews, his aunt. "Thank you, thank you," he says. Over thirty years of trying, and at last they are all together. Old rivalries cast aside; remembered wounds forgotten, for now and for good. And all it took was a few gallstones.

After Cino retired from Waste Management in 1992, he started going back to Italy nearly every year. Money was no longer any object: with the buy-out money and the rent from his buildings, he wouldn't want for the rest of his life. His sons were all gone, off to their own jobs and families. Josephine had also retired, and accompanied him on his travels—they visited her family often, too, in tiny Stella San Martino, where nearly every other headstone in the graveyard reads *Accinelli*. Other times, he went with friends who had asked him to be the executor of their wills, and who needed him to guide them home so that they could die among their people. No matter the reason, he always found a way to make it to Monte Argentario, to see the people who had watched him sail away so many times.

His favorite trips of all, though, were with the boys of Bay Oaks: excitable young men who ran laughing through the Tuscan fields and drank in every drop of sunshine with gusto. These boys were as diverse as Oakland itself: Asian, Latino, black and white; the sons of doctors and garbagemen and janitors; American-born, with no heritage in Italy but the ball on the pitch. But through that ball—through Cino—they found a link to a world they had never experienced.

It all started in 1993. The Bay Oaks Under-16s won their league handily that year, and were invited to an international tournament in Verona. Cino jumped at the chance, and a lightbulb flicked on in his head. Later that day, he called his cousin Alberto Procaccini, who coached a team in Porto Santo Stefano.

"Alberto, guess what? My Bay Oaks boys got invited to play in Verona. We're coming to Italy!"

"That so? Why don't you bring them on by to Porto Santo Stefano, too? We'll put a friendly together."

"You read my mind, cousin!"

Once the wheels were in motion, Cino wouldn't be stopped. He called all the Bay Oaks parents, assuaged fears, sweet-talked reluctant mothers. He organized fundraisers at the Ligure Club, where the boys wore their uniforms and served *frutti di mare* to smiling men and women who slipped twenties into their hands. He assembled the chaperones, bought airline tickets, made group reservations at refined but inexpensive hotels. Then, that summer, they flew to Rome and drove west for their warm-up match against Porto Santo Stefano.

The reception blew Cino away. "I didn't know they were

going to do all that," he recalls with a glow of pleasure. "I thought it would just be a regular pick-up game." Instead, Cino and the team entered town to shouts and applause, and a huge sign strung up near the soccer field: "*Benvenuti, Bay Oaks!*"[108] The boys got off the bus like the Beatles, mobbed with welcoming kisses and morsels of food. The field had been lined with bleachers usually reserved for the Palio Marinaio, in advance of the huge crowd expected for the next day's game. What began as a fun competition between cousins had turned into a cultural event for the whole region.

What an event it was, too. "Their team was good," Cino remembers. "They got the best kids from all over the city, and Alberto trained them well. My boys were a little nervous at first, but then we got on the field. We beat them pretty good." The Bay Oaks players may not have grown up awash in soccer like most Italians did, but they had been playing together all year. They knew their game, they played it well, and the santostefanesi team was no match for them in the end. But that hardly mattered to anyone: it wasn't about winning and losing. It was about sport, about a tradition that spanned oceans and a language that could be spoken without words. The hometown fans cheered just as loudly for a Bay Oaks goal as for one of their own; and, in the end, the players shook hands as confederates, joined forever in that moment.

That night, Cino treated both teams to a dinner on him. As the American players toasted their counterparts (after promising not to tell their moms they got to drink wine), Cino sat with his brother, taking in the few moments he had to truly be at home.

"You know the only thing missing right now?" he mused.

"Don't say it," cautioned Alberto.

---

[108] "Welcome, Bay Oaks!"

"Pino and Mara. If they were here—then, then it would feel right."

Alberto scowled. "You know that can't happen. It just won't work."

"How do you know? You've never even met them!"

"I don't want to go over this again. You know what happened with the money. You know what was said. Piera, she just..."

Cino felt his hackles rise, but he breathed deeply and they settled down again. "He's our brother," he said. "She's our sister. Someday you'll have to face that. *Sempre famiglia.*"

Alberto swallowed his wine and patted Cino on the shoulder. "Maybe for you, brother."

Over the next ten years, Cino took many more Bay Oaks teams to Italy. Every time he came back, he tried to get the family together. But every time, circumstance and stubbornness got in the way.

Finally, he got tired of playing the middleman. He would see Pino and Mara every time he went home, and he would see Alberto and his family, but no more would he ask them all to sit at a table together. In conversations with one, he would not dream of mentioning the other. It was the Italian way of doing things, a way he remembered: if something was too hard or too deep to talk about, just don't talk about it. But after nearly fifty years of bootstrapping himself in America, it chafed at him, and he urged them silently to face the problem head-on. Nothing helped. For once, the card shark seemed to be out of aces to play.

But then, in 2004, an unexpected trump card. Cino's eldest grandson, Christopher, was playing soccer for De La Salle High School that year, and the team got invited to a tournament on the island nation of Malta. Cino agreed to accompany them as a chaperone and liaison, then planned to continue on to Italy for his regular visit. Midway through the games, however, things started to go very wrong. Cino woke every morning with a jabbing pain in his abdomen, which throbbed continuously throughout the day. Every time he ate, or walked, or did anything but lie very still, the pain spiked. And using the bathroom—that was like medieval torture. For a few days Cino tried to ignore it, hoping the pain would go away on its own. But it only deepened and spread, until his breath came like a knife in his side.

"You have to go to the doctor," the other chaperones told him. "We're really starting to get worried."

"Why aren't you at the hospital?!" his wife screamed at him over the phone.

Finally, Cino relented. Barely able to walk, he let one of the chaperones drive him to the nearest emergency room, and even sat in the wheelchair the nurse brought out. He would have made a joke—something like, "Don't tell my wife I let another woman push me around,"—but his lips didn't want to move.

In the exam room, with its dirty floors and curtain walls, the doctor told him that he had multiple gallstones, and would need to have surgery right away.

"No," he said flatly, grimacing with the effort.

"What do you mean, no?" demanded the doctor.

"No...not...here. Not...without...my...family."

"Mr. Chegia, you need surgery immediately. Your family is thousands of kilometers away. I can't recommend that you travel, and, to be honest, I'm not sure you would make it."

Cino smiled weakly. "I'll...make...it," he said. Hours later, he was on a flight to Rome.

Alberto met him at the airport and drove him straight to the hospital in Orbetello: one of the best hospitals in a country with the world's second-best health care system. Vanna sat in the backseat, and they laid Cino down with his head in her lap.

"Call...Jo?" Cino eked out.

Alberto nodded grimly and flipped open his cell phone as he started the car. "Hello, Josephine? It's Alberto. Yes, I have him. We're on our way. It's going to be okay, Jo. I'll call you when he's in surgery—yes, the minute he goes under. Okay, I'll tell him." He hung up and glanced over his shoulder.

"Cino, your wife says that if you die, she'll kill you."

They raced through the hills of Lazio and Tuscany, silent except for Cino's steady moans, which grew to bleats every time they hit a sharp curve or sudden rise.

"You're being too reckless," Vanna clucked. Alberto just gripped the wheel tighter with his eyes on the road. They would get there. They would get there.

They made it to Orbetello and rushed Cino into surgery. Hours later, they wheeled him back out again, groggy and mumbling but alive. They put him into a bed, and he felt his body release a deep tension. Sleep fell on him like a blanket.

When he awoke, they were all there. Standing and sitting, filling the room, squeezing his hands and shoulders and gazing at him with love and concern. *This must be a dream*, he thought. *I must still be under*.

"I'd like to be awake now," he said quietly. There was laughter.

"Cino, you *are* awake," said Zia Faustina. "We're all here for you. Really."

"*All* of you? Even—" he looked up at Pino.

"Even us," Pino said.

Pino looked across the bed at Alberto, the half-brother he had never met—not once, not in 65 years. Their gazes met, and in that moment it seemed as if they passed something between them: an olive branch, a new covenant of friendship for however many years they had left.

"*Sempre famiglia*," Cino smiled. Then the pain kicked back in, and he reached out once more for his brothers' hands.

CHAPTER TWENTY-TWO: THE FINAL CHAPTER

"E basta."[109]

- Common Italian phrase

December 21, 2014. Cino sits in an ornate, straight-backed chair, fidgeting in his best gray suit. Around and around him sit three generations of Chegias, in a circle with one end open. Between them, marble columns reach up toward Roman archways; above, ancient mosaics depict Christ passing down the law, and Bacchus crushing grapes into wine. The circular stone walls are emblazoned with candlelight, and a warm glow falls on the raised altar in their midst. The guests rustle in their fine dress, their voices hushed in the old mausoleum.

At last, the priest arises, dressed in white robes. He steps slowly toward the altar, ascends the stairs, gazes out at the gathered families. He raises his hands. They rise; the piano swells. Into the open archway steps the groom, flanked by his father and

---

[109] "That's enough."

301

mother, rakish in a tuxedo and blond stubble. He takes his leave of them at the altar; they beam wide and blink back tears. He turns—the room turns—the bride enters. She walks slowly and confidently, radiating. Brown curls cascade past her shoulders; even through the veil, her eyes dance in the candlelight.

The priest and congregation raise their prayers to God. The lovers join hands, speak their vows.

"Do you have the rings?" asks the priest.

Trembling, the groom pulls a rose gold band from his pocket. He hefts it and thinks of a year ago, when he got down on one knee and placed in her hand a glimmering diamond promise. "This was my Nonna Josephine's ring," he said then. "My nonno gave it to me. She would have loved you, you know—she would have wanted you to have it. Take it, please; make me the happiest man on Earth."

He catches her wrist, and their eyes lock. She smiles. He slides the band onto her finger. *In nomine Patris et Filii et Spiritus Sancti*, their lives are forever made one.

At the reception, the guests pass baskets of bread and trays of *gamberi*. They shout, they point, they laugh, they drink, they eat, they laugh. Young and old line up to congratulate Cory Chegia and his new wife, Eugenia, on their blessed union.

After dinner, Cino rises to toast his grandson. "Cory, when you told me you were moving to Italy, I thought you were crazy. When you told me you were marrying an Italian girl, I *knew* you were crazy. But now, looking at you two—at your beautiful bride—I guess you'd be crazy not to, eh?" A roar of approval from the red-faced assembly. "To Cory and Eugenia!"

The guests raise their glasses and cheer. Sitting down, Cino catches Cory's eye, and in one look says all he could not in his toast. *Your grandmother prayed for the kind of happiness I see in you now. She's smiling down on us, I know she is.* Cory nods, clears his throat, looks back out over the room. The music picks up, and the guests fill the dance floor with their swaying.

With the Chegia/Procaccini/D'Andrea family back together again, it felt in some way as if things were all done. Everything had been tied up in a neat bow: the kids were all off on their own, Oakland Scavenger was a distant memory, Rockridge Soccer was prospering, and the Italian clubs could take care of themselves. After seventy years of running, fighting, working, grinding, gritting, hauling, shouting, and soothing, Cino could finally rest.

That lasted about three days, and then it was time to find things to do. He and Jo started playing bocce ball with Franco and Madeline, Marge Paoletti, the rest of the gang around town. Cino managed his properties, collecting rent door-to-door like it was *conti* day all over again—fixing sinks and unclogging toilets himself so he wouldn't have to hire help. He bought a candy-apple red Thunderbird, fixed it up, waxed it good, dropped the top and drove Jo to wine country. She smiled as the air rifled her curls.

Mostly, though, Cino went to "church": the Oaks Card Club in Emeryville, where to this day he sits down most afternoons for a "sangwich," a beer, and a few hands of Texas Hold 'Em with the other old timers. They talk about their younger days, about the War, about how much the Bay Area has changed over the years. But, mostly, they play cards, in a quiet sanctuary where they can be with their thoughts.

All in all, Cino's life in the early 2000s was good: simple, paced. It was then that he started writing his memoir, sitting down every so often to unspool a memory from his head and deposit it wriggling onto the page. He loved trying to fit it all together, the puzzle pieces of his past: remembering out who did what to whom, and what happened when, and what the farmer's name was whose oranges he stole. He especially loved the sudden spark of memory as it alighted on an image: the olive trees from the sea, shining like silver; a lone fighter pilot parachuting down through the swollen sky. They burned like torches in a tunnel that stretched back darker and darker, faintly illuminating what was around them. Cino warmed himself by their light.

But good things rarely stay that way for long, and as the years went on, things started to get worse for the people Cino loved. First, it was Franco. Madeline's husband had become Cino's good friend, a big and boisterous man with Cino's keen ability to sniff out a bluff. Quick to smile and sharp with a scowl, he intimidated as easily as he ingratiated—and he loved as much as he ate. He was born in Lucca, came to America when he was six, joined the Army and served in Korea. He and Madeline had five children and fifteen grandchildren. He was a truck driver, a box-shipper, a seller of antiques and flea-market wares. His easy chair was the most hallowed place in the house, his basement was always stocked with wine, and his freezer was full of ice cream and candy. On holidays, his house overflowed with grandchildren, playing with toy guns and Sega Genesis and American Girl dolls, asking their nonno for Pinochle tips. He had a heart of gold, and his family cherished him. But that heart, in the end, couldn't keep up with him, and after a series of illnesses, Franco Petri died in his sleep in 2008.

After Franco was Lamberto Parenti, who had been with Cino since the early days at Oakland Scavenger. They were neighbors, close friends, and Christmas decoration competitors; Lum's wife, Joanne, had been on Cino's first date with Josephine, that fateful day at the movies. He passed in late 2010; one year later to the day, Tony Vignale succumbed to a long illness, surrounded by his family. Cino went to every funeral, consoling the bereaved, reminiscing and joking, sharing his warmth with those who needed it most. Nowadays, he jokes that their spirits accompany him to the card table: "I went to the cemetery and asked those guys for help playing poker," he says. "That day, I won $800! Next day, I bought them all flowers." His laughter is a gesture to his friends and, perhaps, a gesture to the Devil, from the boy who "would have been better off" if he had not lived past the death of his mother.

Watching his friends die was hard, sure. But nothing was even remotely as hard, not even in the same time zone, as the saddening, staggering, shattering walk he took with Josephine in those years.

It started in 2005. Jo had been getting migraines for many years, piercing pains that forced her to sit in a dark room for hours on end. Around then, she started to complain of weakness in her arms and legs, difficulty moving: her gait became slower and her movements less sure. Over the next few years, her body continued to degenerate, until she could no longer grip a spoon well enough to cook dinner for her husband or bake the cakes that her grandchildren loved. Eventually, she grew too weak to walk up the flight of stairs to the bedroom she shared with Cino, and he made a bed for her in their first-floor dining room.

Tragically, Jo's mind went along with her body. Her short-term memory faltered first: she would often forget where she was going or what she was looking for, but still knew her husband well and delighted in visits from her family and friends. By 2007, however, faces and memories had started to fail her. She would forget which son she was talking to, or which grandchild belonged to whom. She was easily confused, and would grow frustrated with her own inability to remember things she had always known. Though she rarely displayed the tell-tale tremors of the illness, by 2007 Josephine's doctors concluded that she suffered from Parkinson's Disease. The disease was advanced, and the outlook was grim: there was nothing her family could do but make sure she was taken care of until the end.

After the diagnosis, Cino made it his mission to look after the woman he loved. Fifty-one years earlier she had swept up his heart, and returned his love in ways he could have never imagined. She taught him English, taught him to dance, taught him to be a good husband and a good father. She was patient, kind, forthright, gentle, infectiously funny, and devoted to the life they built together. She was his home, his partner, and had been taking care of him since he was a young man lost in a new world. The only way he could think to repay her was by guiding her through life's end now.

So, every morning, he awoke with the dawn, cooked Jo some breakfast, sat with her as she stirred in her bed. He helped her get dressed, wash her face, brush her teeth; he sat her down for breakfast, and, if needed, he fed her. Some days she remembered him, remembered their family, looked at him with eyes that saw clearly the world around her. Those days, the biggest problem was explaining to her why she woke up in the dining room. Other days she eyed him warily, like he was a strange man selling perfume on the street—or, worse yet, just stared vacantly off into space. Those days, it was hard to go on.

But he didn't give up: never had, not in anything. He just woke up every day and made sure he was smiling, make sure he treated each morning like it was the first one he'd seen. "You've gotta come see this, Jo," he would say. "It's beautiful out there!" He kept his step light and his spirits high, for his wife and his family and himself. He did all he could for as long as he could, and he made her last years the absolute best they could be.

Eventually, though, it wasn't enough. Eventually the Parkinson's took over completely, and tending to her needs became too much for Cino to handle. The boys told him that she needed professional care, and by 2008 he had to admit they were right. He found her a continuing care community in San Leandro, where she could receive the treatment she needed and still be near enough to visit. He visited her every day. When her condition worsened, he moved her to Oakland Care Center. It was to be her last earthly home.

On June 2, 2010, Josephine Maddalena Accinelli Chegia passed on to the next world. She was 75 years old. Her husband drove over as soon as they called him, and held her hand as he made the arrangements. Her memorial was a week later at St. Augustine's Church on Alcatraz Street, where she had been worshipping since the day she was born. Her children and grandchildren, whom she loved so dearly, gathered around her once more: Joe and Christoph flew in from Hong Kong, Jay and his family from Philadelphia. Friends and relatives poured in to say their goodbyes, to remember how Jo had touched them with her kind and caring heart.

"She had that sort of light about her that brightened a room," they said, "a light from God. May her soul rest with Him now."

As the mourners filed past, Cino couldn't help but think of his own mother's funeral almost 70 years ago. What if the Lord had taken him that day, and his brother along with him? What if the old folks had gotten their wish, and he had never grown up to see war or feel pain or lose his lunch off the side of a boat? What if, when the *Homeric* left port in Alameda, there was no him to jump off it? What a terrible shame that would have been; what a magical, terrifying, spectacular life he would have missed out on. In spite of himself, he looked around—at his sons, at his grandkids, at his nieces and nephews; at the wreath his family had sent from Porto Santo Stefano; at the tears, the bowed heads, the long, warm embraces—and smiled. He was the luckiest man alive.

July 23, 2014. Cino and Alberto Chegia stand at a turnoff on the Via Panoramica above Porto Santo Stefano, gazing out toward Giglio Island. The crowd around them is hushed with something like reverence, and something like that anxious awaiting that comes at the end of things. Off in the distance, a flotilla travels slowly north. Fifteen ships in all, sixteen if you count the huge, ravaged hull being towed behind an ant-sized cutter. After nearly two and a half years, the *Costa Concordia* is on its way home.

"Do you think that's what we look like now?" Alberto chuckles. "Shells of ourselves with all the parts dangling off, that other people have to tow around?"

"Pretty much, yeah," says Cino, throwing his arm around his brother. "But a hell of a story it made, don't you think?"

Alberto smiles and squints his eyes, as the afternoon sun dances across the water. "Let's go get a drinkino," he says, and they follow their footsteps down to find a quiet bar by the sea.

ABOUT THE AUTHORS

Jeff Gilliland thought his great-uncle Cino's name was Gino until he was twenty-four. A native of El Cerrito, Calif., Jeff grew up in the bosom of Italian Oakland, surrounded by his Nonno and Nonna, his Zii and Zie, homemade ravioli at Thanksgiving, and breaded veal cutlets whenever Nonna Mam could be convinced. Jeff holds a Bachelor's Degree in English from Stanford University and a Master's Degree in the Humanities from the University of Chicago; this is his first book. He is honored to have been given the chance to tell this story, and simply asks that his great-uncle not have any more grand adventures in his life, so they don't have to add any more chapters at the end.

Cino Chegia is a proud Italian, a proud American, a proud father and grandfather; a jokesmith, a Juventus fan, and a heck of a card player. If you don't know anything else about him, we haven't done our jobs very well.

Photo by Joanna Jhanda,
Alameda Journal

Made in the USA
San Bernardino, CA
15 January 2018